THE END OF THE HAMPTONS

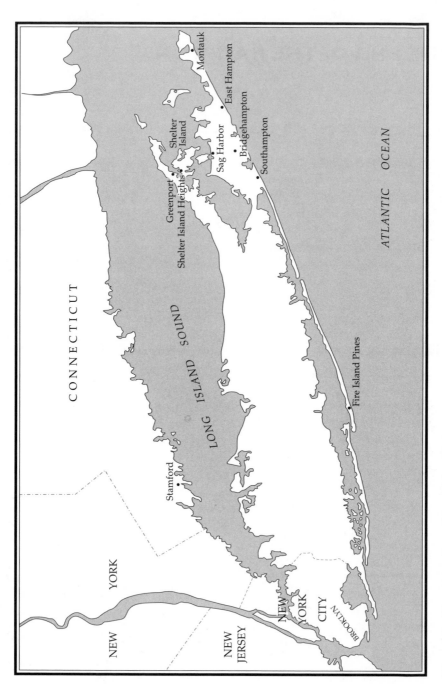

Map of the Hamptons, Long Island, New York.

COREY DOLGON

THE END OF
THE HAMPTONS

*Scenes from the Class Struggle
in America's Paradise*

New York University Press • *New York and London*

NEW YORK UNIVERSITY PRESS
New York and London
www.nyupress.org

Library of Congress Cataloging-in-Publication Data
Dolgon, Corey.
The end of the Hamptons : scenes from the class struggle
in America'sparadise / Corey Dolgon.
p. cm.
Includes bibliographical references and index.
ISBN 0-8147-1958-9 (cloth : alk. paper)
1. Hamptons (N.Y.)—Social conditions.
2. Hamptons (N.Y.)—Social life and customs.
3. Hamptons (N.Y.)—History. I. Title.
HN79.N42H363   2005
306'.09747'21—dc22   2004025133

New York University Press books are printed on acid-free paper,
and their binding materials are chosen for strength and durability.

Manufactured in the United States of America
10 9 8 7 6 5 4 3 2 1

This book is dedicated to Frank Jackson McGuinness, Jocelyn and Daniel Walton, Alex Arch Walton, Charlie David Boyle, Kaylie White Wilson, Magdalena and Ruben Schneiderman, Marina Carmella and Robert Rafaelle Deluca, Stephanie and Deborah Carlin, Bailey Maya Dolgon, and all of the other children of the Hamptons. May they find ways to work together and make a better quality of life for everyone.

Contents

Preface

My wife and daughter and I were returning from a trip to Vermont when we hit a massive traffic jam just north of our home near Boston. It's not unusual to find yourself subsumed by an automotive quagmire in Beantown, so I am well practiced in responding to such situations with the rationalized efficiency of all good twenty-first-century professionals—I reached for my cell phone to check my voice mail. There was a message from a reporter at the *New York Observer*, a New York City weekly that has made a name for itself over the past decade as being somewhat brash and hard-hitting, sometimes left or libertarian-leaning but almost always irreverent and politically incorrect. Apparently, the reporter, Alexandra Wolfe, was doing a story on the Hamptons and had been given my name as someone knowledgeable about the area. I joked, saying that I hoped she hadn't been misled.

We talked for almost an hour on the phone as Boston's "Big Dig"–inspired morass gave me as much time as I needed to chat. Wolfe explained that the paper often did an "end of the summer season" piece on the Hamptons, and this year the editors wanted to focus on the controversial proposal by the Shinnecock Indians to build a casino in Hampton Bays. She said that the article might ponder the question whether the casino would mean an "end to the Hamptons." To this, I responded with a sigh. Again and again, the magic question of whether the Hamptons were coming to an end had surfaced in my research. In fact, people had been predicting an end to the region almost from the moment it had acquired its sobriquet—"the Hamptons." I explained to Wolfe that talk of an "end to the Hamptons" was generally about how successive groups, having conquered the area, suddenly felt inundated by the forces of the new migrations that their own settlement had actually inspired. Whether it was the early Puritan immigrants who grabbed Shinnecock and Montaukett land, nineteenth-century Tile Club artists and the first wave of Manhattan elites who built a summer colony, or the current infusion of the telecommuting hyperbourgeoisie, each group had conquered the land with both great fanfare and more than a little bit of anxiety. This conquest was always followed by a triumphant narrative that proclaimed the "naturalness" of the particular group's success. Change being inevitable, however, these transformations were quickly followed by disappointments (usually brought by newer migrants taking advantage of conditions set in motion by the conquerors themselves). This process was inevitably talked about as the harbinger of the "end" of an era and an "end" to the place. Thus, stories of conquest in the Hamptons were soon overshadowed by tales of the area's demise.

Wolfe seemed interested but believed that the casino issue was too far from being resolved to focus on, anyway. So she inquired about what else I had found in my research. I explained that the central theme in the book I was writing was the impact of large-scale economic and social forces on the cultural politics of the region. Though most people think of the Hamptons as a playground for the very rich and famous, there are many other kinds of people who live there. Native Americans and white working-class people, Latino immigrants and African American workers, middle-class environmental activists and artists, as well as new McMansion homeowners and the ultra rich and famous all breathe the same, often fresh and salty sea air.

Eventually, Wolfe thanked me for my time and asked if it would be OK to call me again before the article was published in case she needed to check facts or quotes. I never heard from Wolfe or the *Observer* again, and when the piece came out a couple of weeks later, I was more than a little bit disappointed. My work had ended up on the editing-room floor before, but usually I could see that my thoughts had at least influenced a reporter to some degree. In this case, however, I imagine Wolfe did feel that the person who had recommended me had misled her.

The article was entitled "Dune, Where's My Hampton? It's Seceding" and focused on a recent effort by a handful of very wealthy Bridgehampton residents to secede and form a microtown called Dunehampton. These "*über* rich," as the article referred to them, were angry over environmental legislation that placed restrictions on shoreline building and erosion control efforts like bulkheads. The article named famous residents like the actor Roy Scheider and the comedienne Caroline Hirsch, who supported the "self-determination" measure, and quoted Scheider as explaining that "events have forced us to form a minor revolution to protect ourselves." In fact, most of the article uses the obvious farce that Southampton Town Council members call "Rich Hampton" to one more time portray the area as dominated by the excess and whimsy of an ultra-elite. The article argues that it's "not enough that there's a VIP tent at every polo tournament, a 'luxury liner' for every jitney and a rope in every club. The elite are determined to find a way to separate their homes from the masses as well. Building a house in the Hamptons may be upper class, but building a village there is *über* class. . . . In a place where status levels have been maxed out in the past decade, where VIP rooms and VVIP rooms have sprung up like dune grass at every event, have appetites for privilege gotten so insatiable that the only recourse is voting yourself off the island."[1]

I had been similarly disappointed the summer before when an award-winning documentary filmmaker, Barbara Kopple presented her cinema verité footage of the Hamptons on ABC. Kopple was famous for documenting working-class struggles in films such as *Harlan County, U.S.A.*, and *American Dream*, and her production assistant (who also interviewed me and must have, like Wolfe, felt misled) had assured me that Kopple wanted to portray as much of the spectrum of lives and experiences in the Hamptons as possible. Instead, Kopple gave us a rather long and boring study of how the very young, rich, and famous also have everyday lives; she offered us a look at Christy Brinkley's daughter's birthday party and a magazine publisher's preparty angst. ABC billed the presentation as "a sexy, true-life look at New York's famous— and infamous—beach resort. The Hamptons are depicted as an enclave unlike any other in America, but also one full of common human experiences, as characters are shown attending weddings and funerals, falling in and out of love, and gathering in a school auditorium for a piano recital . . . it just so happens the person playing the piano is Billy Joel."[2]

"The Hamptons" are undoubtedly a seductive place, but these images betray a social and political reality that is not only about what the rich and famous do behind closed doors—such as create villages or raise their children—but also about the long history of all the East End's people, who have created villages and raised generations from the time of Shinnecock and Montaukett civilizations to the present. One might just excuse Wolfe and Kopple and the dozens, if not hundreds, of others who have also presented the Hamptons as an elite, yet neurotic, theme park for New York City's movers and shakers. But such presentations do have an important political and social impact on the region as they reaffirm the area's sense of place dominated by wealth and privilege.

Many people throughout the Hamptons struggle to create a more just place to live. While all of these efforts maintain links to, and are impacted by, elite migrants, the real stories of the Hamptons must be told from a wide variety of perspectives and cover a broad spectrum of issues and events. I believe that a more accurate and insightful analysis of both historical and contemporary struggles may help further the cause of equality, justice, sustainability, and democracy. These are the stories of the Hamptons that need to be told.

As I finish this book, I am reminded of this year's "end of the Hamptons" story in the *New York Times*. Once more the newspaper ponders how increased traffic and sprawling development begs the "Hamptons Question: Is the Ride Over?"[3] For me, a long ride is over. But, for the people of the Hamptons who, just like their predecessors, must struggle to live together and create a more just and equitable society, the ride has really just begun. I hope this book offers some insight for that journey.

Acknowledgments

To tell this story of the Hamptons required an inordinate amount of help and generosity from a lot of people. I could never thank everyone who has had a hand in giving this book whatever good qualities it has. But I would like to try to thank those who have made the endeavor possible and enriched the narrative in significant ways. I interviewed almost one hundred people in trying to find voices from a broad spectrum of histories, classes, ethnicities, occupations, and political interests. In particular, I want to express appreciation to Mae Anderson, Melissa Arch-Walton, Robert Browne, Vince Cannuscio, Joanne Carter, Wendy Chamberlain, Jim Daly, Quentin Dante, Bob Danziger, Bob Deluca, Bob Fischer, Rebecca Genia, Nancy Goell, Joel Gomez, Julio Gonzalez, Liz Granitz, Jack Graves, Karl Grossman, Elizabeth Haile-Davies, Peter Hallock, George Harney, Katherine Hartnett, Graham and Azba Hotchkiss, Mary Killoran, Michael Knight, Kathi Kugler, Linda Miller-Zellner, Enzo Morabito, Jackie Poole, David Rodriguez, Tony Rosalia, Hal Ross, David Rubin, Carlos Sandoval, Sherry Saunders, Jay Schneiderman, Ed Sharretts, Valerie Suzdak, Kathryn Szoka, Fred Theile, Carlos Vargas, Lou Ware, Cassie Watters, Lori Werner, Meagan White, Mauricio Zuleta, and Michael Zweig. Many of these folks gave hours of their time to me, and I hope, regardless of what they think of the final outcome, they know that I feel a great debt of gratitude for their contributions.

I have to give a special thank you to friends in the Hamptons who hosted my family and me on numerous occasions and made it possible to conduct extended research in one of the pricier ethnographic sites in the world. Tom and Jeanne White, Scott Wilson and Jamie White, Bob and Linda Miller-Zellner, Kathleen Modrowski and Steve Marks, Peter Luibenov and Dawn Haight, Hugh McGuinness and Michelle Claeys, and their families all turned down beds, cooked up meals, and made my family feel welcome regardless of the time of year or tenure of our stay. I would also like to thank Worcester State College for a number of summer research grants that also helped fund the work on this book.

I have been blessed with a host of colleagues in the Hamptons and elsewhere who have given so generously of their time and talents, sharing insights and analysis, reading drafts and revisions, answering e-mails and distress calls. I want to thank Scott Carlin, John Strong, Herb Sherman, Kathleen Modrowski, David Goddard, Catherine Burnett, Karl Grossman, Tim Black, Mary Erdmans, Steve Corey, Jerry Lembcke, Sam Kaplan, and Michael Zweig for their intelligent and compassionate criticism. Family and friends have also acted as readers and commentators, especially Fred Dolgon, Richard S. Milbauer, Russ Haven, Bill Knapp, and Deborah Milbauer, and I want to thank them for helping me in my effort to produce a reader-friendly book.

I have had great help from fine institutions throughout the research and writing process. Many productive hours were spent at the various libraries throughout the East End, especially at the Southampton, East Hampton, Riverhead, and Sag Harbor public libraries, as well as at the Southampton Historical Museum, the Southold Historical Society and Southampton Town Hall. Worcester State College was also generous in granting research funds that made summer research possible. I also received research help from David McAlpine, Cassie Watters, Peter Luibenov, Theresa Dawn Haight, Diana Dayton, Elizabeth Eastin, Emily Oster, Emily Raynor, Dorothy King, Richard Barons, and Jamie White. I must also thank the staff at New York University Press, especially my editor, Ilene Kalish, for their support, enthusiasm, and patience for the project. I owe much gratitude to many people for either granting permission to use their photographs or helping me track down difficult-to-find pictures. These folks include Ron Ziel, Peter Blake, Alastair Gordon, Geoffrey Fleming, David Martine, Richard Barons, David Rattray, Jack Graves, Rivalyn Zweig, Brenda Kenneally, Kathleen Modrowski, and Michaela Kennedy. And the most devout thank you of all goes to my wife, Deborah, and my daughter, Bailey. Both have made sacrifices with great charity and allowed me the time and energy to complete this project. I could not have done so without their love and support, and I hope to compensate their patience and good will sufficiently as I send this work to press.

THE END OF THE HAMPTONS

Introduction

Spending Time in the Hamptons

Going West on Long Island remains in a way a trip forward in time.
The line between rural-resort and outer suburbia is as clear as the line
of smog visible on a sunny day somewhere up toward Patchogue . . .
which is about where the small temples of that late twentieth century
chimera of the tax-conscious outer-suburban, light industry, first appeared. Farther west, in Nassau County, the clock reverses itself, and
one is traveling backward toward the brick warehouses and tall chim-
neys of the late nineteenth century until, through the Industrial Revolution stench of the rendering plants in Long Island City, one sights the
two towers of Babel and the declining years of the Twentieth Century,
the World Trade Center, looming over lower Manhattan. . . . Digging
for the Center's foundations, workmen found timbers of a ship buried
deep in the muck of what was once the east bank of the Hudson. Some
think they were part of Adrien Block's *Tyger*, burned there before he
explored Long Island Sound to Block Island in 1614.

—Everett T. Rattray, *The South Fork*

While the September 11 terrorism attack on New York City has spurred
new worries about the state of the economy and Americans' sense of security, many real estate agents on the East End suggest that the horrific
event might actually turn out good for business as more families, seeking
refuge, move here permanently . . . "for the answer, look to the schools,"
said Diane Saatchi of Dayton Halstead Real Estate in East Hampton.
"School enrollment has skyrocketed around here. These are people who
came out here and never went back and aren't planning to." . . . Cook
Pony Farm has seen an "influx, for the first time ever, of people wanting
to rent a house immediately or buy a house that they can move into tomorrow. . . . Last week, we had our first World Trade Center survivor."

—Steven Kotz, *Southampton Press* (October 4, 2001)

So we beat on, boats against the center, borne back ceaselessly into the
past.   —F. Scott Fitzgerald, *The Great Gatsby*

I

The post-9/11 flood of migrants from New York City to the Hamptons may have made local news, but it certainly was not the first time that signs of urban danger or decay inspired metropolitans to seek the more peaceful, bucolic landscapes of Long Island's East End.[1] The earliest wave of aristocratic "summer people" arrived in search of unspoiled beaches and a calming environment. Urban life's growing chaos and the spreading fears of disease from an increasingly "dirty and smelly" city (especially during the summer months) motivated more and more rich city folks to establish summer colonies in the late nineteenth Century. Over the next one hundred years, various populations came to the Hamptons, some for work and some for play. But all were driven by the attractions of an "anti-urban" landscape that promised a living and a lifestyle markedly different from those of New York City. And, in each case, these social and economic migrations created a struggle between the new and the more traditional populations in the area, ultimately producing a history of conquest and resistance in the Hamptons.

This is the story of how history and geography impact the lives of people and places, shaping their experiences and their identities. But this is also a story about the politics of time and space. While science teaches us that continuous motion is a natural law, human history has demonstrated that most earthly forces and conditions are physically controlled and negotiated by individual and collective action. Thus, people manipulate the actual shape and course of constant change. The history of the Hamptons is a story about the power it takes to shape changes in, and over, time and space.

Those who control the lion's share of power take the lead in inscribing the physical and cultural landscape with their own imprimaturs. But those with limited resources also struggle to survive economically and to establish a sense of social identity and political autonomy. Sometimes the weak succumb, but never easily, simply, or forever. More often, they negotiate the policies and practices of the rich and powerful with their own cultural expressions, social practices, and political protests. The history of the Hamptons reflects these dynamics. It is one of conquests, but it is also one of resistance. Such opposing forces have resulted in a tradition of sometimes subtle dialogue, sometimes volatile conflict, but always a rich variety of mediations and negotiations, adaptations and impositions. In essence, it is a history of struggle.

These dynamics, however, don't necessarily distinguish the Hamptons as unique. According to one of the area's historians, Everett Rattray, "Long Island's inheritance, accumulated over four and a half centuries of European presence and the previous millennia of aboriginal occupation, is a microcosm of the continent's. What happened in this little northeasterly corner of the continent is more or less what happened everywhere else, although not always in the same order or in synchronization with greater happenings."[2] In fact, this book argues that studying Long Island's East End is important precisely *because* the area exhibits social forces and cultural experiences similar to those that exist elsewhere in the region, in the nation, and in the world.

I was first drawn to this project in the winter of 1997 as a faculty member at Southampton College of Long Island University. I became embroiled in a labor conflict when the administration decided to outsource the entire custodial unit, which resulted in nineteen workers essentially being sold to an outside management company. This event revealed that local economic and social changes were inextricably linked to global transformations in corporate culture, labor migrations, and distributions of political power. "Outsourcing" had become a common corporate practice, even among colleges and universities, where increased market flexibility and labor surpluses resulting from deindustrialization and new waves of immigrant populations could be exploited to reduce workers' wages and to bust unions.[3]

The custodians explained, however, that their plight was also steeped in the area's own history of racial and economic stratification. In particular, they documented a history of local labor relations in which people of color had always been relegated to a "mop and bucket" brigade. This dynamic could be traced to the earliest period of working-class formation, when European settlers employed the region's first real wage laborers, mostly Native Americans and freed slaves. Yet, even this historical context had its own ties to the larger social forces of particular periods in regional, national, and world history. For example, early encounters between the Shinnecock and Montaukett Indians and European settlers were influenced by larger international conflicts among European powers (Britain, the Netherlands, and France) as well as by regional struggles among Native tribes such as the Naragansett and the Pequot. The contours of the subsequent local economy and its attendant class structure were linked to a variety of influences: the global usurpation of land by European colonizers, the international slave trade, the rise and decline of the whaling industry, and other moments in history when local activities and global forces converged. In this sense, the story of a place is inevitably the story of many places—the story of its people, the story of many peoples.

To understand what is happening in the Hamptons today requires an examination of the larger social and political contexts of globalization, international migrations, shifting traditional values and identities, and a host of other changes. But it also demands an analysis of contemporary events and forces within a historical framework that is itself a complex mix of changing conditions and human actions. In *The German Ideology*, Karl Marx wrote, "History is nothing but the succession of the separate generations, each of which exploits the materials, the capital funds, the productive forces handed down to it by all preceding generations. . . . on the one hand, [it] continues the traditional activity in completely changed circumstances and, on the other, [it] modifies the old circumstances with a completely changed activity."[4] In other words, the present is simply the most recent set of struggles and conflicts wrested from a history of such tensions, all evolved from the ongoing interactions between human groups (primarily *classes* for Marx) and their social and ecological environments. This is the dance of historical rupture and continuity, of social structure and human agency, of cultural identity and natural ecology.

The Hamptons stand as an excellent place to view such a dance because it is so rich in what Rattray calls "accumulated inheritance." The area is emblematic of our nation's most salient historical themes: early European and Native American encounters; rapid changes in economic development and physical environments; the constant and shifting migration of world populations to the United States; the formation of racial, ethnic, regional, and national identities; and the vast divisions between rich and poor on local and global levels. While Long Island's East End is not the only place where these themes converge, the Hamptons remain one of the most animated and high-profiled sites where modern struggles over power, property, and place expose both complex historical characteristics and possible future frameworks for people's own perceptions of themselves and their worlds.

THE PRESENT IN SEARCH OF THE PAST

This book is not the usual history of a place. I do not try to trace a cause-and-effect outline for the succession of major events or plot the ancestry of various groups and the evolution of their particular travails. The East End and its particular towns and hamlets have already been well chronicled in many more traditional ways. The first Europeans who came to East Hampton and Southampton kept meticulous records, and a succession of historians have used the documents to create well-detailed compilations of early events, especially in politics and culture.[5] Of special note are the major works produced by the historian Jeanette Edwards Rattray. A recently edited collection of her work, *Discovering the Past*, is an excellent presentation of local history that includes vignettes on the early whaling industry and the aristocratic summer colony culture at East Hampton's Maidstone Club. More notable, though, are Rattray's studies of how local villages and landscapes evolved over time, changed by the intersection of global transformations in economy and technology and local negotiations by people who sometimes resisted and sometimes adapted to these changes.

Rattray writes of these forces with a kind of romanticism that is ironically part nostalgia and part boosterism. Although her work exudes a subtext of loss, she always manages to promote the present and to promise hope for the future. Thus, she claims that outwardly "this community remains unchanged," because "[t]he newcomer soon becomes as strongly opposed to any drastic change in East Hampton's appearance as any twelfth-generation descendant of pioneers. He is absorbed, like the invader of old China. He adopts the ways of the old-timers. . . . A passionate devotion to the ideal village—beautiful, quiet, simple, dignified, cherishing its honorable history—seems to develop almost simultaneously with the arrival of any new settler."[6] There is certainly truth to this statement, most obvious in the process of freshly monied migrants becoming antidevelopment environmentalists the moment they've broken ground on their new McMansions. Yet, few groups have come to Long Island's East End without a conqueror's spirit, and each successive wave of "settlers" has had a radical and permanent impact on the physical and cultural landscape.

In fact, those who conquer quickly develop narratives that naturalize and justify their victories, thus shaping the ideological landscape, as well. Early chroniclers of the East End, such as the Reverend Lyman

Beecher, declared that the Town's "success" had been evidence of God's mercy and its settlers' piety. In an 1806 speech entitled "A Sermon, Containing a General History of the Town of East Hampton, L.I. From Its First Settlement to the Present Time," Beecher explained that God had intended East Hampton "as a theatre, on which to make memorable displays of his mercy thro' Jesus Christ. He therefore took care to plant it with the choicest vine."[7]

Toward the end of that same century, the historian George Rogers Howell saw the importance of this theological foundation in the formation of the intelligence and the democratic spirit of Southampton's "founders." According to him, these "men of sterling worth . . . were more than mere colonists—they were the exponents of a new civilization founded on the idea, that under God, men could govern themselves." Thus, God's will and the wisdom of democracy (demonstrated in the settlers' "free charter, their just laws and liberal institutions") legitimized settlement and expansion. More recent historians have focused on the hard work and the sweat equity of early farmers or on the business acumen and entrepreneurship of whaling magnates. Common to all of these stories is the sense that those who triumphed did so naturally, almost inevitably, because of their individual will and their collective virtue.[8]

At the same time that these narratives were created to justify and explain the "legitimate" rise to power of the European settlers, they also started the process of marginalizing and eventually erasing those who had been conquered. While Native and African American communities maintained some history through oral traditions and cultural practices, only recently have historians of the East End effectively recovered the full texture of these groups' early lives and experiences. It is not that these populations were completely ignored in previous work, but stories about them seemed obscured by the cultural perspective of historians who identified with Europeans. A local historian, John Strong, describes such a dynamic as he counters the enduring and popular, yet false, historical impression that Native Americans simply vanished. This "recurring theme," according to Strong, can be traced back to Daniel Denton's claim, in 1670, that Long Island Indians were "decreased by the Hand of God . . . a Divine Hand makes way for them [the English] by removing or cutting off of the Indians either by wars with one another or by some raging mortal disease." Strong argues that this impression is misleading for two reasons. First, "warfare between Native American groups seldom took many lives" (unlike the wars with the English and the Dutch, which were brutal and devastating), and the deadly epidemics of smallpox and cholera "were introduced by the Europeans themselves." Second, Native Americans did not disappear: "they are alive and well on the Shinnecock and Poospatuck Reservations, in small Matinecock and Montaukett enclaves, and in scattered households throughout Long Island."[9]

Strong, along with scholars such as Gaynell Stone and Lynn Ceci and historians among the Shinnecock, such as Eugene Cuffee and Harriet Gumbs, have produced important chronicles of the Native Americans' past in the region. These works not only restore the period prior to European conquest but also provide a more accurate account of how Native Americans survived "settlement" by resisting land usurpation, adapting to changing economic opportunities and political structures, and negotiating new identities while maintaining a strong hold on a sense of cultural traditions.[10]

There is much less scholarship on the history of African Americans on the East End, but the exemplary efforts of Grania Bolton Marcus, Natalie Naylor, and Lynda R. Day, who examine Black history in Suffolk County as a whole (as well as in parts of the East End), bode well for the future endeavors of others who might focus more specifically on African Americans from the North and South Forks.[11] Similarly, organizations such as the Shinnecock Nation Cultural Center and Museum and the Eastville Historical Society have done yeoman's work in compiling material artifacts and presenting exhibits on Native and African American life on the East End. These historical efforts serve as an important corrective to some of Jeanette Rattray's more romanticized claims about continuity and consensus in East Hampton. Some groups, and their cultures and traditions, suffered more than others as new waves of conquerors hit the East End's shores. But, even as historians inform the area's collective consciousness of uncomfortable periods from its past, the significance of history itself has always been an openly celebrated concept among virtually all groups that spent time in the Hamptons.

In fact, the historian T. H. Breen, who once served as East Hampton's "resident humanist," has described the place as being obsessed with history. Partly, this fixation emanates from the constant desire among conquering groups to establish a kind of identity and authenticity by usurping a place's past and re-inscribing it with their own image.

Breen believes this kind of history is really an "empty heritage . . . transformed into a commodity . . . for mobile Americans cut off from a past that can provide them with a secure historical identity."[12] In contrast to Jeanette Rattray's sense that newcomers were simply "absorbed," almost mystically transformed by the power of the place's bucolic charms and idyllic landscapes, each fresh wave of East End arrivistes has actually recast historical narratives to serve its own purposes. For second- and third-generation European settlers in the eighteenth and nineteenth centuries, history legitimized conquest and growth because it displayed God's will and their own virtues. By the turn of the twentieth century, New York's elite had converted the South Fork into a summer colony resort, but they looked to the area's history to give their establishment a sense of authenticity. In East Hampton, they named one of their first major institutions, the Maidstone Club, after the town of Maidstone, in Kent, England, where East Hampton's earliest settlers had originated. In Southampton, Frederic H. Betts called his eighteen-room summer cottage Moncomanto after the Native American who signed the deed with the town's first settlers. By appropriating the past, new settlers could tell stories of the present that inscribed themselves and their status positions on the natural landscape.[13]

For end-of-the-twentieth-century conquerors, history again took on new meanings as elite Manhattanites made their way to the East End year-round. Some have become environmentalists and, in an effort to control the speed and style of growth, promote what the activist Bob Deluca calls "cute country planning." He explains that "people are deluded by architects' pictures into believing that they can have all the retail services and amenities they want and still maintain a rural quality of life simply because they decorate their Blockbuster Videos and bagel shops in earthy tones, with salt-box designs and pitched roofs."[14] Some of the very wealthy have revived the sport of polo and turned the Bridgehampton Polo Club into a site for the sport of *new* kings. Playing polo allows a new bourgeoisie to claim a legacy of wealth and status, legitimizing their ascendancy and demonstrating their fitness to rule as they ride high above the crowd. And some of the wealthiest, like the communications mogul Robert F. X. Sillerman, have been able to "buy" institutions that bestow historical authenticity and cultural capital. Having promised to donate millions of dollars in endowment and offering the potential to raise millions more, Sillerman was chosen chancellor of Southampton College with a ceremonial one-dollar-a-year salary. Although he claimed to receive no benefits other than the "thrill of intellectual discourse," what greater sense of historical legitimacy could there be for a new conqueror than to dress in the centuries-old garb of an academic elite and preside over the presentation of college degrees? Even Sillerman's money, however, could not keep the college fiscally sound in the changing marketplace of higher education. The College is slated to close its doors in September 2005.

But, like the political impact of Native Americans whose reclamation of history has been an integral part of their civil rights struggles, others in the Hamptons argue that to recover a particular heritage can be a form of resistance against new conquerors. For the former East Hampton town supervisor Cathy Lester, history can serve as a kind of "preservation," a potential bulwark against rampant development that threatens to destroy natural resources and privatize public lands and open spaces. Similarly, Helen Rattray (Everett Rattray's wife and recently publisher of the *East Hampton Star*) has declared that history "is the only thing that will save us from becoming the Smith Haven Mall"[15] (once the largest shopping center in Suffolk County). In an introductory letter to a published collection of lectures given in celebration of East Hampton's 350th anniversary, in 1998, village mayor Paul Rickenbach Jr. wrote that "as a community we must never lose sight of our obligation to preserve history and retain as much of our rural character as possible." And for Tom Twomey, the East Hampton town historian, the uniqueness of the town's history is a heritage that must be passed along to make "a better community—a better place to live; now and throughout future generations." Traditional ways of life vanish quickly in the face of rapid growth and development, and fears that the region will lose its "quality of life" or its distinctive local identity create an obsession with history.[16]

Breen was somewhat critical of this obsession, not only for its tendency to turn history into a saleable product, an exercise in self-promotion (an irony given how "selling history" speeds up new development) but also because it rarely recognized the complicated truths that underlie created historical identities. Few neatly constructed narratives of any group's claim to authenticity or birthright do anything but obscure the process of history and the multiple narratives "that humans have always invented to make sense of their lives." Breen did, however, believe that "doing history" could and should be an exercise in preserving some sense of historical identity, regardless of how complex and multifaceted such an identity might be. In fact, he argued that, without preservation, the historical voices of groups that both competed and cooperated in order to survive would disappear under the sprawl of an "instantaneous development" and its attendant, triumphant corporate narrative. The important conflicts and continuities that constitute the past's path into the present would be lost. Breen concluded that his search for historical meanings "in time" was also a search for meanings "*just* in time or in the *nick* of time, meanings revealed before it is too late."[17]

But too late for what? Breen's own work demonstrates that the colonial East End experienced its own rapid changes, brought on initially by massive deforestation and eventually driven by the whaling industry and its links to world trade. The summer colony boom in the late nineteenth and early twentieth centuries initiated an economic development process; soon land would be valued more for its real estate possibilities than for its produce. Similarly, the contemporary shift from seasonal houses or weekend retreats to primary residences has kicked off another major transformation in the economy that has witnessed major cultural and demographic variations. Each period of significant change has inspired a fear that a particular local identity and set of traditions would unravel and, therefore, required a struggle to preserve a particular quality of life before it was too late. Sometimes these expressions have emanated from those being conquered—the Shinnecock, the bonackers (a nickname for early, white, European settlers), or the blue bloods themselves. At other times, voices of doom have come from the earliest waves of conquerors, who worried that their discoveries would lose their charm or value if flooded with newcomers. My point here is that the history of the Hamptons demonstrates, from the particular perspectives of particular groups, that it is always too late. But, from a historical perspective, where the history of time and space is one of constant struggle, it is never too late. This is the kind of history that I am writing.

THE PRESENT IN SEARCH OF THE FUTURE

In this book I look primarily at the Hamptons of today. To do so, I always keep an eye on the past to understand the historical forces at work in shaping the present. Thus, I begin with a historical chapter that focuses specifically on the theme of changing physical and cultural land-scapes. By this I mean that each successive wave of conquerors—the Europeans, gilded-age Manhattan bohemians and aristocrats, twenti-eth-century Eastern European immigrants, post–World War II middle-class professionals, and others—has had lasting impacts on economic and social development, as well as on the land itself. But these changes have also encouraged a variety of forms of resistance, accommodation, and negotiation by those who had previously settled the region. This process of mediation between new ways and old, changing economic and cultural forces and desires to preserve landscapes, traditions, val-ues, and power has characterized the history of the Hamptons from its earliest times to the present.

Chapter 2 examines the contemporary economic, political, and so-cial forces that have shaped the modern-day Hamptons. In particular, I discuss the economic booms of the 1980s and 1990s on Wall Street and their impact on the culture of a new Manhattan bourgeoisie. This group's passion for property and for the cultural capital of a *Town and Country* life eventually combined with desires to live and "raise a fam-ily" in environments away from perceived urban decay. Facilitated by telecommunications technology and up-scaled transportation systems, the Hamptons became "year-round" and attracted increasing numbers of "city people" (and, eventually, up-islanders from Nassau County and Western Suffolk County) to move permanently to the East End. This group of conquerors inspired new McMansion subdivisions and retail outlets that tried to offer both a desired "rural quality of life" and the amenities of suburbia. Meanwhile, the seasonal service economy was transformed into a full-time service economy, and the population rapidly changed to include not only wealthy families with children but also working-class families with children, primarily Latinos from Cen-tral and South America.

The next three chapters look at particular social movements and so-cial forces that represent what I consider to be the most dominant polit-ical and cultural conflicts in the region. In chapter 3, I present the Peconic County Now! movement, a forty-year struggle to effect the se-cession of the East End's five towns, two of which—East Hampton and Southampton—constitute the Hamptons from Suffolk County. Begun early in the 1960s as a response to diminishing political power and in-tensified threats of suburban sprawl, the movement has experienced three major waves of political activity, the most recent of which resulted in a successful referendum for secession in 1997. Statewide political forces have stalled legislation that would allow the five towns to become Peconic County. More significant, though, is how the symbolic importance of Peconic County has changed over time, shaped and reshaped by different demographics to respond to the changing needs of different conquerors and settlers. This chapter traces the movement's evolution and the shifting cultural politics that inspire both support for and reservations about the creation of Peconic County.

Chapter 4 highlights the two most dominant demographic changes in the Hamptons over the past two decades: the permanent migration of both a very wealthy class of New York City professionals and a predominately working-class of Latinos from Mexico and from Central and South America. To demonstrate how these groups work to make homes in the Hamptons, I focus on their use of sports to promote a sense of identity and distinction, as well as to support their integration into the community. The rich have revived an athletic scene where some members prove their fitness and legitimize their ascendancy by playing polo—the sport of kings—while others battle for similar status and a sense of new bourgeois authenticity by participating in the *spectacle* of polo matches under the VIP guest tents. Latino immigrants struggle for their own sense of belonging by trying to integrate traditional forms of culture into their new worlds. While equipped with few economic or political resources, Latinos have come to dominate local soccer leagues and now face open political battles as they struggle to maintain current playing spaces and to develop new fields to accommodate expanding leagues. Polo and soccer represent lenses through which we can witness how new waves of wealthy settlers and working people experience and shape the process of settling in the Hamptons.

Chapter 5 tells the story of a labor struggle at Southampton College, where predominately minority custodians built a coalition with students, faculty, and community members to defeat administrators' efforts to outsource their jobs and break their union. In part, this drama exposes the history of how racial and class identities evolved to create an intensely segregated labor force that persists today. But this story is also an example of how contemporary global economic and social changes are experienced and negotiated by local institutions and communities. The ultimate success of the custodians and their coalition presents possibilities for future action and alternatives to elite-driven narratives about local community and identity in the Hamptons. Most notable about this struggle is the challenge it presents to the continuing stereotypes about who lives in the Hamptons and who has the power to change the public policies that determine the area's future.

The final chapter presents the Shinnecock Indians' ongoing fight over land development next to their reservation, where recent acts of civil disobedience and protest have resulted in court battles over property rights and police brutality. Meanwhile, efforts by the Shinnecock to build a casino on their property have shaken up traditional alliances between government and local developers, as well as recently forged coalitions between Native Americans and environmentalists. While these events take the book full circle, returning to battles over power, authenticity, and place, they also seem a harbinger of things to come as multicultural, multiracial, multi-issue, and interclass coalitions form to protect and conserve cultural heritage and environmental sustainability. At the same time, that the politics of economic development is complicated by new strategies adopted by Native Americans, both locally and nationally. Native Americans' continuing fight for their land and against upscale residential development is both a sign of continued historical struggle and an example of how these struggles change over time, shaped by new economic, political, and social conditions. The ways in which the Shinnecock and their allies deal with these historical ruptures and continuities will impact both the physical landscape and the cultural meanings of local identities, raising important cultural and political questions for the next generation of Hamptons residents.

As always, though, the future of the Hamptons hangs in the balance. How people use time and space purposively will determine what tomorrow's East End looks like. This thematic overview of particular historical and contemporary struggles is not a blueprint for action per se, but I do believe it offers important historical and political analyses that can aid in developing such plans. My personal bias as a scholar and activist has always been to look at history from the bottom up, from the perspective of a historical materialist, where science and action are two integral and intertwined ways to understand *and* reconstruct reality. My own work with environmentalists, youth activists, and the custodial workers in the Hamptons has shaped this research in many ways, reminding me of Marx's statement, that "philosophers have only interpreted the world; the point is to change it." We have much work to do.

I

Waves upon the Shore

Coming to the Hamptons from
Earliest Times to the 1970s

It must amuse the Shinnecock to see local people get excited about the 350th anniversary of Southampton coming up in 1990. Their history can be traced back more than 10,000 years to the first hunters and gatherers who found their way onto the island.
—John Strong, "The Evolution of Shinnecock Culture"

[I]t is ironic that old-timers decry the steady disappearance of the potato fields to development. At the turn of the century the land was given over to diversified farming: the boundaries that marked off a farmer's property were made of privet hedges. Then shortly after World War I, a number of Polish farmers settled in the Hamptons and . . . commenced the kind of farming they had practiced in their homeland. The privet hedges were torn down . . . and the subsistence farming gave way to the vast, unbroken acreage of potato fields. Now, the potato fields are being overrun by [a] modern architecture . . . "of shrill egotism—whose arrogance says as much about its owners' aesthetic tastes as about the extent of their responsibilities to the land on which they have settled."   —George Plimpton, "Introduction" to
The Hamptons: Long Island's East End

It would be impossible to introduce any historical or contemporary study of the Hamptons without starting from the land itself. Natural historians have raved about the many ecological characteristics unique to Long Island's East End.[1] A great glacier's impact on the area's topography left behind a cornucopia of environmental superlatives: soft, sandy beaches and brisk ocean waves, smooth rolling hills and sparkling kettle ponds, thousands of acres of dense pine forests, large expanses of good soil, and calm, protected bays. These geological elements encouraged flora and fauna of all sorts, and fertile hunting and gathering made the region a popular seasonal stop for the earliest Native Americans in the region. Thus, even before the Ronkonkoma Moraine settled into its postglacial shape, human beings had begun to interact with the natural landscape, modifying its processes of change and building their own economic and cultural connections to the land.

The earliest European visitors were similarly impressed by nature's economic offerings, first thriving in hunting, fishing, and agriculture and eventually building a whaling industry that thrust local commercial and social life into the full embrace of a world economy. The Europeans' approach to natural resources differed greatly, however, from the Native Americans' more integrated spiritual and cultural links to land and economy. The historian John Strong argues that the "Europeans dismissed Native American culture with its emphasis on communal values and spiritual harmony . . . [it was] an annoying encumbrance on Europeans' God-given mission to tame the land and to honor God by producing a bountiful surplus of material goods."[2] By the mid-seventeenth century, the landscape of Long Island's East End would be shaped not only by the natural forces of sun and wind and waves but also by the conflicts and tensions among people with avowedly different ideas about how to "use" the land.

Such conflicts over land use and its attendant cultural politics would become a prevailing theme for each wave of new populations to the region. Migrants would come to the East End and, over time, metamorphose from explorers or vacationers, to fur traders or seasonal homeowners, to settlers or year-round residents, to founders or locals, their ultimate goal to become natives. And, while each wave brought its own significant transformations in regional economics, politics, and culture, almost every period of change featured the same discursive tendency—the apocalyptic declaration of an "end to the Hamptons." This chapter traces the stories of these successions, the conquests and resistance that marked these conflicts, and the cultural politics and discourse that shaped each period's own historical narrative.

LOW TIDES: MONEY LENDERS AND KING MAKERS

Native Americans first settled parts of Long Island during the early and middle Woodland Periods, between 3,000 and 1,000 B.C. Although most of these habitats were small and considered migratory, many native peoples settled for varying periods of time near estuaries, harbors, ponds, and other bodies of calm, yet bountiful waters. Eventually, a variety of new technologies (pottery design and projectile points used for hunting), new trade networks, and the development of what Strong calls a "forest-efficient" economic system that provided inhabitants with a source of food, medicines, and the raw materials for basket weaving and textiles all combined to provide a stable habitat for Algonquian peoples.[3]

The area's residents continued to expand and improve these systems and materials of production throughout the late Woodland Period, from 1000 B.C. to around 1600 A.D. Strong claims that "all of the evidence from various sources clearly indicates that the native peoples here had developed a very successful life way in harmony with the environment. They established a balance between domesticated and wild food sources which sustained them through the seasonal round." Close attention to negotiating open spaces, community growth, and changing social practices enabled Algonquians to thrive economically and politically while maintaining a sense of cultural integration and identity with the natural world. Strong concluded, however, that the "rich heritage and landscape the Woodland horticulturalists had received from their ancestors remained intact, but their own descendants would not be so fortunate."[4]

By the early 1500s, European contact began to impact the patterns of economic and social life among the Indians on Long Island. Dutch explorers and traders such as Henry Hudson, Adrian Block, and Peter Barentsen all visited the lands and waters of the Island's East End, and soon a host of trading activities dominated the budding relationship between residents and visitors. The Dutch were the first to invest significantly in the Europeans' "new world," but the English quickly contested land and trade rights. Both groups recognized the economic potential of the fur trade but needed an effective way to rationalize and control economic relationships with Native Americans. After all, Native Americans were not accustomed to a capitalist cash economy or to the ideas of commercial trade for profit. Somehow, Europeans had to communicate a new economic system of production and distribution through some already understandable set of trading practices. Wampum fit the bill.

Made from quahog clam and whelk shells, wampum already functioned as a form of exchange among Indian groups, but it did not dominate or even heavily characterize their economic system. There is little evidence that extensive wampum production predated European contact; it existed as one exchange mechanism among many. In fact, because Native Americans had cultural frameworks for exchange that were fundamentally different from those used by Europeans of the period, scholars have argued that wampum had never represented a form of money per se but had a variety of diplomatic, spiritual, and social connotations for Indian tribes. For Europeans, however, wampum stood as a perfect solution to the need to communicate and eventually impose a different economic system on the area's original residents.[5]

Long Island's East End possessed the appropriate conditions for making wampum, and Europeans provided metal drills called "muxes" to increase production. According to the anthropologist Lynn Ceci, "Europeans used wampum as (1) a trade commodity to be exchanged for the valuable furs of Indians in the interior, and (2) legal tender, because sound metal coinage was lacking in the early colonies."[6] It worked so well, in fact, that it became acceptable currency in both English *and* Dutch colonies. Thus, while strings of wampum may have had a variety of uses as a *kind* of money for Native Americans, they became a major source of economic currency for Europeans who needed to establish a foothold in a traditional "native" economic system at the same time that they promoted a new economy. The beaver trade and wampum production were primary factors in introducing Native Americans to, and ensconcing them in, cash-based commercial capitalism. By the time of the East End's first significant English settlements, in the mid-1600s, previous European visitors had already initiated powerful changes in the land.

Native Americans, however, should not be viewed as either passive observers or ignorant victims in this process. Throughout the 1500s and early 1600s, Native Americans actively participated in commercial and political negotiations with European traders, officials, and militia. While their own set of cultural values and social beliefs could not have prepared them to understand the depth of their eventual defeat by the Europeans, it is clear that many Native peoples participated actively in the changing economic and political systems. Some Indians received many economic benefits from trade relations and appreciated European

This painting by C. S. Reinhart depicts Lion Gardiner at war with the Pequot Indians in 1637. Two years after defeating them in a series of brutal conflicts, Gardiner received land from England's Lord Sterling and became one of East Hampton's founding proprietors. (*Long Island, Our Story*, 1998)

tools and other commodities. This was especially true when they facilitated wampum production, which had become a lucrative enterprise for some Native Americans. Other Native groups believed they could use European allies to help in regional political struggles with other Indian nations. This strategy became increasingly popular, yet treacherous, as the English, competing with the Dutch for power in North America, pursued a much more aggressive military policy for acquiring land in New England and New York.[7]

The most famous example of such strategies on the East End concern the Montaukett Sachem Wyandanch, who negotiated a variety of trading and land deals with the English, primarily in conjunction with military leader Lion Gardiner. After instigating, and then eventually conquering, the Pequots in a brutal war, in 1637, the English proceeded to settle the Connecticut Valley area. According to Strong, Wyandanch saw an alliance with the English as an important strategic defense against the Niantics, who were seeking to bring Long Island and its tribes under their own sphere of influence. Led by Wyandanch, eastern Long Island sachems signed the Hartford Treaty with the United Colonies of New Haven, Plymouth, Massachusetts Bay, and Connecticut, eventually inviting Gardiner to establish a settlement on Manchonat Island—which the English commander immediately renamed "Gardiner's Island."[8]

Within a decade of the treaty that had given the colonial government "exclusive rights of purchase," the United Colonies bought a

The 1948 cover of the *Ladies Village Improvement Society Cookbook* remembers a much less bloody conquest than that depicted in the Reinhart painting. (Photo courtesy of East Hampton Library)

thirty-one-thousand-acre parcel of land between Southampton and Na-peague Bay in an area that would eventually become East Hampton. Again, this deal may have appeared to the sachems as a favorable transaction (they received coats, mirrors, hatchets, knives, and other goods), especially since they thought they retained rights for hunting, fishing, gathering, shell collection for wampum, and other usage. Yet, the agreement did state that Indians *gave up* all rights and interest in the parcel. When the governors sold the land to settlers, the new arrivals as-serted complete political control over the territory. Eventually, the transaction would, in Strong's words, mark a "crucial turning point in the history of the Montauketts": in return for easy access to European goods, they lost almost complete control over their own economic and political affairs. Thus, as important as currency transformation may have been for reshaping Native American culture, ideology, and econ-omy, nothing changed their society more than losing access to, and con-trol over, the land.[9]

An interesting element in this process of land usurpation and change was the role played by Wyandanch and other sachems. Just as wampum had become a mediating mechanism for European economic intervention, sachems played a mediating function for the Europeans' increasing political control. Although sachems did stand as representa-tives for their tribes, they generally ruled through persuasion. The Montaukett and the Shinnecock, like most of the regional tribes, had so-phisticated and participatory forms of self-government that prohibited the kind of oligarchic and authoritarian forms of political control com-mon among Europeans.[10] The historian Jill Lepore argues that the Eng-lish translated the word "sachem" (inaccurately) to mean "King." She explains, "The English called many prominent Indian leaders 'kings,' partly in recognition of the sachems' very real political authority and partly as a result of the colonists' overestimation of that authority . . . 'king' might have seemed a fitting, if not entirely satisfactory, transla-tion of 'sachem.'"[11]

For Europeans, negotiating land deals with Indian groups would have been difficult without an authoritative Native American leader. It was even more logistically challenging to maintain the parameters of these deals following their completion. Many Native Americans did not understand land use restrictions that had resulted from their deals with the English and accidentally broke the new rules. Sometimes, Indians openly resisted these laws. Regardless of the Indians' intent, tensions arose as they frequently violated the provisions of land transactions. The expansion of European settlements and their agricultural enterprises only intensified these conflicts. To effectively enforce property restrictions among Indians, government officials relied on sachems to serve as liaisons to local Native communities. Thus, it is possible that the European "confusion" over the political authority of sachems may have been less about cultural misunderstandings and more about political strategies for control.

Such tactical intentions seem most evident in a 1655 agreement between East Hampton officials and Wyandanch in which the English refer to the Montaukett sachem as the "Chief Sachem of Long Island." Wyandanch had become a crucial partner for the English as an effective arbitrator of local conflicts among Indians and between Indians and Europeans. During what Strong calls the period of "accommodation," a variety of conflicts and skirmishes arose over economic and cultural practices. Expanding animal husbandry among the settlers led to their encroachment on Shinnecock and Montaukett hunting grounds and food storage areas. Europeans tried to impose social restrictions on Native Americans by outlawing powwows and other religious rituals while simultaneously ordering, in East Hampton, that "noe Indian shall travel upp & Down or carrie any burdens in or through our towne on the Sabbath Day & whosoever bee found soe Doeing shall be liable to corporall punishment unto the nature of the offense."[12] Whenever East End Indians either wittingly or unwittingly transgressed European laws or customs, Wyandanch was perceived as a useful mediator who could persuade or convince his people to defer.

Wyandanch should not, however, be characterized as simply a tool of European conquest. Wyandanch often defended Native practices and was a strong advocate in European-dominated settings for the legal rights of the Montaukett and the Shinnecock. He represented local Indians in court and successfully negotiated economic and political treaties that enhanced native residents' share of certain resources. Nonetheless, by the time of his death, in 1659, the period of accommodation had ended and that of subjugation had begun. Dominant sachems were no longer necessary to mediate relationships, since Europeans' ascendant power was now almost complete. Thus, Strong concludes, "The last four decades of the seventeenth century saw a disastrous decline in the Algonquian population on Long Island." As a result of military defeats and disease, the "balance of power shifted to favor the Europeans," who asserted their power and intensified the process of dispossession. Sachems, like wampum, would eventually fade from the center stage of European-Native encounters.

By the end of the seventeenth century and the beginning of the eighteenth, European control over the burgeoning whaling industry had proved to be the proverbial last straw for Native American power. Although local Indian whalers maintained a modicum of negotiating strength because of their position as skilled whalers, the ability of the English to control economic rules and regulations eventually reduced Native Americans to a disempowered working class. The Shinnecock and Montaukett became reliant on an economy controlled by the English, lived on land primarily regulated by the English, and were subject to new hegemonic social practices and values grafted onto the cultural landscape by this European economic and political power. Although the struggles of Native Americans on the East End continue up until today, they are still characterized mostly by the near totality of their defeat. For many, the Hamptons had ended when Wyandanch departed as the last "Great Sachem."

RISING TIDES: THE ARISTOCRACY COMES EAST

The next group to conquer the East End was initially not much interested in the land's economic benefits. In fact, waves of wealthy summer colonists came in the late nineteenth century in search of a place to "get away from it all." Like many a bohemian pioneer, Walt Whitman came to the East End, and his rhapsodies about a relatively "unspoiled" region of "terraqueous" men and women provided part of the clarion call for an adventurous elite in search of a new summer resort. In the mid-1870s, Whitman wrote a series of articles for the *Brooklyn Standard* newspaper in which he described the East End's natural beauty for a New York City audience that had "never seen Montauk with their bodily eyes, or trodden on thy greensward." To counter what he believed to be a misperception that the area was "dry and sterile," Whitman declared it as "fertile and verdant," with rich soil, green and plentiful grass, and bountiful "patches of Indian corn and vegetables . . . within gun shot of the salt waves of the Atlantic." Even to his "unscientific eyes," he continued, "there were innumerable wonders and beauties all along the shore, and edges of the cliffs, . . . earths of all colors, and stones of every conceivable shape, and hue, and density, with shells, large boulders of a pure white substance, and layers of smooth round pebbles called 'milk-stones' by the country children."[13]

More notable, however, is the impact that such a natural state had on the behavior of Whitman and his cohort. Freed from the restraints of civilized, urban life and its restrictive sensibilities, the group of vacationers climbed hills and raced down, "pranced forth again, like mad kine, we threw our hats in the air, aimed stones at the shrieking seagulls, mocked the wind and imitated cries of various animals in a style that beat nature all out." The romp continued:

> We hopped like crows; we pivoted like Indian dervishes; we went through the trial dance of *La Bayadère* with wonderful vigor; and some one of our party came nigh dislocating his neck through volunteering to turn somersaults like a circus fellow. Everybody caught the contagion, and there was not a sensible behaved creature among us, to rebuke our mad antics by comparison.

The East End would come to represent a counterurban landscape where all that symbolized the burgeoning economic and social life of the monied metropolis could be stripped away like sweaty clothes along the sandy shore.

Whitman was not the only artist-pioneer to begin paving the trendy way east for New York City's elite. In 1878 and 1879, *Scribner's Monthly* ran articles about the Tile Club, a noted group of artists from New York City, "at Play" in the Hamptons. Composed of eleven American artists whom the historian Helen Harrison has described as "a bohemian group by conventional standards," the Tile Club came in search of "a wild outpost at the farthest reaches of East Hampton . . . [and] found 'noble amphitheaters of tree-tufted mountains, raked by roaring winds, [which] caught the changing light from cloud-swept heavens; all was pure nature, fresh from creation.'"[14] Quickly, the Hamptons became touted as an "American Barbizon," alluding to the village outside Paris where French painters went to find a bucolic muse. In 1884, the landscape artist Thomas Moran and his artist wife, Mary Nimmo, built the area's first studio-residence. Meanwhile, William Merritt Chase established the Shinnecock Summer School of Art in 1891 and built his own studio-residence nearby. Harrison concludes that by the "turn of the twentieth century, both East Hampton and Southampton had settled comfortably into their roles as artists' retreats."[15]

Although these forays east inspired artists to capture the landscape's wild purity on canvas, it also inspired their (and others') business acumen. Chase's summer classes became incredibly popular, and the resulting financial benefits helped him overcome serious debt. Many of the area's new artists went from having exhibitions at various halls and other open spaces to opening their own galleries. The most entrepreneurial of the Tile Club, however, may have been William McKay Laffan. Laffan worked for the Long Island Railroad (LIRR), which had recently extended its services to eastern Long Island. In a LIRR brochure intended to "promote tourism and encourage settlement," Laffan wrote, "No lovelier stretch of country, none more pleasing to the eye of the artist or poet, none more peaceful and poetically happy in its outward expression, or more varied and interesting in its contour and color, is to be found anywhere along our Eastern Coast."[16] Such descriptions would help the LIRR increase tourism and trade throughout the region.

The historian Alastair Gordon suggests that "Laffan's conflict of interest—between appreciation and exploitation—would become something of a tradition as the area grew in popularity." Certainly, such rhetoric and publicity strategies helped fill the boarding houses and the newly converted "inns" in the early summers of the 1880s. But, given the burgeoning capitalist hegemony of the late nineteenth century, it seems just as likely that Laffan's work in advertising was a harbinger of an increasingly commercialized aesthetic where capturing landscapes was *always* infused with a sense of property acquisition, partly symbolic but powerfully suggestive of a real shift in land use. Those who purchased East End art and became benefactors of this increasingly "landed" set of bohemians filled the parlors of their metropolitan mansions with work inspired by East End muses. The wealthy maintained their parlors almost exclusively for "references to learning, art, nature, and family continuity." Such an aesthetic created a "powerful symbol of [their] shared cultural values." According to *Scribner's Monthly*, the parlor was a place where "no merely useful item is permitted, [it is always overcrowded . . . everything bought for show goes here.]"[17] Initially, images of the Hamptons went west bringing symbols of nature and power

Frederick Betts pursued historical authenticity by naming his summer cottage Moncamato after a Native American who signed the original "deed" with Southampton's first English settlers, in 1640. (Photo courtesy of Southampton Historical Museum)

to the parlors of New York City's elite. Eventually, however, this new bourgeoisie itself would come east.

By the 1890s, the East End was competing with the opulent mansions of Newport, Rhode Island, and with the elite casinos and racetracks of Long Branch, New Jersey, as an up-and-coming summer resort. Yet, what initially made the East End desirable was its distinction as "unspoiled." The art critic Charles DeKay compared the Hamptons to other elite vacation colonies, explaining that "People have so far avoided the absurdity of repeating in Summer the same things they do in Winter." He sighed in relief that one could still "bathe without caring for looks or asking what is the correct thing in bathing suits." Similarly, Laffan exhorted, "These Hamptons are no hackneyed watering-places, and the people who want the glitter and excitement of Long Branch or Saratoga are solemnly warned away from here."[18] The East End not only stood in juxtaposition to the trappings of urban industrial society but also challenged the luxuriant and highly ritualized aristocratic order of other summer colonies. It seemed rugged and unspoiled and promised to be a perfect example of what the rapidly urbanized elite wanted *nature* to be—a real seasonal respite from both capitalist production and elite leisure consumption. Thus, Whitman concludes, "it must be confessed that the east end of Long Island, for summer journey, affords better sport, greater economy, and a relief from the trammels of fashion, beyond any of the fashionable resorts or watering places, and is emphatically a good spot to go to."[19]

But, by the early decades of the twentieth century, the Hamptons had become a *primary* summer place for New York City's rich and famous, and they wanted more than just a respite. As the historian Neston Sherrill Foster described the process, summer visitors went from "borders to builders," acquiring land from both "native" or "original" families and early speculators. Soon the descendants of European "settlers" were advertising in New York City papers to sell property. Some developers had purchased East End real estate as soon as the LIRR reached Greenport, on the North Fork, in 1844. Most serious investors, however, expanded their speculating when the train reached Sag Harbor, Westhampton Beach, Bridgehampton, and Southampton, on the South Fork, in the 1870s. While East End summer "cottages" were still more modest than Newport's Rosecliff or Breakers mansions, they sprouted rapidly in the late 1880s and 1890s. By 1920, however, a marked change had occurred in the "character of the houses erected"; as *Southampton* magazine reported, "people no longer built 'cottages' here but instead built 'summer residences.'"[20] Having conquered the board rooms and banking houses of urban capitalism, New York's elite went east to stay. They no longer bought paintings *of* nature for metropolitan mansions; they built new parlors in the midst of nature itself.

And, as the seasonal population of wealthy metropolitans reached a critical mass, cultural institutions catering to their tastes also dotted the landscape. The historian Robert MacKay claims that Eastern Long Island "met all of the criteria" for becoming *the* primary summer resort, including "ease of access to the nation's social economic and media capital, the development of recreational pursuits for the founding of the leisure class, and a collateral movement that proceeded apace, namely the founding of clubs around these sporting interests."[21] Southampton's Meadow Club opened in 1879 and by 1908 "boasted thirty lawn tennis courts and two squash courts." The Maidstone Club of East Hampton incorporated in 1891, hosted golf and tennis matches, as well as teas, banquets, and a variety of summer social events. That same year, Stanford White, Gilded Age architect extraordinaire, built the Shinnecock Hills golf course and clubhouse. Eventually, summer colony money would finance libraries, museums, and, in 1912, the completion of Southampton Hospital. In 1929, East Hampton's Guild Hall was finished, with a gallery, small theater, gardens, and other cultural amenities. Although the Hall's primary donors, the Woodhouses, wanted it used "by year-round residents, not the summer colony," more than two-thirds of those who joined the Guild Hall committee "wintered elsewhere." The urban elite's seasonal residence was short, but its impact on the physical and cultural landscape would be permanent.[22]

Yet, just as the East End's native population, the Shinnecock, had not been completely passive victims, neither was the next generation of "Yankee natives" without a role in paving the way for new conquerors. Despite their early "standoffishness," "locals" recognized that the summer colony and its burgeoning aristocracy brought in dollars. By 1891, the *East Hampton Star* newspaper ran an article imploring residents not to "spare any efforts to attract the city people to our town. Those contemplating taking summer borders during the coming season are asked to furnish in writing to the nearest station agent, all details—for incorporation in a pamphlet of Long Island boarding houses to be issued by the Long Island Railroad."[23] These tourists promised substantial economic benefits to locals, because they required dawn-to-dusk services: meals, transportation, cleaning and laundering, child care, and so on. Women were especially positioned to take advantage of this seasonal economy as they opened up their homes as boarding houses and catered to the needs of summer visitors.[24]

Eventually, farmers and landowners would make significant sums by selling off property to wealthy urban migrants for their summer cottages. Throughout the 1890s, the *East Hampton Star* even featured a regular column, "Building at East Hampton," which documented the progress of various contractors as they erected bigger and bigger seasonal homes throughout the region. Meanwhile, many of the East End's oldest European-American families started businesses that catered to the service needs of the growing seasonal set. According to Everett Rattray, "the vacation industry raised the demand for architects, builders, carpenters, plumbers, stores and services of every description."[25] In local publications like the *Star*, *Southampton* magazine, and *The Long Island Magazine*, Yankee families such as Bishop and Ellston advertised their painting and decorating shop; Havens and Wilde announced their team of carpenters and builders; R. H. Corwith listed his electrician's business, and Frank Corwith his pharmacy. The summer colony would forever change the Hamptons' economic and agricultural landscape, but not without the active participation of those who had conquered the land before them.

This transformation had a high price, however, not the least of which was increasing development that altered the "isolation and ruggedness" that had attracted the "bohemian pioneers" in the first place. Some of the original summer visitors decried the changes instigated by the rising flood of residential aristocrats and the expanded services they required. A letter to the *East Hampton Star*'s editor protested plans to introduce electric lights to East Hampton, in 1899: "There is no reason because a 'boom' has struck East Hampton, why at once it should be necessary to turn it into a typical up to date American village . . . with arc lights, trollies, cobblestones, and terrible architecture." Yet, this naysayer's prophesy that such trends would be the "last straw," forcing those who loved "East Hampton as it is" to sell summer cottages fast and cheap, could not have been more wrong. Summer residence construction increased during the first two decades of the twentieth century, so much so that both East Hampton and Southampton had regular "datelines" on the society pages of New York City newspapers.

Still, this naysayer's sentiment would become widespread in the face of rapid development as more residents with more money inspired upscale services, merchandisers, and an infrastructure of better roads, sewerage, and electricity. DeKay worried about these "modern improvements," wondering, "How long will Montauk preserve its savage loneliness and grandeur? East Hampton its noble village street? The north woods their shady, sandy solitudes? Sag Harbor its air of an old whaling port?" In response, he suggested forming an organization to "keep some control of roads and bicycle paths and wayside streets [and] have a word to say when property owners through greed or mere lack of sense start to destroy the natural beauty of the country."[26] By the late 1920s and early 1930s, many of the original artists and aristocrats saw the Hamptons as a place that had been irrevocably spoiled by overdevelopment. A new wave of conquerors had conquered but now lamented the impact of their triumph. The Hamptons they had known, or at least wanted to know, were gone.

HUDDLED MASSES ON THE SHORE:
IMMIGRANTS COME EAST

Other forces, however, also transformed the area's economic and social character, as new, less conspicuous conquerors came to the Hamptons. At the same time that New York City's rich and famous imported their cultural tastes and financial power to the East End's physical landscape, the region's largest wave of European immigrants arrived. Between 1880 and 1890, the foreign-born population of Suffolk County doubled from about 5,500 to 10,000. Between 1890 and 1910, it would double again to more than 21,000. The immigrant population nationwide grew so significantly during this same period that the 1910 U.S. Census divided the "native born" white population into three categories: native white persons of native parentage, native white persons of foreign parentage, and native white persons of mixed parentage. The foreign-born population and the native population born of foreign or mixed parentage together accounted for almost 45 percent of Suffolk's 1910 population of immigrants or children of immigrants. By 1920, not only had the region's foreign-born population reached almost 24,000, but native-born children of foreign parents numbered more than 30,000. Thus, the total population of immigrants and children of immigrants (most of whom came from Germany, Italy, Poland, Russia, or elsewhere in Eastern Europe) was well over 50,000, or almost half of the county's population. Many of these immigrants worked for the larger farming families in the area, but others took advantage of the growing, summer colony–inspired service economy that provided opportunities in domestic work, building and carpentry, landscaping, and myriad skilled crafts and seasonal labor.[27]

This new working class's experiences, however, would be greatly different from the conditions that had characterized class formation for an earlier set of Native and African American laborers. Although these new immigrants would face a variety of explicit and implicit forms of ethnic discrimination, the fact that they were white would ultimately prove to be an advantage as they sought to improve their position in a society that privileged whiteness. To transform themselves from immigrant to white American required significant efforts, but these newcomers were aided by many beneficial historical forces. One important historical condition was the potential for economic gain at the beginning of the twentieth century.

Despite the obvious hard work performed by many immigrants, such efforts did not distinguish them from Native and African workers upon whose labor the area's hugely successful whaling industry had been built during the eighteenth century. Instead, specific historical, social, and economic conditions greeted these new immigrants and facilitated their upward mobility. In agriculture, Polish, Italian, and some Jewish immigrants were aided by the availability of relatively inexpensive land and high crop yields and high crop prices that characterized the late 1910s and early 1920s. Numerous articles appear in the *East Hampton Star* announcing, "Farms Still Cheap," "potatoes pay well," "L.I. Spuds Soar to $4.50," and "never before, even in pioneer days, could a man buy a good farm in this state and make it pay for itself as quickly as is possible today." Polish farmers were especially successful in pooling family resources and purchasing large tracts of land in Riverhead and in Bridgehampton. For example, in December 1920, Antone Zaleski, "one of the young Progressive Polish farmers in Riverhead Town," purchased the highest priced farm to that date—eighty acres for $37,000. Another Polish farmer, Dominik Andrewskewiz, bought a forty-acre farm for $18,000. Zaleski's purchase gave him "160 acres of excellent farm land" for someone "only 39 years old."[28]

Italian farmers received significant help from a series of farms developed by Hal B. Fullerton, of the Long Island Rail Road. Initially a publicist, Fullerton wanted to prove that the vast lands along the eastern portion of the LIRR could be economically viable for agricultural production. "The main problem," according to the historian Salvatore LaGumina, "was to induce people to raise crops in sections of the Island that were deemed poor farmlands." LaGumina argues that Italians' success represented two converging dynamics: (1) they had already become a huge part of the low-wage labor force in Suffolk County, and (2) they had experience farming vegetables in difficult soil in Italy. Fullerton favored Italian laborers for his farms because they had proven themselves to be good workers while building the LIRR extensions. After some bad experiences with "native" white workers, Fullerton exhorted, "The Islanders must be replaced by the manual mainstay of civilization; the sons of Sunny Italy must be secured." They, too, eventually, bought their own small farms around Suffolk County.[29]

While some Jewish immigrants purchased farmland as well, many began as peddlers. According to Helen Gerard's extensive oral history interviews of the East End's Jewish community, peddlers came to the rural villages selling goods from backpacks "until they could afford a bicycle, a horse, or a wagon and later a car." With enough savings, these salesmen could open their own stores, and Sag Harbor's Jewish business community was well known throughout the area. But many Jewish immigrants also came to work in the early industries of the East End, particularly the Fahys Watch Case Factory. Harold Fahys, himself Jewish, would send recruiters to Ellis Island in search of skilled Jewish workers. These efforts led more than forty Jewish families to relocate to the town. In 1900, the growing Jewish population established Temple Adas Israel in Sag Harbor. Covering its opening, the *Brooklyn Daily Eagle* wrote, "Twenty years ago, it would have been difficult to find a representative of the Hebrew race in Sag Harbor, but the establishment of Fahys watchcase factory has brought large numbers of Poles and Russian Jews to the village."[30]

Meanwhile, the popularity of the Hamptons with wealthy city folk had literally paved the way for a burgeoning immigrant population to find significant opportunities. Many Italian and other immigrants first came east on construction crews for the LIRR and to build the first major highways heading east from "up-island," such as the Vanderbilt Motor Parkway.[31] As the summer colony moved from renters to seasonal residents, they needed more domestic help, more permanent landscaping, and a host of specialty retailers. Immigrants from eastern and southern Europe provided many of these necessary services and much of the labor. In Sag Harbor, Jewish immigrants became so successful in retail, the *Eagle* reported, that "In business, the Jews have pushed rapidly to the fore [and] control the clothing and fruit trade . . . 15 large stores testify to their industry." Italian farmers opened up nurseries and truck gardens, while others looked for commercial space to establish small restaurants and grocery stores.

Besides representing hard work and economic success, however, these immigrant groups also created powerful social and political networks. Jewish immigrants not only established a synagogue in Sag Harbor but also started the Jewish Association United Brethren which bought land for a Jewish cemetery and sponsored many local programs for themselves and the larger civic community. Both Italians and Poles built their own churches (such as St. Isadore's, in Riverhead, and Our

Lady of Poland Church, in Southampton), as well as ethnic clubs and benefit societies. Perhaps the most important of these groups, however, were political organizations, such as the Italian American Voters and Taxpayers Association of Sag Harbor and the Polish Democratic Club of Cutchogue, on the North Fork. In the towns of Riverhead and Southold, Polish participation in politics increased rapidly during the 1930s and 1940s. As John "Stanky" Stankewicz recalled, "Being of Polish heritage, part of a wave of immigrants that took to farming on the North Fork in the early part of the last century, put you at a distinct social disadvantage. . . . The previous arrivals were only too happy to use the newcomers for cheap labor, but not inclined to allow them into their societies, workplaces and halls of government." The Club began in 1932 when, in exchange for publicly backing the Democratic ticket and forming under a new charter as the Cutchogue Polish Democratic Club, its members were "given" their own Polish policeman on the town force, Anthony Chituk.[32]

In the 1940s, the local Republicans in Riverhead and Southold were forced to place Polish-Americans on their ticket, and, by the 1950s, Poles were regularly elected to town offices. Italians also acquired political influence, especially on the South Fork. With this influence came more official jobs as many Poles and Italians joined previous immigrant groups in winning appointment to local police and fire departments, as well as to other positions in the rapidly expanding civil sector. Following World War II, previously ethnically based social and political organizations died out as more and more European-Americans were welcomed into mainstream groups such as the American Legion and the Veterans of Foreign Wars, as well as the Democratic and Republican parties. Thus, particular types of economic, political, and cultural self-activity among these ethnic groups helped them to assimilate. Still, other structural and ideological forces during the first half of the twentieth century created the context within which immigrant groups could take advantage of such activities to successfully forge new identities as "locals" or "natives"; as one Italian immigrant, Josephum "Jack" Ciochetti, said in the 1950s, after thirty-two years in the community, "I consider myself a 'bonacker.'"[33]

Throughout the United States, the post–World War I period witnessed a massive expansion of the public sector. Public schooling and civil service grew rapidly, in part to meet the increasing needs of burgeoning urban populations. But these public systems that provided for the collective consumption of education, transportation, health care, and other services were also part of an Americanization movement. Partly because of a push from successful radical labor unions and progressive politicians, and partly in response to fears over the cultural and religious differences represented by exploding numbers of new immigrants, the United States launched massive Americanization efforts between 1909 and the early 1920s. According to the historian Roger Daniels, the Americanization Movement:

> was an organized campaign to insure political loyalty and cultural conformity and enjoyed the support of most state governments and three federal agencies: the Bureau of Education, the Bureau of Naturalization, and after its establishment in 1917, the Committee on Public Information. Americanization programs ordinarily went far beyond instruction in English and civics to include training in personal cleanliness, middle class values, and discipline more appropriate to the factory than the classroom.[34]

The Hamptons participated in these efforts to assimilate immigrants, most notably in their support for New York State's "Americanization Sunday" program. In February 1921, the New York State Department of Education asked churches and other civic and secular institutions to recognize George Washington's birthday as "Americanization Sunday." In an interview with the *East Hampton Star*, Long Island's Americanization director, Alfred E. Rejall, explained, "There is perhaps no more fitting time to urge all our citizens to participate in the campaign of Americanization, loyalty and neighborliness. . . . There is no single problem facing our country at the present time of greater importance than that of the assimilation of the immigrant into our national life." Thus, for Rejall and for the movement, American citizenship and local identity or "neighborliness" went hand in hand. He continued: "There are many of your communities which have large numbers of foreign-born people. They work on your estates, on the LIRR, and on your farms and roads; many find employment in your industries which are growing rapidly." Rejall acknowledged that immigrant identities were shaped predominately by their economic positions as workers, but he maintained that the Americanization movement could bring immigrants into the cultural and political mainstream.[35]

Public schools would play a major role in this process. School budgets and classrooms expanded throughout the 1920s and offered students not only classes in civics to promote citizenship but a host of extracurricular activities (especially sports) that wove together a local identity that combined boosterism and civic pride with American patriotism. While New York State legislation provided for official programs such as "Americanization Institutes for training in English and citizenship," schools and communities offered increased support for civic associations and public festivals to promote the integration of Americanization with local identities.[36] In the Hamptons, Polish immigrants became noted for their prowess on the baseball fields, while Italian and German immigrant sons triumphed on the football field. The role of sports in helping immigrant groups to move from successful ethnic enclave to larger civic integration may be best demonstrated in the story of Bridgehampton-born baseball Hall-of-Famer Carl "Yaz" Yastrzemski Jr.

Yaz's father, a potato farmer, was also the star shortstop for the Bridgehampton White Eagles, a team that began at the local Polish-American social club. "We used to hire bands and run dances," recalled Tom Yastrzemski, Carl's uncle and godfather. "We put the money we made into uniforms." As Carl explained, "Baseball was more than an outlet, it was a unifying force. It was a different environment then. . . . We all lived within a few miles of each other. My uncles would come over after work and pitch to me."[37] Eventually, however, athletics not only unified the Polish community but helped integrate the newcomers into the larger East End community. According to the journalist Joe Gergen, Southampton "revolved around sports in the postwar years." Carl Jr.'s baseball prowess brought success and recognition to the area as his Babe Ruth team won the state championship in 1953. At Bridgehampton High School, he led both baseball and basketball teams to Suffolk County championships. From the early 1920s to the post–World War II era, eastern and southern European immigrants benefited from both civic expansion and a growing ideology that connected local pride with patriotism as they sought to successfully assimilate and to achieve economic, political, and social success.

This is not to say that prejudice and discrimination did not exist. The same concerns over cultural and religious differences that fueled Americanization also stimulated a rise in anti-immigrant sentiments and fueled a burgeoning Ku Klux Klan movement in the 1920s. The

The Ku Klux Klan, and its women's auxiliary, parade in Eastport in the early 1920s. Its message linked racial supremacy with both patriotism and local boosterism. (Photo courtesy of Ron Ziel, personal archives)

most notable thing about Long Island Klan activities during this period was their connection of white supremacy to the growing sense of local boosterism and national identity. The KKK held rallies throughout Suffolk County, participated openly in civic associations and community celebrations, and counted three Republican County chairmen among its membership. It sponsored student scholarships and trophies at town fire department festivals in Riverhead and Southampton and ran (unsuccessfully) a slate of candidates in Sag Harbor. It bought gifts of flag poles for several municipalities and sponsored floats during Fourth of July parades. The Klan also tried to fuse its anti-immigrant, pro-white ideology into mainstream Americanism through its support of popular "law-and-order" programs, especially around Prohibition.[38]

One notable event occurred when a "special constable" and Klan member, Ferdinand Downs, was killed by bootleggers in Southampton. According to the historian Frank J. Cavioli, the KKK "seized the incident and converted it into their cause for Americanism." Cavioli explains that 2,250 people attended Downs's burial in East Quogue. One presiding minister "hailed Downs as a martyr," and a cross was burned. Meanwhile, Eastport High School participated in the group's march following the funeral, interrupting the academic day to allow students to "march between two rows of Klansmen" before returning to class. For Cavioli, this event "demonstrated the prestige and power of the Ku Klux Klan on Long Island."[39]

Eventually, Klan support waned, and by the late 1920s, few KKK activities gained much press or popularity. But in their attempts to forge an identity that melded whiteness and Americanness, the Klan was part of a successful ideological and cultural dynamic. In essence, where the KKK failed, more liberal Americanization programs succeeded in establishing the dominance of race in American culture. While the Klan's very narrow identification of patriotism and racial supremacy was spurned, a more inclusive civic identity that allowed new immigrants to assimilate into the dominant culture prevailed. In becoming local citizens and Americans, these immigrants also became white. Polish, Jewish, Italian and other new immigrants were eventually welcomed into the economic, political, and social strata of power in ways that Native Americans and African Americans had never been embraced. While the KKK failed to promote a more reactionary white supremacy, the Progressive Era's embrace of Americanization created a similar local and national identity that linked whiteness and Americanism.[40]

Today, the children and grandchildren and great grandchildren of this period's immigrants remember explicitly the hard work that enabled their families to "make it." While this sensibility often enhances what the sociologist Robert Bellah has called America's "myth of hyper individualism," it is clear that most of the "self-activity" among immigrant groups was collective in nature and that immigrants' practice of mutual support through churches, benevolent societies, social clubs, and economic and political organizations is what created their success. Still, without an expanding set of enabling economic opportunities, civic infrastructure, and cultural identities, it is quite possible that ethnic discrimination would have persisted in more vitriolic and enduring ways, eventually limiting that success. Instead, growing commitment to public education and organized school activities, formal and informal civic associations and events, the desire to harness immigrant political power, and a public discourse about Americanization opened the social, cultural, and political doors for this period's immigrants. The promotion of local boosterism and national identity further created a discursive framework within which immigrants became welcomed as "American" and "native." Even the KKK, in its attempts to discriminate against immigrants, actually enhanced the identification of American-ism with whiteness, a racial identity that these immigrants would claim as their own. In the end, these historical conditions allowed immigrants to fashion a local, American, and white identity that integrated eco-nomic opportunities and civic engagement and that allowed them, alongside the wealthy, to conquer the Hamptons.

All of these identity and cultural politics took place at a unique mo-ment in local history. A class structure based on race had already formed that anointed the descendants of Western European immigrants as the "settlers" and "founders" of the region. They controlled most of the land, the politics, and the economy. The descendants of Native Americans and Africans had become a segregated class of mostly un-skilled labor, although some had risen to the level of skilled, but often highly specialized, craft workers. As new waves of aristocratic migrants and working-class European immigrants changed the area's demo-graphics, new stratifications would be necessary. While whiteness on a national level was fused with a sense of Americanism, on a local level whiteness was divided between those European immigrants who could create *new* white identities and the descendants of the earliest European "settlers" who now claimed "white native" status to distinguish them-selves from both new immigrants and Manhattan's glitterati. In the late nineteenth and the first half of the twentieth century, new waves of human, as well as natural, forces reshaped the contours of the cultural and physical landscape, creating new social conditions out of which people in the Hamptons created identities for themselves and their communities.

HIGH TIDES: LEVITTOWN IN THE SAND

The post–World War II period brought more changes to the region. Global and regional forces produced a more economically, socially, and geographically mobile society. The rise of the automobile and the ex-pansion of highway systems combined with public efforts to build more leisure spots for an increasingly affluent and mobile middle class. In New York, the "power broker" Robert Moses directed planning poli-cies and development projects that brought an urban middle class "back to nature," albeit a more manicured and rationalized version of it. Moses's biographer Robert Caro describes Moses's visions:

He had noticed meadows back in those woods that seemed just made to order for baseball diamonds and level spaces with only a few trees that could be cleared for tennis courts. Why, a portion of the biggest tract, the one between Lynbrook and Rockville Centre, seemed almost made to order for a golf course. And why should people be restricted to looking at ponds and lakes? Why shouldn't they swim in them? Suddenly, the burning eyes were looking at everything on Long Island in terms of parks.

Moses's parks, beaches, and highways converted Long Island, first into an accessible "backyard" for public consumption and, eventually, into literal backyards in booming suburban residential developments. The idea of leisure itself changed, growing in significance as a meaningful, yet separate sphere for middle-class individual and family expression. The importance of leisure activities arose in reaction to the intensifying oppression of daily activities: women grew increasingly isolated in the home; men grew increasingly alienated at work, regardless of their specific blue- or white-collar job; and children were increasingly compartmentalized in standardized programs at school. Leisure in the post–World War II years would not be an escape so much as a new place where one could express one's "real" self. Nature, too, would be transformed—physically and culturally—as it became packaged as the site of this burgeoning middle class's consumption of leisure.[41]

While the growth of suburban life radically transformed Nassau and western Suffolk County in the 1940s and 1950s, the Hamptons, too, experienced the impact of this development and expansion. Initially, the post–World War II move east was led by another wave of bohemian painters and writers, this time driven by European émigrés such as Max Ernst, Andre Breton, and Lucia Christofanetti. Eventually, they were followed by surrealists and abstractionists such as Jackson Pollack, Lee Krasner, Willem de Kooning, and Le Corbusier. According to Helen Harrison, Pollack and Krasner would be a "magnet for their contemporaries . . . acting as unofficial real estate agents for colleagues." Meanwhile, the artist Robert Motherwell experimented in building studios and residences made of war-surplus Quonset huts.[42]

Suddenly, popular magazines and television "discovered" Long Island's East End one more time. Alastair Gordon argues that "eccentric artists made good copy." He continues: "The presence of artists legitimized the place for weekend visitors and established the foundation blocks for a kind of urban culture that would be transplanted from the city to the rural setting. . . . [The area] was being sold as a cultural melting pot." And once again, the initial bohemian pioneers who had arrived *first* (this time in the 1940s and early 1950s) began to decry the "flood" of newcomers in the late 1950s and early 1960s (this time journalists, photographers, editors, psychiatrists, advertising executives, and television people) as inevitably "ruining" the area. The art critic Harold Rosenberg regretted that the Hamptons had become just like New York City, infiltrated by successive waves of new professionals, the worst of whom were "the architects . . . who did the most lasting damage and knew how to ruin paradise."[43]

Unlike the previous wave of Gilded Age seasonal elites whose summer fun had been splashed across the society pages of urban newspapers, a burgeoning television culture promised to make the new Hamptons more democratic and accessible to the masses. Within the context of greater affluence, expanding highway and commuter rail systems, increased leisure time, and a growing public desire for "consuming nature," the East End's summer colony rapidly turned into a "weekend" and "summer tourist" community. The "second home urge" spread east along the Long Island Expressway and the LIRR, and, by the 1960s, the "affordable beach-house market" had reached the Hamptons. The Hamptons seemed to expand in two ways. First, those coming east now came from Brooklyn, Queens, and Nassau County, as well as from Manhattan. Second, more affordable towns like Montauk and Hampton Bays became increasingly popular places for "up-island" vacationers interested in fishing, boating, and beach holidays. New waves of a socially and geographically more mobile, yet frustrated middle class came to "play hard" in the Hamptons.

In part, these new migrants' desires for an active leisure culture were facilitated by new technologies and business plans. According to the sociologists Walter Kuentzel and Thomas Heberlein, the boat-building industry itself had hit hard times after World War II and was seeking new markets. With the development of fiberglass hulls in the mid-1950s, boat manufacturers could "build less costly boats requiring less routine maintenance [and] sailing no longer required great wealth, and was mass-marketed by boat dealers to a broader range of people."[44] For Gordon, nothing epitomized the creation of "Levittown with sand" better than the success of the Techbuilt Company, whose modular beach

Peter Blake Beach House, 1960, a study in antibourgeois modernism for week-end conquerors. (Photo by Ezra Stoller © Esto)

houses had inspired his own middle-class family to buy land and build an "escape house" in Amagansett. One franchiser from Techbuilt, Edward Popisil, met annually with interested New Yorkers at the Plaza Hotel, in Manhattan. Over refreshments, he would explain the various designs and financing plans available to people who wanted to spend summer vacations in the Hamptons but who couldn't afford a summer colony residence or lifestyle. As a realtor, too, Popisil could provide *both* land and home, and he succeeded in selling around fifty Techbuilt houses on eastern Long Island during the early 1960s.[45]

What artist and poet pioneers like Whitman and the Tile Club had started in the 1870s and 1880s had eventually resulted in a boom in summer cottage construction for the first wave of wealthy Manhattan blue bloods. But the second wave of bohemian painters and writers, in the 1940s and 1950s, resulted in a different sort of flood. Changing class structures and technologies democratized the region's accessibility for both an urban and a suburban middle class. And the new professionals brought with them different expectations for a summer vacation. Gordon explains:

The sixties weekend had little to do with traditional notions of rural re-
pose. Instead, it represented a frenetic set of recreational options and
social opportunities. The dividing line between rural and urban became less and less clear. Everyone wanted to get away, but while so
many more were heading east to escape the pressures of New York
City, city and country began to merge in unforeseen ways. . . . The east
end could no longer be perceived as a string of small villages with
lovely beaches, rustic windmills, and eccentric artists. With more
houses, more media coverage, and extended highways, it was something different. The area had become the modern phenomenon known
as "The Hamptons."[46]

The evolving social meanings of "weekends" and "summers," just like
the shifting cultural notion of experiencing "nature," eventually
changed the East End and created a new "Hamptons."

For others, however, the new Hamptons meant the end of another
old Hamptons. Once again, previous migrants found the flood of new
arrivals distressing enough to warrant apocalyptic visions. The *East
Hampton Star*'s "Summer Colony" column officially declared 1969 "the
end of the summer colony."[47] Some of the strongest voices declaring the
end of the region's traditional culture and landscapes were the very
artists and writers who had come to the region in the years after World
War II. Peter Matthiessen, a writer who had come to the area during that
period and who worked for years with the haul-seining commercial
fisherman known as "baymen," lamented the changes that occurred
throughout the 1960s:

With the sudden rise in the value of the land, the peaceful atmosphere
of the South Fork began to change. The change developed like faraway
massed clouds in the northern sky, the first iron weather of winter
storm. Sagaponack was now the closest public beach to Sag Harbor,
and traffic down its main street increased quickly. Within a few years
the old Hildreth Store expanded its services to accommodate the
swelling rise of tourists, and the old village's quiet days were over. A
new rash of real estate speculators, entreating others to "share our heritage," discovered Sagaponack, where the smaller local farms, unable
to compete with huge agribusiness in the West, or survive the growing
tax on land inheritance, had begun to die. Even the oldest family farm

in the United States was sold off by the squabbling heirs, with most of the money, it was said, gone to lawyers.[48]

Just as past waves of conquering and conquered had performed the dance of historical rupture and continuity, so too would this new migration inspire another round of cultural and social politics about what would be gained and what would be lost on a newly changing landscape.

But Gordon and Matthiessen go too far in presenting the area's bucolic landscapes as fully transformed by the 1960s and 1970s. Well into the 1970s and 1980s, the East End remained much less developed than any other part of Long Island; it still possessed lovely beaches, rustic windmills, wide expanses of farmland and woods, and centralized commercial districts, primarily within comparably small villages. More notable, though, was how the power and permanency of these most recent changes in the land encouraged a strong environmental movement dedicated to the preservation of open space and planning for controlled growth. New coalitions formed to protect the local ecology. Similarly, both old and new migrants began promoting the importance of conserving and celebrating "traditional" cultures; in fact, this new "local" identity would offer a vitriolic response to the onset of increased middle-class tourism and weekend residents. While the "original" white native families remained entrenched in their positions, second-generation immigrants would now jostle to become "local," trying to distinguish *themselves* from the new and more "crude" waves of "city people" who brought a more "frenetic" and intrusive sense of metropolitan life.

Ironically, some of the greatest supporters of "saving" both traditional landscapes and cultures were those who had recently relocated to the Hamptons—not just the artists and writers or the flood of weekenders from the newly monied professional and middle classes but those New Yorkers who would make the East End their primary residence. Perhaps this could be considered the next bohemian wave, composed of people like Hal Ross, an economist and political operative, and Nancy Goell, an advertising executive, both of whom were attracted by the area's "peaceful surroundings and natural beauty." Soon after arriving permanently in the early 1970s, they got involved in local environmental politics—Ross through the East Hampton Democratic Party and Goell with the environmental organization Group for America's South Fork. While both participated in successful organizing campaigns that helped build coalitions among varied groups, it became clear that those who had migrated to the area not for the season or for weekends but to start a "new life" wanted to protect their conceptions of "natural landscape" and "rural character." What for Gordon (and many of the previous waves of conquerors and settlers) had already disappeared was for newcomers like Ross and Goebel still the dominant character of the area and possible to save. Their struggles to preserve the landscape fused with their own sense of creating a local identity.

And these struggles have characterized much of the social and political landscape during the past twenty-five years in the Hamptons. New people riding the waves of an expansive global economy continue to arrive on the shores of the East End. The rest of this book examines some of the cultural and political dynamics of these trends: the still prevalent agriculture fields transformed into farm views for mushrooming McMansion subdivisions and their telecommuting, exurban renegades; the Peconic County separatist movement that repackages old myths of rugged, Yankee independence as new myths about rural landscapes and lifestyles of the rich, famous, and somewhat socially responsible; a new crop of postindustrial aristocrats imposing the physical symbols of their wealth and culture on the area's potato-cum-polo fields and glossy society pages; the new Latino working class struggling to maintain a sense of dignity and identity in an increasingly hostile environment; an older Native and African American working class, also fighting for workers' rights and participating in social movements that challenge some of the traditional racial and class barriers in the area; and, finally, a contemporary land conflict between Shinnecock Indians and contemporary developers who hope to turn another swatch of land into a place where new migrants can become locals.

Yet, the Hamptons of today are not completely different from the Hamptons of the 1600s. The *New York Times* columnist Peter Cooke has gone so far as to quip: "Much of world history, if not all of it, can be seen as the Hamptonization of one place or another. English money Hamptonized the South of France. The Czars Hamptonized Tsarskoye Selo. The Pharaohs Hamptonized the lower Nile. . . . Boom follows bust; one man's beach is another man's blot upon the pristine sand." Cooke may, in fact, be right. But conquest is more than just an issue of bad taste or artistic differences. The history of the Hamptons has always been about power and the ability of those with power to use their resources to re-shape the land—economically, politically, and culturally. Contemporary struggles still represent the conflicts and tensions between waves of new and old, rich and poor, powerful and not-so-powerful. How people continue to fight for the power to impose their own sense of identity and quality of life on the social and political landscape will shape the contours of future struggles.

2

Houses in the Fields

New York City Moves East

What has happened in the South Fork over the last five years is not really any different, in fact, from what has happened in much of Manhattan. . . . Should development be allowed to continue on the argument that the land belongs to those who can afford it, that the best future for any community, rural or urban, is the one that occurs naturally when the free market is allowed to prevail?
— Paul Goldberger, *New York Times*, September 4, 1983

Maybe the whole thing was one of God's warnings. Why didn't he and Judy and Campbell get out of New York . . . and the megalomania of Wall Street? Who but an arrogant fool would want to be a Master of the Universe—and take the insane chances he had been taking? Why didn't they sell the apartment and move out here to Southampton year round?   — Sherman McCoy in *The Bonfire of the Vanities*, by Tom Wolfe (1987)

[The return of homeless people and squeegee men] suggest[s] to me that dealing with quality-of-life issues is like dealing with a garden lawn. Unless you constantly mow it, it's going to grow back.
— Eli Silverman, professor of criminal justice, quoted in the *New York Daily News*, August 13, 2000

Since 1996, our own district population has increased by approximately 20 percent. The Internet has fostered an employment mobility that has contributed and will continue to contribute to our own growth. . . . [F]amilies are moving out of New York City and up island to settle down in our area. They are attracted by the lifestyle.
— Candace Porter, publisher, *Landpaper*, summer 2001

Long before the Twin Towers fell on 9/11, New York City residents had tried to escape their apocalyptic fears of urban life.[1] In the late nineteenth century, concerns over congestion, filth, and crime inspired wealthier residents to create what Leo Marx called a "middle landscape" somewhere between the chaos, garbage, and immigrant-dense metropolis and the "uncivilized," "provincial," and "poor countryside."[2] Members of America's new ruling class found Long Island more appealing than their estates in Newport and their bungalows in Bar Harbor, Maine, primarily because of the Island's proximity to the city. As Baxandall and Ewen write, "their Long Island estates were ideal for the spring and fall season and many winter weekends."[3] Despite the cultural attractions of the city and the economic need to remain tied to city life, concern over urbanism's characteristic social problems led more and more people of means to seek refuge outside the city core.

While panics about the dangers of urban life sometimes appear to be cyclical, the post–World War II, white, middle- and upper-class exodus from New York City has had only a few interruptions. Bob Moses's parks and Bill Levitt's mass-produced "little boxes" inspired massive surges of midcentury suburbanization. The farms and fields of Nassau and western Suffolk counties would be overrun by subdivisions and strip malls, eventually becoming one of the nation's largest "nonurban" Standard Metropolitan Statistical Areas. Subsequently, this eastward sprawl would reach the Hamptons. But the relationship between New York City's elite and the reshaping of the Hamptons as an upscale suburban or "exurban" landscape is complex.

In part, the process represents forces fueled by a rapidly changing global economy that featured major financial market booms and an increasingly bifurcated economic growth pattern with big winners and big losers. Geographical shifts in economic production, labor markets, and worker migration also resulted in huge demographic swings such as growth in permanent residency among both wealthy whites and working-class Latinos. Add to these factors an intensified set of media-hyped urban horrors and new bourgeois fashions and lifestyles, and it becomes apparent that the Hamptons now stand at the juncture of contemporary social transformations. It is a place where people simultaneously flee from the ashes of the old economy and seek out the promises of the new economy.

Upscale urban flight and fluctuating class identities among the professional elite have resulted in a chaotic convergence of old and new. On the one hand, rural landscapes are reshaped by McMansion subdivisions clustered along the outskirts of old potato fields, while farms are more likely to raise horses for polo than crops for sale. These new landscapes represent the changing economy as agricultural land use shifts from producing vegetables to providing vistas. Yet, at the same time that old ways of life are supplanted by new residents and a new economy, the present wave of conquerors embraces nostalgia for traditional landscapes and ways of life, pledging their support to save the natural environment and cultural traditions. In fact, it seems that the very quality of life that wealthy newcomers want is partially wrapped up in maintaining a sense of the past. But, preserving "rural lifestyles" and "traditional values or character" looks increasingly impossible as migrants want all the "charm" of the past but demand the conveniences of the present.

Meanwhile, the same economy and technology that created both the newcomers' wealth and their ability to live in the Hamptons year-round have also intensified new immigration patterns. More and more Latinos from Central and South America (as well as Mexico) are moving directly to the Hamptons, filling the need for low-wage labor in construction, landscaping, and the growing service sector. Although these new workers facilitate and subsidize the cultural lifestyles of the area's wealthy residents, they also require adequate housing, health care, education, and other social services. The region's inability to meet the needs of these workers as residents has resulted in the kinds of urban problems that many bourgeois newcomers were trying to escape. Along with a bounty of natural beauty and rich history, the new Hamptons landscape also abounds in irony.

EMPIRE IN THE REAR-VIEW MIRROR

Long Island grew up rapidly as Moses and Levitt designed and manufactured a residential mecca for post–World War II white working- and middle-class residents. But it was New York City's steady economic, social, and physical decline that continued to fuel the migration from Manhattan to the "'burbs" long after the initial American dreams of Levittown life subsided. The persistent growth of urban ghettos and white flight in the 1960s and 1970s caused major financial shortfalls in New York City and serious cuts to city services. Strikes by police, fire fighters, teachers, hospital employees, and sanitation workers combined with deteriorating roads, bridges, schools, and other public buildings to foster the picture of a city literally falling apart. When, in 1975, the *Daily News* announced that the federal government would not rescue the city from default with its now famous headline "Ford to City: Drop Dead," many in New York believed the city already had.

The massive displacement of poor people following gentrification, deinstitutionalization, and the Reagan-era dismantling of the welfare state pushed New York into even more of a tailspin by the mid-1980s.[4] Despite a Wall Street boom, homelessness and poverty increased, and massive debts threatened to send New York City towards its second economic default in a decade. Mayor Ed Koch's (1977–1989) revitalization plan was clear—"kill it to save it." "Hizzonah" Koch engineered a serious shift in budgetary priorities away from capital investment in social services and public programs and toward private real estate development and prisons. He created massive tax and land giveaways to rich private-sector investors who destroyed low-income housing and renovated blighted areas by building upscale apartments and luxury office suites, eventually privatizing more and more public space.[5]

While the rich made out like bandits (sometimes literally), the poor got poorer.[6] Two local journalists, Jack Newfield and Wayne Barrett, contend that the "boom of the 1980s bypassed whole chunks of the city." During Koch's reign, the number of people living below the poverty line in New York City increased from 17 to 25 percent, and the homeless population grew to 60,000. Newfield and Barrett explain: "the high school drop out rate rose to 54 percent, AIDS became a plague; crack became an epidemic. . . . Manhattan was fast becoming the Ethiopia of the housing market, with a famine of rental apartments for the middle class and the working class starving for shelter. A city of scarce resources, dependent on its government to be honest and frugal, New York increasingly began to resemble a Dickensian city of extreme paradox."[7] Although Wall Street triumphs resulted in private investments for ever more gaudy and grandiose remakes of Gilded Age exhibitionism, the real show on New York City's streets looked much more like Hogarth's Gin Lane than Dickens's Drury Lane. Such, at least, is the claim of Tom Wolfe's fictional character, Gerald Steiner, a British-born media baron whose *City Lights* newspaper (a takeoff on

Rupert Murdoch's *New York Post*) covers the major plot line of Wolfe's best-selling 1987 novel, *Bonfire of the Vanities*. After listening to his reporter describe an encounter with "every sort of vice" in the stairway of a Bronx tenement, Steiner responds, "It's bloody Hogarth . . . Gin Lane. Except that it's vertical."[8] The building in question is home to a young African American teenager who gets run down by a wealthy Wall Street broker and his mistress, lost in the Bronx after taking the wrong exit while returning from Kennedy Airport. The incident sparks the novel's main series of events, which unravel to reveal the depths of New York City's decay. For Wolfe, the city is a divided world of racial segregation, economic extremes, and almost debilitating fear. Even "Masters of the Universe" (a nickname given to Wall Street's highest rollers) cannot avoid being pulled down into the detritus of late-twentieth-century capital exploitation, racism, aggressive ambition, and brutal despair.

In many ways, however, the novel's main character *is* New York City. Wolfe himself stated as much in a 1987 interview with the *New York Times*. He explained that, "although there is a central character, I always wanted in a way for the main character to be New York, and the way the city dominates its players and drives them to do reckless things." Frank Conroy referred to this kind of presentation as "Dr. Wolfe's urban laboratory of horrors," where the main character, Sherman McCoy, is a "carefully bred white rat . . . destined to run mazes and endure shocks for our edification and amusement."[9] New York City, then, is a sort of Skinner box for documenting social behavior. Wolfe contends that "people are always writing about the energy of New York. What they really mean is [people's] status ambitions. . . . That's the motor in this town. That's what makes it exciting—and it's also what makes it awful many times." While New York exerts the pressure, the drama emanates from the human response to it. But the driving force in the end, according to Wolfe, is power: "Money alone won't do . . . the ultimate certification of your status is seeing people jump, and New York is a city set up to see people jump."[10]

But, as many of the novel's critics have pointed out, the book is really about white, professional New York. No African American (or other minority) characters are ever given the position to narrate events or articulate their conditions. Despite the satiric scrutiny with which Wolfe depicts much of white, wealthy, professional New York, it is always *their* story. As Richard Eder describes it: "In the author's bonfire, everybody's vanities burn, but the vain themselves do not all burn equally. Some are allowed a glass of water."[11] Thus, when the criminal justice system's racialized class realities are exposed by Assistant D.A. Kramer's reference to minority defendants as "chow" and his admission that "It was not pleasant to go through life telling yourself, 'what I do for a living is, I pack blacks and Latinos off to jail,'" Wolfe never bothers to contest these images or to humanize the voices of nonwhite or working-class characters. In essence, Wolfe's novel about white New York depicts, and ultimately reifies, the complex structural and ideological systems that maintained the separation between "civilized Manhattan" and "the jungle."

Wolfe's book appeared at a particularly vulnerable moment for most New Yorkers. As bad as the city's bifurcated economic growth had been in the mid-1980s, the stock market crash of October 1987 resulted in worse circumstances for even more city residents. Suddenly private-sector investments disappeared: luxury office space and apartment vacancy rates, as well as unemployment and homelessness, hit post–World War II highs. Between 1985 and 1992, the *New York Times* alone published almost five hundred articles on homelessness, street crime, and an overall decline in the city's "quality of life." In June 1990, the *Times* columnist Ewa Zadrzynska wondered whether censoring the lyrics of 2 Live Crew's *Nasty as They Want to Be* made any sense in a city where homeless street people mistake "a crate on the sidewalk for a toilet" and brush their "hair with a metal fork."[12] Even *Time* magazine dedicated its September 16, 1990, issue to wondering whether New York City had become "the Rotting Big Apple." *Time* reported that almost two-thirds of New York City residents polled "would leave the city if they could choose where they would live."[13]

Politically, the social scientists Arian, Goldberg, Mollenkopf, and Rogowsky explain that the overwhelming media coverage of intense experiences with symptoms of urban decline resulted in New York voters turning toward promises of protection and security. According to a *New York Times*/CBS exit poll, the primary concerns of the city's electorate in 1989 were drugs (25 percent), crime (20 percent), and homelessness (19 percent). Given these statistics, Arian et al. point out that the victory of the Liberal-Democratic mayoral candidate David Dinkins was partial at best. They wrote: "Rudolph Giuliani came within a hair's breadth of making his own kind of history, becoming the first Republican mayor of New York in a quarter of a century . . . he would only have

had to recreate the relatively conservative white Catholic-Jewish alignment that has, to varying degrees, constituted a political majority in the
New York City electorate . . . [a] coalition that Edward Koch assembled,
and that Giuliani came so close to reassembling, remains implicit in the
New York City electorate."[14]

In 1993, Giuliani would defeat Dinkins, primarily by remaking just
such an alignment out of the 58 percent of voters who believed the city
to be even less safe than in 1989. Giuliani successfully realigned the
Koch coalition by creating an atmosphere where middle- and upper-
class white New Yorkers could vote on their racialized fears and animosity over a "loss in quality of life" while never openly having to
admit the racist implications of whom they blamed for its demise. New
crackdowns on poor people and people of color would be a major part
of restoring quality of life through Giuliani's "get tough on crime" approach.

The geographer Neil Smith has explained that the cultural and political significance of the mayor's "zero tolerance" policy was spelled
out in "Police Strategy No. 5," a document dedicated to improving
quality of life and "reclaiming the public spaces of New York." Smith
argues that the manifesto articulated two things: first, "a visceral identification of the culprits, the enemies who had indeed stolen the city
from the white middle class; and second, a solution that reaffirmed the
rights of the white middle class to the city." He concludes:

> Rather than indict capitalists for capital flight, landlords for abandon-
> ing buildings, or public leaders for a narrow retrenchment to class and
> race self-interest, Giuliani led the clamor for a different kind of re-
> venge. He identified homeless people, panhandlers, prostitutes,
> squeegee cleaners, squatters, graffiti artists, "reckless bicyclists," and
> unruly youth as the major enemies of public order and decency, the
> culprits of urban decline generating widespread fear.[15]

Ultimately, Giuliani enlisted longstanding emotional and social
baggage—fear, insecurity, and racism—to conflate physical and emotional safety and to create an argument in which, as Smith puts it, "the
symptoms *were* the cause." Initiated in 1994, Strategy No. 5 resulted in
the sentencing of thousands of petty criminals to long prison sentences
and the removal of thousands more homeless people from the streets,
sometimes to shelters, sometimes to prisons, and sometimes dumped in

whereabouts unknown. By "sanitizing the landscape," Giuliani promised to revitalize the metropolis as a "new city on the hill."[16]

By the late 1990s, Giuliani and others claimed victory and heralded serious improvements in the quality of life for New York's entitled middle and upper classes. A 1997 performance by the satirical musical group Capital Steps paid homage to the City's "perceived *improvements*" by voicing sarcastic reservations "that without its ubiquitous squeegee men and rampant graffiti, the city isn't as easy to disparage." They sang, "Nobody likes New York if there's no cause to complain," adding that the city could return to a more lampoon-friendly condition if only New Yorkers would "stop voting for mayors like [Giuliani]."[17] By 1999, according to Smith, even the "erstwhile liberal galleries applauded. . . . 'We're not suicidal liberals anymore,' announced one community activist turned anti-homeless crusader."[18]

But the signs of urban decline never disappeared completely—they were only temporarily obscured. Herr Giuliani's militia merely created a privatized, security-style landscape where architecture required higher walls and stronger fences; parks, street corners, and ATM machines needed constant police presence; and public life in general was dominated by what the sociologist Sharon Zukin calls the "aestheticization of fear."[19] Meanwhile, as poverty and homelessness continued to increase, no amount of policing could keep squeegee men and homeless people off the streets and out of the public eye. Although New York City cops claimed staggering increases in arrests for "quality of life crimes" between 1997 and 2000 (including a 15 percent increase from 1999 to 2000 alone), the *Daily News* reported that city residents were feeling a "subtle change" in the summer of 2000 that reminded them of the "bad old days" of urban blight. The paper explained, "To some, it's just a feeling, perhaps fueled by recent shootouts. . . . Others talk of random daytime attacks—like the mobs that assaulted 56 women after the National Puerto Rican Day Parade, or the two women attacked by brick-wielding homeless men this year—that seem to hearken back to a more menacing time."[20] Perhaps for the professional middle and upper classes, quality of life in the city is always under attack.

In the decade between 1990 and 2000, more than 16,000 new householders moved to the Hamptons. These people came primarily from New York City; some were from the suburbs of Nassau County and western Suffolk County, where Manhattan's urban sprawl had already brought with it the city's social problems. While many of the metropolitans who came to the East End were still seasonal residents, they began to spend more and more of their time away from New York City and its diminishing quality of life. In 1997, a *Times* reporter, Bruce Lambert explained, "People who began as occasional summer visitors are staying longer, into the 'shoulder seasons.' Part-time residents are becoming year-rounders. Renters are becoming owners."[21] According to Enzo Morabito, an East End realtor, more and more professionals began organizing offices in the Hamptons during the 1990s. He said, "they [New York City professionals] took advantage of better transportation, telecommunications, and would come out on Thursdays and leave for the city on Mondays. . . . Eventually they wanted to be here as close to full time as they could."[22] The only permanent solution to the persistence of Tom Wolfe's jungle was to escape, not just for the summer and not just for weekends but permanently, or at least as permanently as possible.

FROM "A PLACE" TO "THE PLACE" IN THE HAMPTONS

In 1998, Steven Gaines wrote the much publicized *Philistines at the Hedgerow: Passion and Property in the Hamptons*. While he avoided some of the gossipy qualities of previous "tell-all" Hamptons tales,[23] his focus on the rich and famous seriously skewed the area's portrait. Gaines argued that "Hamptons land lust" drove post–World War II changes on the East End as an increasingly new and status-hungry urban bourgeoisie sought an adequate showcase for its power and wealth. He declared:

> As the go-go eighties stock market pushed the Dow Jones toward the 2,000 mark for the first time in history, freshly minted millionaires were being pumped out daily. They were the cream of the baby-boomer generation: spoiled young urban professionals—stockbrokers, lawyers, junk-bond kings, financiers, and self-styled corporate raiders. The crop of brash "Masters of the Universe," as Tom Wolfe called them in *The Bonfire of the Vanities,* was seeking not only second homes but an arena within which to compete socially. . . . To own a home in the Hamptons was to have *arrived* . . . pockets stuffed with cash, a generation of arrivistes invaded the East End in numbers never before seen.[24]

This interpretation does have some merit, and I discuss various aspects of this "set's" cultural politics in chapter 4. But it is an error to represent today's Hamptons as simply an extension of Wolfe's Manhattan to which geography's primary role is to allow people with power to "express themselves" or "see people jump."

Gaines's perspective suffers from a few major flaws. First, he almost completely overlooks the fact that much of the area's *initial* postwar growth came from a burgeoning middle class as well as from a newly monied bourgeoisie. Second, he ignores the conditions that initially inspired *both* middle- and upper-class New Yorkers to perceive the Hamptons as more than just a site for leisure culture or as a secondary circuit for real estate investment, or simply as a status symbol. Thus, he misses the eventual transition of wealthy urban migrants from seasonal to year-round residents. Finally, Gaines completely ignores the burgeoning Latino population that has filled the low-wage, unskilled service and construction sectors. The contemporary Hamptons landscape is characterized by a growing number of migrants from all sectors of the economic spectrum who seek a particular and improved "quality of life" and increasingly make the area their primary place to live.

Gaines does acknowledge that the 1950s and 1960s saw massive growth throughout the South Fork, explaining that East Hampton's population grew 68.3 percent between 1950 and 1970. In fact, residential construction reached significant boom proportions throughout the area by the mid-1960s. In East Hampton, the number of housing structures more than doubled from 1960 to 1980, growing from just over 5,000 to well over 11,000. The 1970s saw an even greater increase as 3,300 more housing units were built, thus increasing stock by another 30 percent in only ten years. In Southampton, the boom had started even earlier as houses built between 1940 and 1960 increased the number of available units by almost 60 percent from 5,400 to well over 12,000. Between 1960 and 1980, this number doubled again to almost 25,000 housing structures in the town. In the 1970s alone, more than 7,000 houses were built in Southampton. Thus, about the same time that Nassau County and the western parts of Suffolk County were becoming icons of post–World War II suburban development, the Hamptons, too, experienced rapid residential construction, economic expansion, and the beginnings of what would eventually be called "exurbanization," a process defined by J. John Palen as "upper-middle class settlements . . .

in outlying semirural suburbia—the area outside the second ring of densely settled subdivisions."[25]

Thus, when Gaines contends that the area's increasing population represented a migration of "common millionaires," he ignores the point that Alastair Gordon makes very clear, that "many of the same individuals who had been able to get their first mortgages through the G.I housing bill could [by the late 1950s and early 1960s] afford to build a second home far away from the noisy city."[26] Meanwhile, the construction industry quickly recognized (and responded to) the potential for a "lucrative new market." Carl Fischer's Soundview Estates and Macy's "Leisurama houses" provided hundreds of reasonably priced summer homes, some on third-of-an-acre plots and selling for as little as $11,000. As discussed in the previous chapter, Techbuilt beach houses combined William Levitt's rationalized production and marketing systems with a European modernist aesthetic to provide hundreds, if not thousands, of middle-class New Yorkers with the ability to buy second homes in the Hamptons.

The middle-class character of this growth is reinforced by the portrait created at the village and hamlet level. Between 1970 and 1980, for example, Southampton's greatest population increases and its greatest number of housing starts occurred in the traditionally working- and middle-class communities of Hampton Bays, Riverside, North Sea, Noyak, and Shinnecock Hills. These sections represented almost 70 percent of the town's growth, accounting for almost 6,000 of the municipality's 8,112 new residents. Similar trends took place in the Town of East Hampton. As the population increased 32 percent (from 10,980 to 14,029) between 1970 and 1980, almost the entire growth occurred in the historically working- and middle-class communities of Montauk and Springs, which accounted for 2,200 of the town's 3,049 new residents. While the median incomes of individuals and families that built homes on the East End between 1950 and 1980 may have been higher than those of the average American, of the newcomers the majority were solidly middle- and upper-middle-class people who sought less expensive sections of the Hamptons and simply took advantage of postwar prosperity to participate in a growing national trend toward building vacation homes.[27]

Many of these second-home owners, however, also thought of these structures as potential sites for retirement. According to a 1967 *House*

Beautiful survey quoted by Gordon, almost 30 percent of homeowners planned to retire to their vacation homes, and more than 50 percent planned to buy vacation homes with retirement in mind. These national trends continued throughout the late twentieth century and had a large impact on once-seasonal vacation meccas like the Hamptons.[28] Census data show that one of the fastest-growing population groups relocating to Southampton and East Hampton during the 1960s and 1970s consisted of people age 55 and older. Especially notable were people age 65 and older, whose numbers increased by almost 150 percent in East Hampton and by more than 200 percent in Southampton between 1960 and 1970 alone. A 1995 study by the Southampton College Institute for Regional Research found that "nearly one-third of current full time residents started as seasonal residents."[29] Thus, by the 1950s and 1960s, what had initially been vacation homes soon became the places where New York City (and even Nassau County) doctors, lawyers, and teachers and other civil servants looked to retire year-round. By the 1970s, both East Hampton and Southampton planners worried about the area becoming a "retirement community," and planning documents from both towns considered what kinds of permanent infrastructural changes such populations would require.

But those who shifted from seasonal renters or vacation homeowners to year-round residents were not only retirees. Population data shows that the second largest age group that came to live in the Hamptons between 1960 and 1980 was between ages 35 and 44. Liz Granitz, an economics professor at Southampton College–Long Island University, and her family rented houses in East Hampton during the early 1960s and bought a house in 1969. Her mother eventually decided to move the whole family to the East End after her father died. Hal Ross, a political consultant and retired bond trader, had also vacationed in the Hamptons during the 1960s and bought some land for a summer home in 1972. Following his divorce, he moved in year-round. Nancy Goell, a former magazine editor and president of the Group for the South Fork, and her husband met in the Hamptons in 1960 and built a house for summers and weekends just a few years later. Attracted by the public schools and the "natural beauty," they made the area their primary residence in the early 1970s. Jim Daly, a business consultant and former economics professor at Southampton College, had been spending summers in Montauk during the early 1970s when he heard about a job opening. He jumped at the opportunity and became a full-time resident in 1976. Each of these individual stories follows what the East End researchers Kevin McDonald and Nancy Kelley describe as a pattern where "renters become buyers" or where "second-home buyers have evolved from strictly summer residents to year-round weekenders to full-time residents."[30]

Postwar booms in the defense industries led to job growth in eastern Suffolk County as Brookhaven National Laboratories and Grumman Allied Industries developed large facilities in towns bordering the Hamptons.[31] Younger migrants also found work in professional occupations linked to a growing leisure industry that created not just seasonal work but full-time positions in hotel and restaurant management, financial support industries, and other commercial and public relations ventures. In the early 1960s, C. W. Post opened up a branch campus of Long Island University in Southampton, which eventually hired 150 full-time faculty and about as many staff and administrators. Other colleges and universities sprouted up in the area, including the State University of New York at Stony Brook (1962) and the Suffolk Community College campus in Riverhead (1971). Both grew exponentially during the period to meet the increasing numbers of postwar students taking advantage of massive federal grants and increasing middle-class affluence by seeking higher education.

With the year-round population increasing and seasonal visitors using their second homes more frequently and for longer periods of time, the area's commercial centers and civic infrastructure also expanded. The five largest retail centers on the South Fork were built between 1970 and 1978. Three major supermarket franchises located stores in Westhampton Beach (National and A&P), Southampton Village (A&P), and Hampton Bays (IGA) in 1970, with the first two locations undergoing major expansions within just a few years. Public school enrollments increased, too, reflecting a growing population and creating a need for more teachers, administrators, and related school personnel. Town governments in East Hampton and Southampton, as well as municipal governments in Sag Harbor, Bridgehampton, Hampton Bays, and Montauk, also added new employees to meet the burgeoning demand for services.

Growth continued throughout the 1980s and 1990s, but with a demographic shift. Southampton's population rose more than 25 percent between 1980 and 2000, from 43,136 to 54,712, more than double the projections of town planners and organizations like the Long Island

Lighting Company (LILCO). East Hampton grew almost 40 percent during the same period, from 14,029 to 19,719. Of Southampton's 35,838 housing structures tabulated in the 2000 census, almost one-third were built between 1980 and 2000. Of East Hampton's almost 20,000 homes at the turn of the twenty-first century, 42 percent were built during those same previous two decades. But the socioeconomic status of the new migrants rose dramatically during this period. Between 1980 and 2000, the income levels of new homeowners rose more than 50 percent in both Southampton and East Hampton. These newcomers were increasingly year-round residents. According to the 1995 Southampton College study, not only were almost a third of current year-round residents former seasonal migrants, but also the same number of current seasonal residents already "plan[ned] to live in Southampton full time sometime in the future." In fact, "the strongest conversion from part to full time occurred among those who arrived in Southampton Town between 1980 and 1989, when four in ten made the transition."[32] While the 1980s migrants were much better off financially than those from the previous two decades (thus lending some credibility to Gaines's insight about the impact of new Wall Street fortunes), the fact that 40 percent were actually relocating full-time suggests that more was at stake than just status competition.

According to a draft of Southampton's Comprehensive Plan in 1999, the profile of the town's residents had become more "complex" than simply traditional, year-round residents and summer-only weekend visitors. Along with "snowbirds" and "extended weekenders who might split their residence year-long between a house in Southampton and a pied-à-terre in Manhattan," a variety of changing conditions allowed more and more people to spend more and more of their residential life in the Hamptons. Innovations in telecommunications and transportation increased the ability of even modestly wealthy professionals to maintain primary houses in the Hamptons while performing most of their business in New York City. The expansion of edge-city sprawl and high-tech suburbs created major economic development throughout Nassau and western Suffolk counties, allowing software designers and financial agency executives to live in the Hamptons and commute relatively short distances down the Long Island Expressway to their primary places of business. By the late 1990s, few people could ignore the impact of the area's burgeoning year-round population driven by increasingly wealthy newcomers with cultural tastes markedly different from those of their predecessors.[33]

Over the past decade, the *Southampton Press* and the *East Hampton Star* have reported on rapid rises in both public and private school enrollments and the increasing need for expanded social services and public infrastructure for an upscale population. The *New York Times* documented the shift from battles over local shopping malls in 1985 to what one year-round resident referred to, in 1989, as "the Carmelization" of the Hamptons. Susan Seidman complained that "the city people who come out for country weekends all year round" yuppified the Hamptons, and "the few days a week they spend here" came to dominate the commercial landscape of village main streets. In 1992, a *Philadelphia Inquirer* reporter discussed an even more disturbing trend, the onset of upscale factory outlet stores. Fearing what the author called "the Jersey Shore Syndrome," residents worried that the traffic and overcrowding caused by an increasingly middle-class population might scare away locals. Phyllis Estey, a seventeen-year resident of Amagansett, complained about traffic and parking "already worse than anything she experiences in Manhattan where she and her husband keep an apartment on Central Park West." Sounding like the current wave's siren for impending Armageddon, Estey exhorted, "Can you imagine? The people who live here year-round now want to run away during the summer."[34]

Of course, they didn't. In fact they just kept coming. By the end of the twentieth century, the area's transition represented a new phenomenon on the American geographical landscape—the creation of an upscale exurban community where suburban sprawl is reconfigured by a convergence of unique economic, political, cultural, and historical forces. Contemporary land use politics now feature coalitions of wealthy landowners and environmentalists who, in part through zoning policies and in part through market forces, restrict the development of working- and middle-class subdivisions and department store outlet malls in favor of three- to five-acre residential plots. They quaintly design commercial centers with upscale merchandisers and carefully preserve a sense of historical identity by "saving" traditional landscapes and cultures at the same time that their own migration threatens to seal the fates of dying landscapes and ways of life. Thus, the Hamptons have become one of the nation's poster communities for McMansion landscapes where wealthy migrants become local residents by building houses that conquer the land and adopt authenticity by appropriating images of the past.

SUPERSIZED LIVING IN THE HAMPTONS

In August 2001, the staff of the *East Hampton Star* got into a disagreement about the definition of a "McMansion." Some focused on the specific physicality of such structures—their excessive square footage, their disproportionate size to the lot they occupy, or their "fast food"–like qualities of rapid production and "cookie-cutter" design. But the publisher Helen Rattray wondered whether those who complain about "McMansions in our midst" aren't just being "snobs." Comparing new supersize homeowners to previous waves of wealthy migrants, she considered how locals responded to summer colony houses at the turn of the nineteenth century. Rattray asked, "Did East Hamptoners chortle about the so-called 'cottages' in the same way we carry on about McMansions? Or, nurtured for generations by the beneficent land and sea, [they] may have been satisfied to consider wealth and its manifestations simply as something apart from their own way of life." Rattray believed locals were content in knowing that "theirs was the good life."[35]

Despite the wide range of characteristics that McMansions seem to possess, most architects, scholars, and critics seem to agree on the basic elements of these fashionable houses. McMansions range from 3,000 to 7,000 square feet or more and are erected on relatively bare lots that have either been clear-cut of trees or occupy old farmland. These structures are generally wood shingled and symmetrical, with a gambrel roof, several gables or dormers, expansive porches, "soaring" entryways, a multicar garage, some kind of stone or brick veneer, and at least one Palladian window. Inside, according to *Home Monthly* magazine, a McMansion features a large and luxurious kitchen with granite counters, lots of built-in features, a breakfast area, several guest rooms, many fireplaces, and a large mixed-use open space known as a "great room."[36] Some have described McMansion subdivisions as "Levittowns for the overclass," where enclaves feature huge "hulking houses cheek by jowl." In response to one such Bridgehampton residential spread, a Hamptons realtor quipped, "There ought to be crime scene tape strung across the entrance to Erica's Lane." Perhaps the most fit-

Parrish Pond McMansions: "Little boxes" of more than 4,000 square feet standing cheek by jowl. (Photo by author, 2004)

ting definition of a McMansion might be similar to former Supreme Court Justice Potter Stewart's definition of obscenity: critics know one when they see one.[37]

While many McMansions "grow like topsy" in corner clusters of cul de sacs or in croplike rows set back from main roads, the latest trend to threaten the perceived rural charms of places like the Hamptons is the "tear-down." With less and less open space available for developing "spec houses" of starter-castle proportions, wealthy urbanites looking to invest in large, expensive homes buy smaller houses on half- to three-quarter-acre lots and then tear down the existing house. In 1998, the *New York Times* reported that the trend was irritating wealthy suburbanites from Ridgewood, New Jersey, to Westport and New Canaan, Connecticut, to the East End. Hamptons realtors told *New York* magazine that people increasingly had to purchase smaller, "contemporary-style houses" built during the 1980s Wall Street boom and raze them in order to create the "palaces of their dreams." As the reporter Alex Williams wrote, "This is how a three-to-four bedroom house in the 1,800 square foot range surrenders to a hulking six-bedroom, 5,000–6,000 square foot behemoth."[38]

But no residential building has inspired more hyperbole than Ira Rennert's planned 110,000-square-foot complex, called "Fair Field," in Sagaponack. Rennert, a billionaire whose money comes primarily from buying and selling chemical and coal companies and cashing in on junk bonds, has designed a "home" that will feature almost 30 bedrooms, 40 bathrooms, a 164-seat theater, a restaurant-size kitchen, and an entire English pub reconstructed piece by piece from its historic location in Britain. Rennert's Bridgehampton neighbors, under the guise of a newly formed Sagaponack Homeowners Association (SHA), filed lawsuits to stop his construction, calling the compound "a blight on the quaint character of the community." Although they lost the case, residents are trying to incorporate Sagaponack as an independent municipality in order to better control local land-use decisions. The group, however, may not fair any better against Rennert than environmental activists and the EPA have in attacking his Magnesium Corporation of America for polluting the communities around its major plant in Utah. According to Chip Ward, founder of Utah's Citizens against Chlorine Contamination, "Rennert's company slips through the cracks of just about any environmental legislation there is. . . . My own feeling is that you would be hard pushed to find any company anywhere in the world that has less credibility than Magnesium Corporation, or anything else owned by Rennert."[39]

Of course, Rennert's house is no run-of-the-mill McMansion, and his claim that it is solely for use as a "single-family residence" stretches the term's definition, if not the imagination. But such a comparison does suggest that more important than definitions or descriptions of McMansions is what they represent about the surrounding area's changing physical and cultural landscape. For most recent bourgeois migrants to the Hamptons, these large buildings are no mere trophy houses; they represent changing land-use patterns that are found in ex-urban areas around the country. On the one hand, houses have become *the* major investment vehicle for professional and upper-middle-class families. According to the geographer Tom Daniels, the convergence of this investment pattern with the perception that the countryside is a "safer, cheaper, and more rewarding place to live" than cities or traditional suburbs has resulted in new homeownership strategies: "a. buy as much house as possible; b. maximize the federal mortgage interest deduction; c. build up equity in the house while paying off the mortgage; and d. buy or build a house in the countryside where the appreciation potential is high."[40]

On the other hand, more than fear and economic investment fuels the demand for freshly built big houses. Census, ethnographic, real estate, and public and private school data all seem to confirm a changing portrait of the East End's wealthier migrants. The largest increases in population between 1980 and 2000 have been in the 35–54-year-old age bracket, with the next largest age group composed of children and teenagers ages 5–17. Both public and private school statistics demonstrate huge increases in student enrollment, especially during the 1990s. Most of these students were children of parents who had recently moved into the area. The significant increase in the cost and size of new houses built during the past decade or so suggest that, regardless of Ira Rennert's vision of family life, McMansions do, to a large degree, represent the single-family residences of people who increasingly live year-round on the East End. And, while many of these newcomers may see their purchases as potential retirement homes, of greater concern is the possibility of making a home in the Hamptons right now.

Many older couples have purchased large homes in hopes of facilitating big gatherings of children, grandchildren, and extended families. Others see these houses as simply great places to "hang out" with groups of friends. The most notable characteristic of almost all the McMansion owners interviewed for this research is that, far from seeing their homes as symbolic "starter castles," they perceive them as places to be used throughout the year, either as a primary residence or "as primary a residence" as possible. Unlike the summer colony elite that pursued Hamptons "land lust" at first for its rugged, anti-urban charms and eventually for its social register, contemporary conquerors are making their presence felt in less elite, yet more dramatic fashion. As the Hamptons have become "year-round," new residential patterns and the day-to-day lifestyles of recent migrants have had an overwhelming effect on the physical landscape.

One place to observe these changes is on Southampton's and East Hampton's roadways. More than ever before, traffic patterns have shifted from a seasonal crunch to a persistent weekend problem to a daily crisis of standstill proportions. Part of the traffic, especially on weekday mornings, consists of trucks and vans related to construction, landscaping, and other residential services—what one village resident refers to as a "trade parade." But, continuing automobile congestion throughout the day comes directly from the increase in year-round, residential people out and about, transporting children to school, commuting to work, shopping, and conducting errands. According to the Federal Highway Administration's 1995 National Personal Transportation Survey, New York State households averaged five car trips per day of about ten miles each. Bob Deluca, president of the Group for the South Fork, a regional environmental organization, claims that every new household in the Hamptons now generates an average of ten vehicle trips per day. This figure includes not just resident trips but all of the increased service and commercial travel related to larger populations. The Group estimates that the more than 1,000 new houses built on the East End in 2001 will result in more than 3 million additional car trips a year. The number and the duration of these trips are partly a result of the lack of public transportation and the centralized village settings for local commerce. A Bridgehampton resident, Fred Havermeyer, described the overall effect as "an invasion . . . the traffic is strangling us. This isn't the beautiful village it used to be. You can't see it for the cars. You can't get here if you want to, and you can't get away."[41]

The massive impact of traffic and a variety of other issues stemming from a growing year-round residential density have also resulted in greater social and political interests in environmental issues, especially as they relate to the politics of economic development and regional identity. From the early 1970s on, environmental organizations and local neighborhood groups formed to address land-use policies of all sorts. The Group for the South Fork, the Peconic Land Trust, Save the Peconic Bays, North Fork Environmental Council, the Long Island Pine Barrens Society, the Riverhead Foundation for Marine Research and Preservation, Sustainable East End Development Strategies (SEEDS), the Southampton Trails Preservation Society, PEACE (Protecting Every Aspect of the Environment), the South Fork Groundwater Task Force, and Amagansett Springs Aquifer Protection, as well as active chapters of regional and national groups such as the Long Island Progressive Coalition, the Greens, and the Nature Conservancy are only some of the groups organized over the past few decades to try to restrict or control the environmental effects of rapid growth. The irony of local environmental politics emanates from the fact that much of the support for controlled growth or antigrowth politics comes from the same group of new residents who benefit from and contribute to the kinds of residential and commercial development that threaten coastal waters, wetlands, aquifers, and open spaces.

The original Shinnecock and Montaukett Indians' concern for the environment arose from the almost total integration of their economic survival and cultural practices and their physical surroundings. Although original European "settlers'" approach to the environment was dominated by capitalist exploitation or profit-driven "use-value," they also demonstrated a significant interest in maintaining at least a productive, if not always healthy, environment. To some degree, the early farmers and fishermen of the East End were the precursors of the area's present "wise-use" movement, promoted by some environmentally conscious developers, builders, and other businessmen. This contemporary group recognizes that the area's economic growth and commercial success are, in large part, tied to its natural landscape. As McDonald and Nagle Kelley wrote, in 1994, "On the East End, we recognize that scenic beauty, heritage and environmental quality are good for business. . . . Realtors and restaurateurs and resort owners all realize that they must protect the 'product' they are trying to sell."[42]

Yet, recent environmental protection and preservation efforts have been largely (albeit not exclusively) led by newer residents, not by "native" populations or local businesses. Although some groups can trace a few of their members' roots in the area back generations, the majority of support emanates from people who have migrated within the past few decades and whose agendas come from a combination of "nimbyism", economic self-interest, and a general sense that the time to stop development and preserve the natural landscape began the moment they arrived. Even the Sagaponack group opposed to Rennert's project is composed mostly of people who have come to the Hamptons since 1970, "Johnny-come-latelys with their own megacottages," according to one critic.[43] Some environmental efforts do reflect a more traditional sense of environmental movement politics as organizations campaign to protect clean drinking water, halt the destruction of wetlands, and stop chemical waste contamination from places like the nearby Brookhaven National Laboratories. But many environmental protests derive from the desire to protect economic and cultural capital. If Daniels is right about the rationale for exurban residential development, then both land values and social values are a huge stake in the battle to control growth. People who pay close to a million dollars for a house want property values to remain high. People who purchase homes with "farm views" don't want new housing structures to impede their vista. People who want the country charm of small commercial hamlets don't want to drive by Golden Arches and strip malls on their way to Main Street.

This kind of environmental protectionism is often explained within the economic and social construct of "the second-home owner." McDonald and Kelley warn that "the more suburban it becomes, the less the East End will be seen as an appealing place to purchase a second home or primary residence." In a letter to the *Southampton Press*, Hal Ross echoed these sentiments, writing that the area's "economic base rests on the 40-plus percent of our houses that are owned by second-home owners. They are here (and in ever-increasing numbers) because of the special characteristics with which most of the East End is blessed —our rural, unpolluted quality of life, natural beauty of the fields, waterways, beaches, woodlands, 350-year historic and small-scale hamlet centers, open spaces, wood-shingled houses and all the rest. . . . Destroy the basic characteristics of the East End, and second-home owners will flee."[44]

The land, however, no longer produces much in the way of subsistence, nor does it provide the raw materials for agricultural industries, with the exception of upscale consumer goods and services like vineyards and horse farms. Instead, the land is most valuable as the site of highly regulated, upscale real estate development and must be protected in order to maintain a new economy, not old ways of life. Thus, despite the sense of nostalgia for a "rural quality of life" long gone, the key to the "second-home-owner" discourse is its potential to mediate the contradictions between supporting economic growth based on real estate development ("in ever increasing numbers") and preserving environmental landscapes and historic or quaint cultural appeal.

Such rhetoric, however, feeds a sharp dichotomy between myths about the area's rural authenticity or, as Ross calls them, "basic characteristics," and fears of uncontrolled urban or suburban sprawl. This contrast permits Ross, for example, to elicit a double threat: if "controlled growth" isn't pursued immediately, the Hamptons could lose both the second-home economy and the sense of natural beauty and historic charm. But Ross's commentary is steeped in a kind of nostalgic portrayal of "rural" and "unpolluted" qualities of life and landscape. His letter reflects (almost word for word) decade-old documents from the Peconic County secession movement (see chapter 4). While the Hamptons may still be more rural than the suburbs of Nassau County and the streets of Manhattan's Upper East Side, it seems implausible to call most of the area "rural" or the commercial centers of Southampton, Bridgehampton, and East Hampton "small-scale hamlets." Yet, both nostalgia and fear combine to create a kind of middle ground where the continuous migration of second-home owners who increasingly make the Hamptons their primary residence can simultaneously claim a connection to both nature and history by supporting controlled or anti-growth policies. In essence, new McMansion owners acquire a kind of geographical and moral legitimacy by identifying with a natural and historical image of the past, appropriating a perverse version of the "good life" that Rattray thought would always satisfy "native" residents. But that good life is gone.

EVERYTHING NEW IS OLD AGAIN

The power of such nostalgic perspectives on the area's natural environment and quaint folkways has always been more a romantic packaging of anti-urban, cultural capital than an actual documentation of what the landscape is or was. From John Howard Payne's "Home Sweet Home" (Payne's family was from East Hampton) to Whitman's "From Montauk Point" to Thomas Moran's "A Midsummer Day, East Hampton" to Irving Ramsey Wiles's "Scallop Boats, Peconic," artists have imbued East End landscapes with what the historian Helen Harrison called an "antique rural charm." Writers and painters tried to capture the land and sea as they saw them in an attempt to represent what was natural and authentic about both the physical environment and human nature. But such conceptions of what is *natural* and *authentic* always represented a culturally imposed view of nature juxtaposed with the growing pervasiveness of a rationalized industrial development and the seeming chaos of the city. And these artistic renderings were always intended for a bourgeoisie that sought cultural legitimation for its eastward migration and its physical conquest of the land.[45]

Today, artists, environmentalists, and their patrons are romanticizing a new juxtaposition of physical landscape and human development —this time nature versus postindustrial urban nightmares and a new economy driven by the real estate industry. But, this time, they are also trying to claim a kind of "stewardship" over an ecology and a history they have proclaimed as natural and authentic. This view is supported by photographic projects such as Kathryn Szoka's *Vanishing Landscapes* and Wendy Chamberlin's *True East: Farming Ancestral Lands on Long Island's East End.* Szoka began the *Vanishing Landscapes* effort in the late

1980s already cognizant of how "open spaces and farmlands were disappearing." In hopes of preserving the "spiritual relief and natural soothing" of the East End's "quietude," Szoka juxtaposes such geographical places with what she refers to as the "failed community" of the city. Yet, the city is represented not in and of itself but by its wealthy refugees and the "sprawl" they bring, which intrudes on the East End's bucolic landscapes. Chamberlain's juxtaposition is more implicit, but she, too, declares the importance of educating the public (primarily newer urban migrants) about the area's agricultural legacy, because "people [come to the area] and live right next door to these farms and don't know their work or culture."[46]

Both photographers also fear the loss of an authentic "kind of honesty and ability to trust." For Szoka, the traditional values of farming culture are represented in the self-service honor system used by some of the remaining small farm stands. Chamberlain, who spent countless hours working and living with selected farm families, explains that by integrating herself into, and being embraced by, the lives of these people, she learned "a lot about ethics and morals." She contends that farmers have "passed on basic qualities and values . . . and if your word was good, that was what was important." Chamberlain sees a kind of volunteerism and civic service as key to this set of authentic values. The farmers represented a "different culture . . . one in which service to the community is taken for granted and volunteering for the fire department or as an EMT is almost a given." Both contrast small-town, traditional values with those of commercial developers and urban transplants.[47]

Szoka is perceptive in recognizing the way that, as the landscape is transformed into an object to be bought and sold, subdivisions and new residential roads are being named for the physical landscapes they've replaced. Thus, she notes that streets such as Whispering Fields Court and Farm Court, as well as dozens of development clusters given monikers such as Rover Circle Farm and Roses Grove Knolls, are doubly tragic because they first destroy nature physically and then pervert it culturally. But in aesthetically juxtaposing vanishing landscapes and recent real estate trends, Szoka, too, romanticizes a "natural environment" that derives its significance primarily in contrast to postindustrial production, sprawling development, and city life. Thus, her conception of nature is not so much that of Whitman's or Moran's "wild," "unspoiled," or "untouched" landscape where the natural world is to be discovered and emulated. It is an ecological and ideological vision of an already domesticated, harmonious integration between humans and the earth, best represented by agriculture and the farmers who work the land. She claims that farmers find "a way to live more harmoniously with nature and landscapes." Barns, "nestled within the environment," become "spiritual icons" because they are "functional and efficient, not dominant."

Chamberlain also romanticizes an agricultural state of nature, comparing her experience of entering East End farms to "walking into the Museum of Natural History." She claims that one "can't divorce the natural world from the spiritual world" and explains that her visits to the farms "restored a sense of perspective and I would become calm." Again, agricultural land use represents an idealized integration of human existence and nature in which farms are portrayed as authentic sites for material and spiritual production. To be fair, Szoka admits that such a view may be overly romantic, and, to her great credit, her recent environmental work is linked to a much broader social justice agenda that includes building coalitions with Latino, African American, and working-class groups around issues such as affordable housing. For Chamberlain, her depiction of *True East* inspired her to open a landscaping business through which she tries to educate a predominately wealthy clientele to be "respectful of property and the environment . . . to get them involved in the landscape and make them better landlords and caretakers." In trying to preserve the historical legacy of East End farmers, Chamberlain now tries to help better integrate new and old landscapes, "dealing with the inevitability of change while also hoping to save what farms still exist."[48]

But, as these photographic essays attempt to document a historical process, it is the ahistorical aspects of the *Vanishing Landscapes* and *True East* projects that seem most troubling. After all, it was European farmers, driven by Protestant rationality, righteous and racist arrogance, and entrepreneurial ambitions, who destroyed the "natural landscapes" first embraced by the area's Native Americans. Farming resulted in massive deforestation, which decimated the Shinnecocks' and Montauketts' traditional culture and economy. Szoka thoughtfully theorizes that perception can be "very insidious" as it adjusts "rapidly to development and what might be shocking for a day or a week or a month after a year isn't really noticed."[49] Such an insight, however, must be brought to bear on her and Chamberlain's own projects; a critical reading of the past exposes one person's landscape of spiritual healing and harmony as being perhaps, in Walter Benjamin's words, another's "document of barbarism."

The overall problem with such romanticizing, though, is not just its skewed view of what nature was before and is now but also its implication that, by representing and preserving it, one becomes a part of its sought-after authenticity. Thus, in the process of saving such landscapes, the artist (or patron or environmentalist) becomes rooted in the land and its legacy. By investing time, money, or creativity in such endeavors, new migrants adopt a sense of historical and moral legitimacy as the rightful heirs and stewards of older environments and cultures. Not only can conquerors protect their investments at the same time that they impose their own lifestyles on the social and physical landscape; they now do so within an aesthetic and narrative framework in which they, too, are authentic. Only they can save the Hamptons because they have become the Hamptons.

Similar cultural and political processes can be seen in recent attempts to preserve other ways of life in danger of disappearing. A prolonged campaign to save the baymen from "extinction" has been under way for almost two decades. These traditional fishermen, using large nets, small boats, and a variety of "low-tech" means to catch coastal fish, from striped bass to scallops and clams, have lost their livelihood to the onset of brown tides and other forms of pollution, increased sportfishing and coastal development, and severe government restrictions on commercial bass fishing. Peter Matthiessen's 1986 elegy to the baymen, *Men's Lives,* offers a sympathetic portrait of the bonacker culture's demise. It inspired serious attempts to raise money and support for these fishing men among the Hamptons' more celebrated residents, culminating in Billy Joel's 1990 "Concert for the Bays and Baymen," at which he sang his own ode to the bonackers, "The Downeaster Alexa," which concludes:

> *I was a bayman like my father was before;*
> *Can't make a living as a bayman anymore.*
> *There ain't much future for a man who works the sea;*
> *But there ain't no island left for islanders like me.*

In 1992, Joel, along with other celebrities, local politicians, and baymen themselves, committed civil disobedience to protest bans on commer-

Billy Joel arrested with baymen and others for violating a New York State law banning the catching of fish with haul-seining equipment. (Photo courtesy of *East Hampton Star,* 1992)

cial bass fishing by casting nets into the waters off East Hampton and violating the law that prohibits "catching bass by means other than angling." In explaining his support for the baymen, Joel, who grew up in Nassau County and moved to the Hamptons in the 1980s, explained, "These guys represent something unique. . . . They are the real Long Island, the Long Island that keeps disappearing." He continued, "The baymen are an old community fighting for their survival . . . [they] are the essence of this area. . . . They are living history."[50] For Joel, the baymen, like the disappearing agricultural landscapes and the farmers who worked them, are imbued with an authenticity essential to local ecology and identity. Lewis Greenstein, former dean of Southampton College's Friends World Program, went so far as to explain that preserving the baymen's "unique local heritage is clearly desirable. . . . We should protect the indigenous traditional enterprises [for] as the century and the millennium come to a close, it's important to look at issues such as natural resources."[51] Here the baymen themselves *become* natural resources, to be protected like the environment.

Baymen, like the indigenous farming culture, are aesthetically packaged to represent a particular set, or at least sense, of community and values. Ann Chwatsky, a photographer, believes that her pictures of "old-time" Sag Harbor residents such as baymen and duck carvers portray "real people" and represent a sense of "community" and "continuity." She explains that, "for all of us coming from other places, [we] have this longing for small town security . . . the photographs of baymen and farmers are icons."[52] The juxtaposition of newly arrived "city people" with "real" natives shapes the entire exhibit, giving Chwatsky's interpretation of "community" and "authenticity" its significance. Baymen themselves contribute to this cultural positioning, enhancing their own status and support among a new set of local conquerors. For example, Arnold Leo, president of the Baymen's Association for more than twenty years, claims that the "baymens' way of life is based on community values that are very old and which formed an important part of the fabric of American culture. To live simply, work hard, help thy neighbor, be at one with one's fellow man and with God, to be a part of nature—these are the strands of the fabric." History, ecology, and theology all come together as the baymen's story becomes a kind of regional jeremiad for newcomers to admire, lament, and ultimately adopt as their own story.[53]

Joe Pintauro, a playwright chosen to adapt Peter Matthiessen's work for the stage, takes the iconography one step further in claiming that baymen represent an almost absolute or pure authenticity. He contends that these fishermen are "simple people, the original people who lived out here before any of us and haul seining is their method. It's difficult, primitive, and beautiful." Pintauro seems to spiral into a kind of nostalgic, Luddite-like abyss as the baymen eventually evolve into a mythological everyman:

> relating to the plight of blue-collar workers and the victims of urban gentrification . . . and to the steel mills in the Midwest and the coal mines in Wales . . . when men of craft and industry are mistreated and wiped out or laid off in record numbers by the capitalist monster, leaving workers and their skills in the dust of profit over everything, the artist must make a statement about how important it is to preserve a style of life so that we don't lose everything to computers.[54]

Somewhere in this mixing of metaphors, this amalgam of revolutionary rhetoric and liberal pabulum, is the aesthetic repackaging of history and struggle as "lifestyle." In the end, as the working class loses yet another battle in a string of capitalist slugfests, the artist steps in to make a statement about preservation, not revolution. And the working class—in this case, the baymen—becomes little more than museum exhibits for the educational and spiritual enrichment of those newcomers with the intelligence and sensitivity to appreciate history and nature. In essence, the baymen bestow upon their audience of new migrants their historical identity, authenticity, and moral legitimacy.

Yet, like Wyandanch and the Shinnecock, who negotiated treaties with the British, and the nineteenth-century boardinghouse operators and craftsmen who serviced New York City's elite summer colonists, and the twentieth-century farmers who sold parcels of land to pay off debts or to increase wealth, the baymen participate in negotiating the terms of their own demise as they try to shape their own fate. Wayne Grothe, president of the Southampton Town Baymen's Association, linked the fishermen's survival to the beauty and cleanliness of the bays themselves and quoted a "fellow baymen turned conservationist" who linked his own survival to that of the bays themselves, asking a summer resident, "Do you want your children to swim in water you can't eat the shellfish?"[55] Perhaps Tom Lester, though, best embodied this balancing act between being reduced to a nostalgic icon and promoting one's own historical identity as authentic, therefore claiming status as legitimate heir to the area. According to T. H. Breen, threatened by the rapid pace of change, Lester "loudly celebrated" bonacker culture and crusaded for the survival of the local baymen. Yet,

> Many people in East Hampton see Tom Lester simply as the quintessential Bonacker, a romantic survivor from an earlier, perhaps simpler, time. The last of the Baymen. A symbol rather than a man. And though he plays the part with skill, Tom and Cathy [Lester, his wife] seem to know full well when he is being patronized. They sense that the great network of old families is actually a very fragile thing on which to place their hopes for the future of East Hampton. They have seen too many local people—members of the ancient clan—auction off their own heritage.[56]

The threat of rapid social transformation leaves baymen with two basic choices: either to sell out to the conquerors or to market support for their own survival like an elixir to new migrants anxious over their own lack of historical and cultural identity. In either case, the baymen must accept at some level the inevitability that bonacker culture's very future will be directed primarily by those most responsible for its demise.

Even real estate agents try to repackage themselves as "environmentally friendly" and rightful moral leaders in the community. Similar to Chamberlain and Leo's contention about the "community values" represented by the bonackers, Melanie Ross, president of Cook Pony Farm Real Estate, emphasizes the agency's beginnings in the 1940s in a "quiet and unsophisticated" Hamptons that possessed a "deep sense of community." She recounts the legend of the company's founder, Ed Cook, who would pay the bills of local fishermen who couldn't make their insurance premiums, telling them "not to forget him when they had a good catch." She concludes, "He took care of them and they of him. Each was a part of this wonderful community and did what they could for each other. It's those roots that helped build Cook Pony Farm and continue to support our sense of community."[57] But just whose sense of community does Cook Pony Farm really represent?

Breen, too, notes how the East Hampton Ladies Village Improvement Society (LVIS) has worked hard to "assure that East Hampton's storied charms will not be disturbed by the pressures of contemporary growth and development." But whose stories are these? The original LVIS was composed of some of the wealthier summer colony women who supported road improvements and "historic preservation" efforts to maintain the architecture and appearance of Main Street. From providing watering carts to keep the dust at bay to planting trees and purchasing old-fashioned paving stones, the LVIS created their own vision of what a "charming community" catering to their class should look like. Thus, Breen concludes, "we must ask what is the connection between history and identity, between style" and what he calls "imagining a community."

The process of imagining a community is ultimately a political one, and the history of the Hamptons, both past and present, is the history of just such struggles over who gets the power to imagine what kind of community. The struggle continues today as those with wealth, prestige, and political power physically dominate the landscape by building McMansions and encouraging upscale commercial development. But such triumphs require new narratives, new stories that help recent conquerors not only justify their reign but naturalize it in such a way that the Hamptons becomes their community culturally as well as economically. What better stories to relate than those of environmental protection and historical preservation? When Hal Ross invites the Town of Southampton to protect "our rural, unpolluted quality of life, natural beauty of the fields, waterways, beaches, woodlands, 350-year historic and small-scale hamlet centers," he has already changed and repackaged history and nature to his own specifications with the simple pronoun choice of "our." Or, as George Orwell wrote, "Who controls the past controls the future. Who controls the present, controls the past."

THE BEGINNING OF THE END, OR
THE END OF THE BEGINNING?

For every new group of migrants that vows to protect the quality of life in the Hamptons, there are those who decry their arrival as representing the East End's demise. The current period is no exception. At the conclusion of *Philistines at the Hedgerow,* Gaines declares that the area's latest skirmish in the eternal Them-versus-Us struggle is already over. The invaders, this time composed of loud, celebrity nouveau *very* riche, have won. The way of life that "locals" and "natives" wanted to protect has already disappeared. Gaines explains that "The establishment can hold off the newcomers for only so long. . . . Eventually you have to come to terms and make friends. But once you do, the newcomers' ills kill you."[58]

But even Gaines's "new arrivistes" period has already been declared over. In *New York* magazine, Alex Williams and Beth Landman Keil wrote a definitive piece on Lizzie Grubman, the daughter of the billionaire music attorney Allen Grubman, who drove her SUV into a crowd of patrons and staff at an East End bar and sparked months of "rich girl goes bad" stories for the New York paparazzi. According to Williams and Landman, "The Grubmans, as much as anyone, are responsible for the modern Hamptons, in all their obsession with wealth and celebrity and their thrilling, stupefying social excess . . . [but], in a crash that broke ankles and pelvises, and spilled cocktails and launched upwards of $100 million in law suits, [Grubman] may have ended a

The Manhattan socialite Lizzie Grubman,
whose SUV accident, according to *New York*
magazine reporters, "broke ankles and pelvises
[and] may have ended a whole Hamptons era."
(*New York* magazine, 2001)

whole Hamptons era."[59] Or, it may be that endings and beginnings in
the postmodern world are all premature.

Perhaps the most fitting, yet virulent, of the doomsday forecasts
comes from the artist Miles Jaffe's Web site, www.nukethehamptons
.com. Here Jaffe, son of the famous architect Norman Jaffe, has enabled
anyone with Internet access to destroy part (or all) of the Hamptons
with just a few clicks of a mouse.[60] According to the *Southampton Press*,
Jaffe's Web site "is a plebian cry of outrage against wealth, conspicuous
consumption and the changes it has wrought in his beloved home—
changes so drastic that he's willing to destroy the Hamptons to save it."
Jaffe himself claims that the area is in "deep trouble," explaining that
"When I came here 30 years ago this was a rural community, we bal-

anced tourism and agriculture and sustainable lifestyle. . . . Now there is no balance, lifestyle is king. People have to have a 12,000-square-foot house and a fleet of exotic cars." Jaffe had always thought of himself as "living in the country," but, he now declares, "the Hamptons is not the country, it's suburbia, intense suburbia."[61]

The Hamptons may not be what one traditionally thinks of as suburbia, but then neither are the suburbs anymore. Many stretches of Nassau County and western Suffolk County are barely distinguishable from the stretches of Brooklyn and Queens that precede them along the Long Island Expressway. As Palen has written, the "suburbs are no longer sub. . . . Once overwhelmingly residential, suburbs now dominate the metropolitan business landscape . . . not only hous[ing] the bulk of retail trade, they often have more office workers and office space than the traditional downtowns."[62] But, with more and more upscale subdivisions filling the potato fields, more "sophisticated" chain retail stores nestling in between the local boutiques and farm stands, and more cars, trucks, vans, and other "land yachts" packing the back roads, the Hamptons are certainly more suburban than ever before.

In the end, however, whether one refers to the Hamptons as suburban, exurban, outer urban, or something else, what seems clear is that the quality of life once sought by middle-, upper-middle-, and upper-class urban migrants is disappearing, regardless of how many environmental organizations they join or how many retrospective exhibits they capture on film or on the stage. The very development these conquerors inspired initiated trends that eventually seemed to threaten both the physical landscape they sought and the cultural images they hoped to appropriate. But the double irony now emanates from the fact that such development has converged with larger economic, political, and cultural forces to bring to the Hamptons the very same social problems that urban refugees fled in the first place.

During the summer of 2002, Southampton police conducted what they called "Operation Crackdown," to stifle the growing crack cocaine trade in the area. According to police chief James Overton, the project was only the culmination of an intense eighteen-month effort that resulted in more than four hundred arrests. Earlier that spring, residents of Bridgehampton had met to discuss the drug trade that seemed prevalent in an area known as Huntington Crossway, just a few miles north of the bustling downtown strip. In both cases, local residents criticized the police efforts as ineffective, racist, and driven by political and economic self-interest. Of "Operation Crackdown," residents noted that police seemed interested only in the Flanders, Riverside, and Northampton hamlets—notably the poorest and most African American neighborhoods in Southampton—because of public outrage over "street dealers." Many contended that the arrests would be just a "band-aid" and that little would change until more was done for the area's youth. They complained about the Town's lack of interest in building a community center in the hamlet, explaining, "Kids need a place where they could go to do their homework instead of sitting on the streets and selling drugs . . . there's no other avenue for these kids right now."[63]

The Bridgehampton gathering was even more volatile as African American residents criticized the meeting's organizer, a local realtor, proclaiming, "This is not about kids or drugs; it's about property values and money." Bridgehampton School Board member Vivian Graham condemned what she called "opportunism," declaring, "I am sick and tired of this. . . . When you want development, you come into our community. But when we wanted to build a gym for our kids, to get them off the street, you voted down the budget." Bridgehampton is another hamlet in the town of Southampton that has a majority African American population and a history of racial animosity over disinvestment and disenfranchisement. Residents complained that police focus only on young African Americans but asked, "Who supports the drug trade —rich people. The people who buy drugs are not pulled over." Now that Bridgehampton has become trendy for McMansion subdivisions and upscale commercial development, residents note that "it's funny that all of the people here of a certain ethnicity [white] are realtors . . . you think that you can just move out the color and build as you please."[64] Residents worry that drugs and crime will be used to justify the gentrification of their historically black neighborhood. Fears of displacement and homelessness may not be unreasonable, given the lack of affordable housing and the area's rising homelessness problem.

In the fall of 2002, the Tuckahoe School complained about the influx of thirty unexpected new elementary grade students (almost 10 percent of the school's enrollment) because twenty-seven of them came from homeless families whom the Suffolk County Department of Social Services had resettled in nearby motels used as emergency housing in the Shinnecock Hills and Tuckahoe neighborhoods. As homeless populations have increased over the past two decades, more and more Suffolk

County families have been moved to facilities in the Hamptons. In fact, five hotels in Southampton are used as emergency family shelters, and over the past few years, nearby residents have complained bitterly about the impact of such facilities on their neighborhoods. One neighbor of the Hampton Bayside Motel explained that he was "concerned about vandalism, theft, and the quality of life he's entitled to." Another man who lives near the Olympia and Southampton Bays Motels claimed to be "constantly chasing away residents of the motel" from his property (including a couple he found having sex in a car parked in his driveway) and complained that "the value of our homes are diminished and threatened."[65]

Nowhere are the problems of poverty, homelessness, and racism more significant than among the region's burgeoning Latino population. Between 1990 and 2000, the Latino population in Southampton grew almost 300 percent, from 1,201 to 4,700, and now accounts for almost 9 percent of the total population. In East Hampton, Latinos now make up almost 15 percent of the population, having increased in number from 812 to almost 3,000 between 1990 and 2000. While such rapid increases impact a wide variety of social services and civic institutions such as schools, hospitals, and housing, the Hamptons have also experienced new waves of ethnic and racial hostilities, particularly around issues such as overcrowded housing and an influx of day laborers. A recent proposal to construct a community center with day-care facilities in Montauk has encountered stiff opposition. According to David Rattray, of the *East Hampton Star*, a caller explained his opposition: "Latinos, he told me, were the root of most of the problems facing Montauk and then proceeded to list a few: higher taxes, a language barrier, and the conversion of several prominent motels into illegal apartment housing. The day-care center would be for them, the children of Latino immigrants who live five to a room and, with Mom and Dad both working, don't have anyone to watch their children."[66]

Similar sentiments have been common in reaction to the growing numbers of predominately Latino day laborers who often congregate in the early mornings outside local delis, convenience stores, and, especially, the Riverhead Building Supply store. An East Hampton resident circulated a petition to address the problem of "illegal" immigrants, explaining that the "'uncontrolled influx of illegals in the last five years' has caused an increase in litter, crime, taxes, insurance, and health-care costs, as well as a decline in property values and the excessive need for

A group of day laborers wait for work across from Riverhead Building Supply Company, in East Hampton. (Photo by author, 2004)

affordable housing."[67] Southampton, too, has faced issues of discrimination as calls for the increased hiring of Latino teachers and for adding more bilingual personnel to Southampton Hospital have been met with apologies by the press and derision from public officials. By far, however, the most volatile racial situation has developed in Farmingville, a community that borders on Southampton Town. Here, a local group known as Sachem Quality of Life has joined forces with some of the most reactionary organizations in the United States to stop immigration "by any means necessary."[68]

Among the reported incidents in Farmingville are the beating of two Latino workers by white supremacist youth and a promise by local politicians that their constituents would be "out with baseball bats" if "attacked" by an influx of "illegal aliens." Certainly, the situation in the Hamptons is much more "civil," and, in fact, many local groups and individuals have spoken out against such incidents as the East Hampton petition. But, as the documentary filmmaker Carlos Sandoval has argued, "We [in the Hamptons] are shifting the costs of our McMansions back on places like Farmingville . . . we shift onto them the burden of taking care of our day workers. . . . Contractors go to places like Farmingville to pick up supplies. They pick up workers just like another commodity."[69] While some of the best work for Latino day laborers is in the Hamptons, affordable housing and other services there are almost nonexistent. Expanding economic development, driven by an upscale real estate industry and all its attendant services, will continue to create a demand for a relatively low-wage skilled and unskilled labor force. Latino workers will continue to be attracted directly to the East End to provide their labor power, but, as Sandoval explains, "We [in the Hamptons] don't welcome them with places to live."

More and more, though, Latinos are relocating to the Hamptons on a year-round basis. They, too, are looking for a better quality of life, and, like the middle- and upper-class migrants from New York City and "up-island," they want to make a home in the Hamptons. Maintaining the area's natural landscapes and historical charms, however, seems less important to them than finding good work, decent housing, adequate healthcare, schools for their children, and the social networks that help them establish identities in a new world at the same time that they preserve a sense of their own cultural heritage and legacy. Future debates in the Hamptons about affordable housing, school budgets, and undocumented workers will undoubtedly be, in part, about what kind of quality of life Latino workers and their families will eventually experience. But such debates will take place within a consistently changing, complex matrix composed of groups whose interests conflict and

In Southampton, 7-Eleven management posts signs to dissuade the hundreds of workers who wait each morning to get picked up for hire in the store's parking lot. (Photo by author, 2004)

coalesce in a cultural and historical mating dance of geographical convergence and convenience. As the economy of the early 2000s declines, the Hamptons may become even less "civil" toward Latino workers. The next historical dance will be complex, but its steps will determine what kind of community the Hamptons become.

Demographic, economic, and social changes have affected the sense of local identities created by various groups over the long history of migrations to the Hamptons. As members of both the newest and the largest demographic groups—the very wealthy and Latino immigrants —become year-round residents and assert their own identities within the local landscape, the Hamptons themselves will undergo transitions shaped by new economic forces, new political allegiances, and new cultural dynamics. History and geography will continue to shift and change as the impact of global transformations is reflected in the waves of new people who come to the Hamptons and in those who have already established themselves as part of the local landscape.

The process of claiming a local identity as "native" is a complicated one that represents the area's always changing historical consciousness and cultural politics. These dynamics play themselves out in many venues, but one of the most interesting and representative has been the East End's four-decade struggle to secede from Suffolk County and to form an "indigenous" Peconic County.

3

Peconic County Now!

Whose Quality of Life Is It Anyway?

Newsday, the business associations—the Long Island Association, all of these people—[are] trying to promote super-industry. . . . [Long Island] gets saturated and they've got to give it another shot in the arm, and then it's saturated again and then another shot in the arm. And I don't think you can keep on living that way. . . . That's why they want to build a bridge [to Connecticut] . . . more parking lots, more pavement, more of everything we don't want.

—Evans K. Griffing, founder of Peconic County independence movement

In short, the East End is still a rural area with farming, fishing, tourism and second homes as an economic base, which depends on its small villages, open spaces and environmental quality for its economic health. It has little in common with the remainder of Suffolk County, which is suburban, commercial and industrial. . . . Peconic County [is] the best means of protecting the rural character and natural resources of eastern Long Island from the destruction by the suburban sprawl.

—Peconic County Now! legal brief, 1997

If you've put a "Peconic County NOW" bumper sticker on your SUV and think it refers to the local chapter of the National Organization of Women, you're definitely NOT a local.

—*Southampton Press* editorial, May 25, 2000

Even if you told people their taxes would double, they'd still vote to secede.   —George Guldi, Suffolk County legislator

from Southampton

On Election Day, November 4, 1996, an overwhelming 70 percent majority of voters in the five towns of Eastern Long Island supported a referendum to secede from Suffolk County and to form Peconic County. A local state assemblyman, Fred Thiele Jr., one of the biggest supporters of the initiative, credited the victory to "literally hundreds of people who got together on cold winter nights [going door-to-door] from Montauk to Eastport to Wading River." As chairman of Peconic County Now!, an incorporated organization set up to promote secession, Larry Cantwell argued, "It's not just a pipe dream. It is a mandate from the people of the East End for a new county." For Peconic County supporters, the referendum was the culmination of forty years of struggle.[1]

The fight to secede has accompanied some of the most prolonged periods of rapid change in the area's history. But these changes have also inspired what the historian T. H. Breen calls an "obsession" with history itself. For newcomers, asserting the primacy of history lends a sense of legitimacy and even authenticity to their new claims. Even the discourse around environmentalism is wrapped in a historical cloak; saving "vanishing landscapes" promises to promote both ecological and cultural preservation. This kind of historical consciousness dominates McMansion landscapes as farms are protected to preserve open spaces and farmers to provide small-town values and local charm.

Others, however, argue that historical recovery could fuel resistance to such landscapes; Tom and Cathy Lester, discussed in chapter 2, hope that recovering "their heritage" might stop the privatization of public lands and the devastation of traditional ways of life. Breen believed that their insecurity about protecting the area's "quality of life" was evidence of a "full-scale social crisis." He wrote:

> East Hampton is totally obsessed with change. The community has in recent years experienced a dramatic, often wrenching, transformation. For many people a familiar world seems to be coming apart. A failure to address the problem of development, they argue, threatens to leave East Hampton looking . . . much like any other American town. At stake is a distinctive historical identity.[2]

Still, Breen recognized that the history of the Hamptons is ultimately a contested one that offers few clear and convincing narratives

PECONIC COUNTY <u>NOW</u>

INSIDE: 5 MAJOR REASONS TO CREATE PECONIC COUNTY NOW

1996 Peconic County Now! campaign poster. But *whose* East End would be saved? (Poster courtesy of Hal Ross, personal archives)

to support any group's claim to authenticity or birthright. Thus, he opted for a more "hermeneutical history" that "explores the creation of *truths*" and that sorts through the "conflicting perceptions" and multiple narratives "that humans have always invented to make sense out of their lives."[3]

Nowhere is the politics of Hamptons history and identity more notable than in the Peconic County Now! movement. The drive to form a more "indigenous" Peconic County is steeped in the same kinds of identity politics that Breen found in East Hampton's obsession with its own past. Despite the wide variety of individuals and interest groups that sought to create Peconic County, they seem to share a common paradigm that there is *something* unique, authentic, distinct and, ultimately, valuable about the East End that needs to be simultaneously protected, defended, and promoted. According to one Peconic County leader, Hal Ross, "the primary reason to create Peconic County is to preserve and maintain the distinctive rural character, the 350-year historical and cultural identity, and the natural beauty of the East End."[4]

Because of its link to authenticity and identity, Peconic County attracts more than just bonackers and blue bloods. Many wealthy Manhattan migrants who now make the Hamptons their primary, year-round residence have signed onto the movement. The running joke that everyone who crosses the Shinnecock Canal Bridge wants to blow it up behind them is, in part, inspired by the seemingly common practice among recent home buyers of turning into vociferous antidevelopment activists as soon as their own contractor has hammered home the last nail. This metamorphosis translates easily into support for Peconic County. Many environmentalists who believe that "up-island" developers and politicians threaten the preservation of regional open spaces and natural resources generally align themselves with secessionists, too. Conservative, antitax activists (linked primarily with older white natives and newer libertarian dot.comers) like Peconic County's promises to keep tax dollars low and local. Promoters of local democracy and "home-rule" doctrines see separation as a way to enhance participatory practices and "good government." Almost everyone seems to find some reason to support the creation of Peconic County.

This chapter examines the history and politics of the Peconic County movement. In particular, I look at how the idea of secession has come to represent a shifting sense of identity among the area's changing demographic groups. Although the idea was initially steeped in a kind of nativist, antidevelopment form of resistance, it now represents a confluence of interests among diverse class and political constituencies, all of whom share a similar desire to identify the East End as a place of distinction and themselves as indigenous to it. Central to this convergence is a substantial yet sometimes obfuscated discourse about the area's geographically and historically unique "rural quality of life." These stories, and their claims to an authentic cultural identity, are powerful narratives framed by the reality of aesthetically stunning ocean beaches, sprawling, sun-drenched fields, and dense, deer-filled woods. Ultimately, though, these same appealing narratives about a place of distinction and its natural beauty threaten some of the movement's own goals of environmental protection, economic sustainability, and political democracy. After all, the more distinct the area's image, the greater the pressures for continued upscale residential development, new shopping centers, and higher taxes to provide necessary social services.

Perhaps more notable, though, is that the sense of exclusivity inherent in the idea of Peconic County raises the stakes for already marginalized populations. Many working-class people and people of color wonder whose Hamptons a Peconic County would represent. Ultimately, it may be that the vision of Peconic County not only represents a romanticized historical narrative but also betrays the real history of constant demographic integration and transition. Despite a history of conquest and resistance, the Hamptons possess a past of adaptation and diversity, cooperation and mutualism. The complex history of struggle and unity could offer an alternative view that gives the region its most authentic sense of place. While Peconic County doesn't openly support discrimination, its claims to a particular authenticity and identity do obscure the rich legacy of the area's human diversity; it is this diversity that must be preserved and promoted to offer a truly distinct and sustainable vision for the future.

HISTORY: PECONIC COUNTY THEN

The idea for a Peconic County took shape in the early 1960s when, at the urging of Evans K. Griffing, the Shelter Island town supervisor, East End leaders responded to a newly proposed Suffolk County charter that would change the area's governing structure. The County Board of Supervisors was originally composed of the ten town supervisors, each one receiving the same individual vote regardless of the size of his or her town. Thus, Shelter Island, with a population of 1,300 in 1960, had the same political clout as Islip, with a population of 173,000. To many regional government advocates and pro-development forces in Nassau and in western Suffolk counties, the area required a stronger, more centralized administrative system to facilitate economic growth and its attendant infrastructure of public services. More important, the much less populated East End and its supervisors were staunch opponents of pro-development policies such as countywide sewage systems and highway expansions.

Alicia Patterson, publisher of *Newsday*, Long Island's major daily newspaper and a pro-growth booster, became a driving force behind the promotion of a new Suffolk County charter. Along with Alan Hathaway, the paper's managing editor, she argued that the County's form of government had not changed since the 1700s and that a "unified county government" was required to plan rationally for serious growth. In addition to bringing together a host of town-specific departments into a countywide system, the charter, in its most significant change, would provide for the election of a county executive who could break ties between the five western, pro-growth town supervisors and the five East End, antidevelopment supervisors. According to the *Newsday* historian Robert Keeler, when Griffing and his East End bloc promised to stand in the way of the charter, Hathaway decided it would be necessary to commit "political murder" and went after Griffing.

To do so, Hathaway enlisted the well-known reporter Bob Greene to promote the charter, first by trying to negotiate with Griffing, and finally by trying to defeat him with a pro-charter candidate when he ran for reelection. Greene remembers negotiating with Griffing one evening while sipping scotch on Shelter Island:

> We were really searching around this whole night to try and find some way in which everything could be satisfied and he would not be politically hurt, in his terms, and also that the East End wouldn't be screwed. . . . But the point is that, no matter how you did it, the East End was going to be screwed . . . and we both came to this conclusion.[5]

Although Hathaway and Greene failed to defeat Griffing's reelection bid, their continued pressure for the Charter paid off as the East Hampton supervisor, Richard Gilmartin, defected from the East End bloc and the County Board passed the charter in 1958. Later that year, the voters of Suffolk County overwhelmingly approved the legislation that created a county executive, to be elected at-large countywide.[6]

Further erosion of East End officials' local authority occurred following pro–civil rights rulings by the U.S. Supreme Court in the early 1960s. Relying on the principle of "one-man, one vote," U.S. federal courts mandated that Suffolk County create a new legislative body that reapportioned representation on the basis of population, not township designations. A five-year struggle over reapportionment proposals finally ended in 1969 when County officials approved a plan to abolish the Board of Supervisors and to establish an eighteen-member, part-time county legislature composed of district representatives.[7] The new districts left the East End with only one-and-a-half representatives out of eighteen. East End leaders recognized that this shift impacted their own power, as well as their constituency's ability to shape local affairs and land-use policies and to control taxation. It also contravened the principle of home-rule held so dearly by local politicians. Griffing argued that the East End towns had become "step-children" of the county. He explained:

> It's like hollering in a rain barrel. You can't accomplish anything with your vote. It's opposed by the [legislators'] votes at the other end of the County. They're not concerned with what goes on here. I have a feeling that we're being taken to the cleaners . . . this is when we began to go downhill.[8]

The charter and the new legislature became symbols for the kinds of social change that threatened the East End's control over a "traditional and local way of life." In response, Griffing says, "as soon as we saw the erosion approaching, we realized that the only salvation was to separate." Together with Steve Meschutt, Southampton town supervisor, and Norman Klipp, Southold town supervisor, Griffing created the Peconic County idea and began organizing support through lectures and local publicity.

Yet, the concern of local politicians was not just about losing power per se; it was about what the loss of that power would mean. For many on the East End, the Suffolk charter represented the inevitable onslaught of suburban sprawl and marked what the local journalist and historian Karl Grossman says was the "handwriting on the wall." For more than a decade, Long Island planners and politicians discussed the impact of massive migration from Manhattan, its attendant problems of automobile traffic, residential overcrowding, and waste disposal. As early as the 1950s, fears of rampant suburbanization sparked debate over the need for a rapid-transit system to ease the inevitable burden on Robert Moses's expanding Long Island highway system. As Robert Caro described:

> Low-density subdivision had already inundated two-thirds of Nassau County. But the rest of Nassau and most of vast Suffolk County still lay largely unsubdivided—unshaped; great chunks of Long Island were in 1955 still a tabula rasa on which a design for the future could be etched with the lessons of the past in mind . . . [but] once the Long Island Expressway was built, no change would be possible. Construction of the great road would open up the entire Island for develop-

ment. As it pushed through new farm country—even *before* it pushed through the country, as soon as the announcement was made that the push was imminent—the country would fill up with subdivisions.[9]

Robert Moses would have nothing of mass public transportation. To ease congestion, he suggested making the road even bigger. As the writer Karl Grossman puts it, "It was a clarion call."[10] But Moses-inspired highways and their tributary ticky-tacky subdivisions and strip malls were not the only development interests in the game. Griffing argued that it was really a convergence of profit-driven leaders from business, government, and media that directed the development frenzy. As one Suffolk legislator points out in *Power Crazy,* Grossman's book about the Long Island Lighting Company (LILCO), "LILCO and its conduits in the Long Island Association [LIA] and the construction trade unions —all major contributors to both parties—managed to buy silence from town and county governments."[11] The LIA represented a fairly typical, post–World War II pro-growth machine, its engines emanating from links to national and international politics through LILCO director (and the LIA's seventeenth president) William J. Casey.[12] Led by Moses, Casey, and *Newsday,* local and regional business interests combined with a national power elite to boost defense-related industries on Long Island, such as Republic Aviation Corporation, Grumman Aircraft Engineering Corporation, and Brookhaven National Laboratories. As pro-growth supporters built the financial, residential, and commercial establishments to facilitate this industrial growth, Nassau and western Suffolk counties set Atlantic regional records for industrial expansion and commercial development in the 1960s.

While the loss of legislative power and the fear of both industrial development and suburban sprawl may have been behind the idea of Peconic County, the drive for a more autonomous and indigenous set of political borders also germinated in the collective sense that East Enders had about their own history and identity. Evans Griffing drew this distinction very clearly. He explained:

> The people of Eastern Suffolk are more self-employed . . . than people numerically in the western county. We have a great deal more independence and self-dependence . . . people at the west end . . . are simply employees of corporations. They don't have to make decisions that are vital to their very existence. Out east, agriculture and small busi-

nessmen have to make decisions to determine whether they're going
to survive or not. . . . [W]e have the nucleus of a very decent, fundamental county on the five eastern towns because of the simple independence of the individual.[13]

Not only do the East End's historical identity and distinction origi-
nate in the nation's own creation myth of self-reliant settlers who tamed
the land with their hard work and strong values, but also Griffing im-
plies that this heritage legitimizes the political autonomy of the area.
Much of this self-reliance could be traced back to the "basic individual
ruggedness" of Griffing's descendants, the New England Yankees who
migrated to Long Island in the 1600s. For him, "as soon as you become
dependent on somebody else for everything, you lose some of your
own reliance." He continues: "Today if the lights go out, we're a mess.
Years ago if the lights had trouble we had kerosene lamps, we didn't
have a catastrophe. And your furnace didn't stop. You had coal in the
bin or wood in the shed. We didn't have a dependence on a centralized
source of energy."[14] Echoed in Griffing's heroic nostalgia are the voices
of Crevecoeur's American farmer, whose "industriousness" and "individualism" combined to create "the American," a new man who had
passed "from involuntary idleness, servile dependence, penury, and
useless labour . . . to toils of a very different nature, rewarded by ample
subsistence."[15]

But this individual passion for industry and self-reliance also fueled the kind of unrestrained growth that was now threatening the idyllic life of the yeoman farmer. As the historian John Strong has written,
"it was European technological superiority that led the newcomers to
conclude that they were destined to take over all of the land. It was just
a matter of time. They believed that the land was theirs by natural right
because they could harness the natural resources and make the land
productive."[16] The Yankees themselves had originally conquered the
Native American "wilderness" in part because the Indians' open fields
and spaces seemed "boundless" and "unimproved." Entitlement to the
land required maximum utilization, and, according to the Yankee busi-
nessman William Wood, the Indians' land "had become 'all spoils, rots
. . . marred for want of manuring, gathering, ordering, etc. . . . Like the
'foxes and wild beasts,' Indians did nothing 'but run over the grass.'"[17]
More than three hundred years later, the Yankees' own sense of place—
now defined as "traditional" or "rural" or "agricultural"—was being

threatened by another wave of rationalized economic development and political conquest. These ironies and contradictions haunted the idea of Peconic County, a place where certain kinds of historical identities might be preserved at the same time that uncomfortable tensions might be submerged.

Despite early support for secession throughout the East End, some local legislators questioned its effectiveness. H. Beecher Halsey, of Westhampton Beach, had reservations about the financial aspects of separation and called for a feasibility study.[18] Most resistance, though, came from western Suffolk administrators and legislators, who feared the loss of regional control and of the tax base. Lee Koppelman, the Suffolk County planning director, sympathized with the preservation instinct but argued that supervisors already had the power to regulate economic development through the local comprehensive planning process.[19] The county executive, John V. N. Klein, argued that such a split could not be fairly negotiated, would result in the duplication of numerous building and services, and would leave both sections of Suffolk County in financial ruin. Klein threatened to use "every legitimate device available" to stop the secession, echoing the words of his predecessor, H. Lee Dennison, by exclaiming that Peconic County would secede "over my dead body!"[20]

The largest stumbling block, though, was a New York State constitutional requirement that any new county have a population large enough to qualify the area for its own state Assembly district. In 1960, that number would have been around 100,000; by 1970, the number was up to 121,000; in that year, the East End towns had only 85,000 residents. Efforts to create Peconic County were resurrected in the early 1970s, though, through a proposed constitutional amendment, but state voters opposed the 1973 ballot question by a wide margin. While western Suffolk voted against the measure because of the obvious implications for its tax base and its political clout, others around the state apparently worried about a possible domino effect—an avalanche of other county secessions. Yet, according to Ed Sharretts, then a leader in the Peconic County effort, the bill did not lose because of its implications for other areas. The ballot initiative received little publicity, and voters tend to say "no" to most "top-of-the-ballot" questions. And Griffing, who now realized that "dark clouds" of growth and development would carry with it the "silver lining" of increased population, remained optimistic. He argued that, by 1975, the area would have enough population to secede. For the time being, he explained, "The attempt is futile, as far as accomplishment goes, but we are keeping the egg warm so it will hatch one day."[21]

The issue of Peconic County received renewed support in 1980 as census data showed that the East End's population had grown to exceed 100,000 at the same time that overall state population had decreased. Thus, a local state assemblyman, John Behan, submitted a bill calling for a referendum on secession in the five East End towns. Opponents demanded that all ten Suffolk County towns be included in the referendum, assuming that western Suffolk would want to keep the tax-rich and service-poor East End within its jurisdiction. As the conflicts intensified, the issue of financial feasibility reared its head again, and debates arose over exactly just how much a new county might cost its residents. Peter Cohalan, the Suffolk county executive and a self-proclaimed "opponent with an open mind," issued a report titled "Impact of Proposed Peconic County." The document declared that "the inescapable fiscal conclusion is that separation would mean a tax increase for the new county." Cohalan did not rule out creating a Peconic County and made it clear that he would support whatever voters decided. He continued, however, "If the people feel strong enough for separation, then certainly that commitment should include the willingness to pay for it."[22] But Cohalan did not advocate the creation of Peconic County, and the idea again faded from the political landscape. Despite periodic references and bumper stickers, little headway toward actual secession occurred throughout the 1980s. Still, Griffing's egg continued to incubate.

HATCHING A NEW MOVEMENT

Fred Thiele Jr. was born in Sag Harbor in the 1950s, the son of second- and third-generation working-class immigrants from Poland and Portugal. He grew up interested in politics, explaining that, "When I was ten years old I had a Bobby Kennedy bumper sticker on my bike." Following his graduation from Albany Law School (part of Union University), he returned to the East End to work with the area's state assemblyman, John Behan. In the 1980s, Thiele became the town attorney for Southampton and the attorney for the East Hampton Planning and Zoning Boards. His focus, however, "was always on politics and eventually running for public office."[23] In 1987, he ran for the Suffolk County legislature and won, serving two terms in office until 1991. By his mid-thirties, Thiele, a liberal to moderate Republican, had a comprehensive knowledge of East End politics and a formidable ability both to understand complex economic and social issues and to communicate them in an accessible way to his constituency. An intelligent and personable politician, Thiele was poised for success.

Hal Ross had grown up in Brookline, Massachusetts, and, after years as an economist and Democratic Party activist based primarily first in Montgomery County, Maryland, and then in Stamford, Connecticut, he moved to East Hampton in the early 1970s. He quickly became involved with the town's local Democratic Party, in particular with a group of women activists led by Judith Hope who were interested in running for office to protect, in Ross's words, "the area's rural quality of life." Like the rest of the East End, East Hampton had been a traditional Republican stronghold, and few people gave the Democratic upstarts much of a chance. Yet, they ran a campaign focusing on what the *East Hampton Star* and local polls had suggested was the area's primary concern—the environment. Ross is careful to explain that the group didn't use the word "environment"; it had polled people "and found it was too narrow a term." Instead, the candidates talked about preserving and conserving the area's distinct "quality of life." With a platform that stressed "up-zoning" and open spaces and campaign propaganda that frightened the public with photos of Coney Island superimposed onto East Hampton beaches, the Democrats won. When Ross moved to Southampton a few years later, he was able to repeat his success by helping to elect the first Democratic town supervisor in decades.[24]

By the late 1980s, both Thiele and Ross had grown discontent with their respective parties. Thiele felt "disrespected" and "slighted" by local Southampton Republicans, who had become entrenched and arrogant. Thiele had expressed an interest in running for town supervisor but had been rebuffed. Ross was not happy with the leadership of the Democratic Party, which he felt had created only a narrow base of blue-collar and patronage-related support that "couldn't get anything done." Ross told the chair of the Southampton Democrats that, if he didn't change the status quo, "I'll have to form a third party." Only a few days later, according to Ross, "the Lord came down and gave me Fred Thiele." Together, in early 1991, Ross and Thiele created the

Southampton Party, committed to the kind of environmental "quality of life" platform that Ross had promoted in East Hampton and that Thiele had wanted the Republicans in Southampton to adopt.

Against the odds, the Southampton Party won election to the Town Board of Supervisors in 1991. Despite running on a relatively liberal, pro-environment/controlled-growth platform, it also gained support from independent Republicans who were disaffected with a party leadership that had encouraged rampant development and, in the perception of many, had mismanaged government funds to support investments in growth. Ross and Thiele were also able to put together a slate of candidates and supporters committed to the kinds of environmentally based, quality-of-life issues that Ross had helped infuse into the East Hampton Democratic Party. And Thiele was the perfect candidate to adopt a relatively liberal agenda but also to garner the support of Republicans. Thiele explains, "I had a reputation as an eclectic politician who was fiscally conservative and very good on taxes, but very good on environmental and social issues, as well." The real success of the party, however, was its ability to capture a sense of local identity that transcended or transgressed party loyalties and created a constituency based on the idea of keeping Southampton "Southampton." For Ross, the campaign had become a kind of "crusade," evidenced by the turnout (in excess of 50 percent) for a town in which it is rare to get a 40 percent turnout. In the face of increasing fears over unrestrained growth and mismanagement, the Southampton Party based its appeal on a certain sense of place and local identity that was founded on a historic, predevelopment notion of what the area was, as opposed to what it might be or, for some, had already become.

As town supervisor, Thiele began working with other East End towns to forward preservation efforts and a limited growth agenda. Most notable was his partnership with another disaffected Republican, Tom Wickham, who had established a similar third party named United Southold, in the North Fork town of Southold. Along with other East End officials, Thiele established a variety of local landmark preservation projects. He acknowledges that the platform and strategy of the Southampton Party certainly influenced a renewed interest in Peconic County, but he contends that such a revival would not have been possible without a growing sense of regionalism among East End legislators. Thiele explains:

> You had a host of elected officials in all of the towns that seemed to
> have a broader, regional view. Even non–Peconic County supporters,
> like Tony Bullock in East Hampton, had a more regional view. . . . We
> were already working together on things like the Peconic Estuary and
> the Pine Barrens. The natural next step was to say that we are working
> on all these regional issues; why not resurrect the granddaddy of all re-
> gional issues—Peconic County?[25]

The growing regionalism was undoubtedly driven by land-use politics as every town on the East End faced increased development pressures linked to the same forces discussed at length in chapter 2. But
much of the research and analytical groundwork for a revitalized
Peconic County movement was developed in the early 1990s as part of
an East End Economic and Environmental Task Force report commis-
sioned by then-Governor Mario Cuomo titled "Blueprint for Our Future: Creating Jobs, Preserving the Environment."

The report began by laying out much the same argument that the
new Peconic County supporters would eventually put forth. The task
force explained that the East End of Long Island had a different history,
culture, and character from the rest of Long Island. From its earliest
links with small-town New England Protestants, as opposed to New
York City commerce, to its continued "rural lifestyle and environment,"
task force members asserted, the region faced a special problem in its
need to "enhance the economy of the East End of Long Island without
threatening its fragile environment." Thus, the report promoted the argument that the East End's "high quality environment . . . must continue to be perceived as unique and unspoiled" and that the region
must "maintain, if not enhance, its local character and appeal."[26]

These are the themes that Hal Ross and Fred Thiele Jr. employed to
build the new Peconic County movement. Time and time again, Ross
explained that the idea of Peconic County is a "simple one: to preserve
the rural nature of the area." Thiele echoed this statement, explaining
that widespread support for Peconic County is, and always has been,
based on a wish to protect quality-of-life issues. The report helped to
raise these issues within a context of the need to generate a sustainable,
regional economy on the East End. By promoting environmentally sensitive industries such as agriculture, fishing, wineries, and recre-
ation/second homes, the authors argued not only that it would be possible to "strengthen the East End economy without adversely affecting

its environment" but that environmental preservation itself was necessary for generating economic growth. Commenting on the booming $10
billion investment made by second-home and recreational "users" of
the region, the authors cautioned that, "like other investments, this one
could turn sour if the reason the second homeowners have invested so
much on the East End disappears. If the beaches of the East End become
polluted, or if agriculture and fishing vanished, these second homeowners would have no reason to maintain their investment on the East
End. . . . The East End economy would crash."[27]

Once the Economic and Environmental Institute demonstrated that
the East End could "preserve and protect" the area's "rural qualities"
while still promoting economic development, Thiele and Ross believed
that the next step toward establishing Peconic County had to be an ex-
ploration of just how much it would cost its residents. Again, Cuomo
and the five East End towns put up money for more research—$100,000
to the Institute for a Peconic County feasibility study. Although some
(such as Lee Koppleman, former executive director of the Long Island
Regional Planning Board) criticized the report's findings, few have
challenged the comprehensive nature and the integrity of the study.
Ross speaks with great pride of the dozens of volunteers who contributed to the research in a committed and objective way. Liz Granitz,
professor of economics at Southampton College and a local resident,
got involved in the feasibility research, in part because she "didn't want
to engage in having a County and having a huge government structure
which would then increase taxes just to have more bureaucracy. . . . you
had to have a cost-benefit analysis and it had to be realistic."[28] Released
in August 1995, the feasibility study declared that Peconic County
would be financially viable. In fact, the report explained that a new
county would result in an overall savings for residents, in part because
of the disproportionate amount of tax dollars contributed by East End
towns to Suffolk County compared to the tax dollars the towns received
from the county. The rest of the savings would come primarily from, in
Ross's word, "downsizing the structure of County government," something that would inevitably result in reducing social services.[29]

Armed with the study's findings and a deep conviction that
Peconic County could be the key to "saving" the East End, Ross, Thiele,
and other major advocates such as the East Hampton town attorney,
Larry Cantwell, formed the nonprofit organization, Peconic County
Now, Inc. For Thiele, this new group meant moving from the citizens

advisory committees that had provided the policy conclusions for the feasibility study to channeling "its members and their energies into an entity that will do public education and lobbying for a new East End County." In January 1996, they began an intense campaign, reaching out to every nook and cranny of the East End. Thiele, Ross, Cantwell, and others spoke to community organizations, church groups, chambers of commerce, and a variety of business and civic institutions in public forums at town halls, libraries, church basements, and school gymnasiums all over the North and South Forks. They also developed a legislative strategy that succeeded in getting the state Senate to pass legislation providing for a regional referendum on Peconic County in November of that year. Although many people contributed to the campaign, Thiele was the movement's acknowledged leader, both spiritually and in labor power. Not only did he make more speeches and chair more meetings than anyone else, but also his own history and identity as a local success story and representative of the community gave Peconic County a sense of authenticity and possibility.

Meanwhile, Hal Ross, as chair of the group's Public Education Committee, prepared "The Case for a Peconic County." In this document, used by a host of speakers in formal and informal settings, Ross laid out the "Five Reasons to Support Peconic County Now." They included giving the area more local control; saving the area's "rural quality of life and traditional economy"; reducing county property taxes; creating a smaller, more efficient government; and developing a fair settlement for both counties. Soon these declarations found their way onto posters, flyers, handbills, and advertisements and were repeated in editorials, press releases, radio interviews, and a host of other forums around the region. Ross concluded the document by explaining that, if an initial, nonbinding referendum was passed by a significant majority of East End voters, then a second binding referendum could be forthcoming pending approval from the state legislature. He cautioned, however, that "a *simple* majority is not sufficient reason to proceed ahead on such a serious matter." As the November 1996 elections neared, Peconic County supporters knew they would win the referendum, but they could not be certain about the extent to which their platform's major plank—to preserve the area's rural character and quality of life—had won the hearts and minds of the East End population.

Yet, the Peconic County of the 1990s was significantly different from the Peconic County of the late 1960s and early 1970s. Now, secession was not antigrowth per se but was being recast as supporting "sustainable economic development and environmental preservation." This recent incantation was not the movement of old Yankees hell-bent on saving home rule and keeping the city's professional managerial elite from the gate. Instead, it preached an economic growth strategy based on the "second-home industry," the very people Griffing and his cohort had thought would threaten the East End's native spirit of laissez-faire independence and rugged autonomy. Thus, the Peconic County Now! movement contained its own historical contradictions: it cloaked the new political entity with a cultural nostalgia for "rural lifestyles" at the same time that it linked the county's economic success to the kinds of development that continued to supplant those lifestyles. By the time of the 1996 referendum Southampton and East Hampton alone had more than 40,000 more residents and more than 30,000 more houses than when Griffing first proposed the creation of Peconic County. Some wondered just what was left of the old East End to preserve.

THE GROUP FOR THE SOUTH FORK AND AN
ENVIRONMENTAL QUALITY OF LIFE

Ross was, however, confident that supporters had framed the Peconic County issue in the best way they could. After all, survey after survey had demonstrated that the one issue East End people cared the most about was the environment.

No other formal organization in the area had been as successful in creating environmental awareness and intervening in land-use issues from an ecological perspective as the Group for the South Fork. Originally known as the Group for America's South Fork, the organization was founded in 1972 with a grant of $150,000 from the Whitehall Foundation. Ross himself admits that much of the East Hampton Democratic platform in the early 1970s emanated from the teachings of Ian Marceau, the first executive director of "The Group." Marceau led a seminar at Southampton College and "re-educated us on environmentalism," says Ross. "He taught us that when you develop a field, change a road, you can never go back—that does it—it's irreparable. . . . It changed my belief that economic development is always a good goal."[30]

The Group's founders were an ad hoc bunch of local residents, many of whom had recently moved to the area on a year-round basis.

They were angered by a series of East Hampton town planning decisions that threatened the natural resources, as well as by what they perceived to be the area's environmental character. In fact, the issue that inspired their first meeting was a plan to build a major shopping center in
Bridgehampton. The Group's main interest was not to stop growth per
se, for many of the initial members were themselves recent migrants. As
one founder, Nancy Goell, explains:

> We wanted to *control* growth . . . we wanted development that would-
> n't be harmful to the community, that would not destroy the farmland,
> the wetlands, the beaches, the aesthetic quality of the villages. The in-
> tegrity of the villages here greatly depends on the open spaces be-
> tween them. I don't know, sometimes people shy away from saying
> that the aesthetics are as important as anything else. I don't. I think the
> visual character of this place is what makes it so attractive to so many
> people.[31]

Although the Group failed to stop the shopping center, it eventually
succeeded in raising money, hiring Marceau, opening an office, building a membership, and establishing the organization as an important
local player in land-use politics.

The Group was quite successful in the early years, in part influenced by the larger national movements that had spun off from Earth
Day in 1970.[32] This growing consciousness and environmental awareness merged with the evolving concerns over land-use issues and gave
the Group and its efforts strong credibility and legitimacy. From its inception, however, the Group identified itself, and environmental issues
in general, with the "distinctive quality" of the region. In one of its first
newsletters, the Group explained, "It's called the Group for *America's*
South Fork because the South Fork of Long Island . . . is unique in the
U.S. It's an area of beaches, marshes, woodlands, ponds, and potato
fields, which [has] played a basic part in the history and culture of this
country."[33] Thus, environmentalism in the region was more than just a
consciousness about pollution and sprawl; it was bound up in a sense
of local and historical identity.

The Group's interest in linking the local area to a national movement also represented a change in the regional population's own consciousness, or at least the consciousness of its new residential demographic, now dominated by a wealthier, more professional, and more

THE GROUP FOR THE SOUTH FORK

The Group for the South Fork's "Signs of the Times" links historical nostalgia with the desires of new migrants who buy authenticity along with their produce. (Poster courtesy of Group for the South Fork; original photos by Rivalyn Zweig)

politically sophisticated urban class. These migrants brought with them a metropolitan sense of political organizing and campaign marketing. Yet, they also had a different idea of who they were as "locals," and this alternative identity helped to create a philosophy of environmental preservation that was not hostile to growth but was critical of the kinds of development that threatened the very "environmental quality of life" they sought in moving to the Hamptons year-round. This shift is evident in the Group's belief that somehow the Hamptons belonged to a larger population outside the local area. The Group explained, "Only 100 miles from New York City, this relatively unspoiled area serves as an essential, open-space recreational area for many thousands of urban dwellers."[34] Most new residents had once been these New Yorkers, enjoying the Hamptons for their "unspoiled" (read "nonurban") landscapes. Despite (and, ironically, because of) increasing suburbanization, the Hamptons now belonged to them, too.

In order to promote a controlled growth agenda, the Group established a multilevel strategy. First, it developed a research and education agenda that would provide the information necessary to raise the area's environmental consciousness. Next, it became a watchdog organization whose members attended meetings of local governing bodies, planning committees, and zoning boards and informed the community about the relevant decisions being made. Finally, the Group used its education, research, and communication networks to intervene in policy making by lobbying and organizing members to make their voices heard on environmental and land-use issues. Sometimes political intervention took the route of "assisting" town boards with research on development projects that threatened natural resources such as barrier dunes and wetlands. On other occasions, such as the case of Gansett Dunes, in East Hampton, where the Group's advice was ignored and the town approved the building of thirty-five houses on shoreline dunes despite the environmental devastation it would cause, the Group took legal action and sued the town's planning board. And, sometimes, when political pressure was needed most, the Group organized large turnouts for meetings to demonstrate that public sentiment supported its environmental agenda.

Throughout the mid- to late 1970s, the Group succeeded on a variety of issues. Both East Hampton and Southampton continued to pass upzoning legislation, moving thousands of acres from half-acre and one-acre plots to one-acre and two-acre plots, respectively, as well as restricting some new housing structures to three- and five-acre plots of land, thus reducing population density and maintaining open spaces. The Group was instrumental in derailing the development of many hotel, condominium, and subdivision projects (such as its eventual victory at Gansett Dunes), while forcing many other developers to modify their original plans in order to protect wetlands, barrier dunes, and other natural resources. And the organization created farmland preservation programs to help save the dwindling number of traditional farmers.

Perhaps the Group's greatest achievement, though, lay in the increasingly popular paradigm that linked consciousness of environmental issues to local identity. In 1979, its executive director, Nancy Goell, wrote:

> When the Group for America's South Fork was formed seven years ago all agreed that our primary goal was to preserve farmland and open space. Aesthetically the loss of farms means the loss of the rural quality of life which is of such a value to this area, and the loss of agricultural industry which brings fifteen million dollars each year to the South Fork. Unless the governments of the South Fork produce a comprehensive policy to preserve the agricultural industry and maintain the farmland, the battle to keep this area's rural character and to keep the economy sound will have been lost. . . . Our citizens must speak out, attend planning board and town board meetings, decry the subdivision and development of our farms and demand action to stop it.[35]

Once again, the "rural quality of life" and "rural character" became the driving force behind local identity—to such an extent that environmental issues were as much about this identity as they were about ecological sustainability and natural resources.

And, despite the Group's success in stopping and modifying myriad development projects, it proved to be much harder to actually control growth regionally. While the housing boom of the late 1960s and early 1970s did fall off in the mid- and late 1970s, some of that decline could easily be accounted for by the economic downturns of that period. When the economy rebounded in the late 1970s and early 1980s, housing in the Hamptons boomed again. Still, the Group remained an important player in land-use politics, and it continued to grow in membership and influence. Not only did it participate quite noticeably in the

Water Mill's newest shopping plaza, anchored by a Blockbuster Video, sports the kind of "cute country planning" that Bob Deluca calls a "half-assed cartoon of the country." (Photo by author, 2004)

East End's Economic and Environmental Institute, but it even became a benefactor of one of the summer season's more notable charity events—a fundraiser hosted by Peter Jennings, of ABC News, a summer resident.

Throughout the 1990s, the group continued to chalk up victories on a variety of issues. With Fred Thiele and the Southampton Party running the Southampton Town Board, the Group's agenda had great influence. Not only did the town improve its farmland preservation and upzoning policies, but Thiele helped pass the Group's most controversial plan—a land transfer tax that would take a 2 percent cut from new home purchases costing more than $250,000 and second purchases of more than $100,000 and put the money into a fund for purchasing farmland and open spaces for parks, recreation, and preservation purposes. And, while the Group itself did not take a position on Peconic County, it was clear that many of the environmental and "rural quality-of-life" issues that revived support for Peconic County were supported and promoted by the Group.

By the late 1980s and early 1990s, however, the demographics of the new housing boom were becoming clear. Changing development patterns, driven by new technologies and cultural tastes, were creating a whole new set of land-use pressures. First, the summer season seemed to expand as second homeowners showed up on weekends well before Memorial Day and stayed to see the leaves turn color well after Labor Day. Soon they came also for holidays like Thanksgiving, Christmas, and New Year's week, and for spring breaks, Easter, and Passover. Driven by the advent of telecommuting technologies, supported by more frequent runs by the Hampton Jitney and other luxury bus lines, and eventually served by a growing number of private schools, more and more second homeowners became primary residents. The increasingly year-round character of this population did more than just impact the number of new residential structures being built on the East End. The Group for the South Fork's current president, Bob Deluca, claims that a new cultural paradigm had spread along with the changing demographics. He calls it a "cancer of convenience":

> We move to a rural destination to get away from people and things that represent an urban culture to us, and suddenly we have to have the same things. Maybe we have a pitched roof on the Blockbuster Video, but we have to have the Blockbuster Video. I better be able to have a McDonald's, and I better be able to have a Pizza Hut, and I better have a Midas Muffler because it's three dollars cheaper, and I want a superstore K Mart because I can get a roll of toilet paper for a nickel less. The paradigm of convenience and discount shopping . . . pushes and pushes and pushes at the seams of the planning that determines the future of the landscape.[36]

While some of the Manhattan migrants of the 1960s and early 1970s had founded the Group particularly to ward off such developments, a new bumper crop of year-rounders now seemed hell-bent on bringing with them the amenities of city life. Still, the development needs and tastes of this new population did not require the eyesore megaplexes and strip malls that overran Nassau County and western Suffolk in the first decades after World War II. These new migrants were not the apathetic, middle-class "employees" that Griffing had disparaged; they were elite financial managers and publicity moguls, dot.com entrepreneurs and music industry executives, media personalities and real estate mavens. The amenities had to be upscale.

The East End became a site for the convergence of a variety of economic and cultural trends. The push for upscale development, particularly the amenities to facilitate a wealthy, second-home and year-round population, combined with an increasing opposition to "suburban sprawl" and a romantic vision of rural aesthetics and quality of life to inspire what Deluca calls "cute country planning." Retail developments would be slightly smaller and less intensive; the retailers would tend to be more boutique-like or gourmet specialty shops; and the structures that housed them would be built with soft woods and decorated in earthy tones. These projects still threatened the actual ecology of the area, diminishing open spaces, encouraging more automobile traffic, increasing solid waste disposal problems and pollution, and facilitating the further development of the area. Even the aesthetics, according to Deluca, are absurd. Despite the salt-box delicatessens and pitched-roofed pizzerias and video stores, "there is nothing on the East End that looks like this in nature. There was never any little farm community that turned into a Blockbuster Video and a bagel shop anywhere." He contends that the planning process has reified an aesthetic sense of nostalgia:

> you can be deluded by landscape architect pictures that you are really creating a cute country setting . . . maybe it's a little more aesthetically pleasing than a strip mall, but will anyone really go there with their children and open up a picnic basket and feel that they're in the country? No. The only difference between it and a strip mall is a little more grass, some Victorian lawn ornaments, and hipped roofs that serve no potential purpose.

Quoting the geographer Howard Kunstler, Deluca concludes, "What we've created is a half-assed cartoon of the country."[37] The Group for the South Fork continues to wage battles on environmental issues, but as the farmlands they fight to preserve achieve their highest value because of the vistas they provide instead of the crops they produce, the substantive reality behind protecting a "rural quality of life" is transformed. Although the East End's agricultural industry remains some of the most productive in the state, what's actually produced has shifted from potatoes, cauliflower, and other row vegetables to vineyards, horse farms, tree farms, and upscale subdivisions. The economist Michael Zweig explains how this dynamic works on the East End's North Fork. "In Southold," he contends, "agriculture is not just about aesthetics—it's an economic development strategy—a viable industrial program." Yet, he continues, "the complication is that the people who are going to do the farming are different people, and there is a tremendous amount of resentment among the traditional, long-term, resident farmers." The resentment intensifies because those who develop vineyards are not local, and they have a lot of money. Zweig concludes that "the long-term consolidation of agriculture out here under these circumstances requires a change in who the actual investors are in the land, and that is a political problem."[38]

On the South Fork, however, this political problem has been overwhelmed by the rise of upscale subdivisions and commercial development. While environmental concerns remain salient, while the "natural beauty" is still preservable, and while the desire to "save" some of the land continues, the notion of a "rural quality of life" becomes increasingly more of a romantic vision of the past than a real possibility for the future. Fears of suburban sprawl have been partially realized. Thus, although one can still juxtapose what is now western Suffolk suburbia with East End exurbia, what would be Peconic County is already a vital economic center for Suffolk County. The main roads leading west to east through Southampton and East Hampton are jam-packed Monday through Friday mornings between 6 and 9 a.m. regardless of the season, and all day long during the summer. The same is true between 4 and 7 p.m. in the opposite direction. The Group for the South Fork fought valiantly to save farmland, but much of it has been preserved as farm views for new McMansion migrants, not as workable soil for working farms. Farmers may not be museum pieces yet, but the "traditional rural character" they represented has left them with little purpose other than to serve as an icon for a romanticized movement. Perhaps nowhere is this dynamic more obvious than in the fact that many farmers resist upzoning and other development restrictions supported by the Group for the South Fork and many Peconic County advocates.

The irony, given these development and demographic changes, is that Peconic County became a more popular idea during the 1990s, even as the impact that it could be expected to have diminished. Thus, despite the impossibility of keeping the area "rural" in a traditional sense, the desire for such an image became even stronger. As the geographer and local activist Scott Carlin has noted, "Peconic County is the antidevelopment development strategy; it's a way to save farmland and make money at the same time."[39] The point here is not that the Group for the South Fork's continued struggle for environmental protection failed—it has succeeded in many ways. But its successes could not stop upscale residential and commercial development and the cultural changes they ignited. In fact, as Appendix K to the "Blueprint" explains, "the more a community does to enhance its unique set of assets, whether natural, architectural or cultural, the more tourists it will attract. . . . Make a destination more appealing and people will stay longer."[40] In the Hamptons, people are staying year-round, in part because environmental advocates have succeeded in warding off the worst forms of residential and commercial sprawl. The Group could continue to fight for the environment, but the quality-of-life issues, especially those presented in the context of historical and traditional identities, could not be maintained. Similarly, while a Peconic County might legitimately create a more local county government that would be more accessible to its constituents and might even be able to regulate growth more effectively than Suffolk County's legislators, the rural quality-of-life issue had already been defeated.

WHOSE PECONIC COUNTY IS IT?

The changing economic and cultural character of the landscape has informed many of the voices critical of the idea of Peconic County. Roger Wunderlich, editor of the *Long Island Historical Journal*, devoted part of the spring 1997 issue to the question of secession. He featured one piece that advocated the secession of Peconic County, written by Fred Thiele Jr., and another piece, written by Lee Koppelman, against it. But, in his introduction to the debate, Wunderlich wrote:

> In their deeply felt conviction that their area is distinctive, Peconicans tend to fasten the label "suburban" on western Suffolk. Although often employed by commentators, "suburban" is an anachronistic word for Long Island, the kind of designation that lingers on long after its meaning is obsolete. Dashing Dan, the symbolic commuter, now represents fewer than one in five Long Islanders, the vast majority of whom work as well as live here. We have been in the post-suburban era for decades, self-sufficient instead of dependent. Rather than flowing towards the metropolis, traffic originates in the city, with Peconic the destination instead of the point of departure. A growing number of

Manhattanites owns or rents East End property, especially in the Hamptons.[41]

Here Wunderlich echoes the geographer John Palen's claims that "economically as well as demographically, suburbs are no longer sub. . . . Outer cities, edge cities, technoburbs, suburban cities . . . are coming to dominate the metropolitan landscape."[42] The diversity of the area's economic and demographic links makes it difficult to classify the East End as "rural" in any traditional sense.

In some ways, the region stands as an extraordinary suburb for Manhattan's elite who now telecommute or ride luxury buses or even helicopters into the city for board meetings or theater dates. In many ways, though, the area has become a traditional suburb for upper-middle-class professionals from Nassau County and western Suffolk. In 1999, the *New York Times* built the circumstantial case that the Hamptons had been taken over by up-island suburbanites. A *Times* reporter, Bernard Stamler, spoke to a special-events planner who claimed that almost a third of her guests were now coming from "up-island, something you never saw a few years ago." Restaurant owners confirmed that increasing numbers of reservations were coming in with "516 area codes" that cover Nassau County and unfamiliar numbers from "way past Shirley," in western Suffolk. Marina managers claim that almost 25 percent of local slips belong to people from Nassau. Stamler concluded, "Most Long Islanders now live and work on the island, pushing residential and commercial development farther east than many imagined possible 20 years ago."[43] As Palen suggests, the East End has itself become an economic center of activity that rivals the traditional suburban idea. Although Wunderlich himself remained neutral regarding Peconic County, he did not accept its "antisuburban" narrative as a legitimate justification.

Ed Sharretts was a long-time supporter of Peconic County. He signed on early in the movement, became Peconic County Committee chairman in the late 1960s, and was instrumental in organizing for the 1973 referendum campaign. But he, too, now says, "It's too late for Peconic County." Sharretts cites rampant development, the loss of working farms, and major highway traffic as three major reasons that even secession would not help restore the area to how it looked in the 1960s and early 1970s. He explains that "when farmers can sell their land for millions more than they could make growing potatoes, they sell. Even the old guys who try to hold on eventually die, and their families sell." Sharretts once thought local control might help stop some of the worst kinds of sprawl, but, he now he says, "too much has changed in the last forty years for us to go backwards. The East End is not rural anymore, no question about it." While the wealth and power of recent migrants keeps the area less densely developed than Nassau and western Suffolk—and Sharretts applauds the successful protection of open spaces—he laments that "the idea of Peconic County was to stop it a long time ago and that didn't happen."[44]

Koppelman makes a related point about the impact of recent development and demographic changes have had on the economic viability of a Peconic County. Koppelman claims that the Peconic County feasibility study demonstrated that the county would enjoy increased revenues from a growing second-home population at the same time that it would face a reduced need for public services. But, as he explains, "No consideration was given to the fact that seasonal housing has shown a tendency to be converted to year-round use. Even if more houses would be viewed as a plus, any increase in permanent residents inescapably would result in the need and demand for more public services."[45] Similarly, Southampton town officials have been forced to address the growing shortage of relatively moderately priced housing. For the most part, the adult children of working and middle-class residents cannot find adequate housing stock available for less than $400,000. Teachers, small-business owners, and government employees have all clamored for affordable housing. In a recent forum sponsored by the East End chapter of the Long Island Progressive Coalition, Kathryn Szoka, an organizer, listed the average house prices in the region and explained that "many of the people who make up our community can no longer afford to live in our community."[46] Both East Hampton and Southampton legislators are scurrying to find solutions to a low- and moderate-income housing crisis, and Assemblyman Thiele has proposed a transfer tax that would place one-half of 1 percent of the price of all new and luxury homes sold into a fund for developing affordable homes. But it is hard to imagine that a new Peconic County could solve such a problem without developing programs that would require greater revenues.

"Affordable housing" itself is a relatively exclusive concept that, for all the good intentions of legislators and activists, rarely includes the housing needs of the area's lowest-paid workers.[47] For decades, the

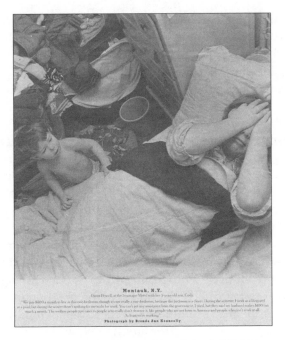

This photograph appeared in a March 2000 *New York Times Magazine* article entitled, "The Invisible Poor: 21st-Century Nativism among the East End's Poor." (Photo by Brenda Ann Kenneally)

homeless population of the Hamptons was small and relatively invisible, often perceived as consisting of poor people from western Suffolk who had been transferred to emergency shelters and transitional housing (usually former low-rate motels) on the East End because there were no vacancies up-island. Now, however, the increasing year-round population and the skyrocketing housing costs have created an indigenous problem with homelessness. The Suffolk County Department of Social Services claims that the average family of four requires an annual income of almost $50,000 in order to afford the least expensive housing rentals available—and prices for most housing throughout most of the East End costs more. According to Lori Wehrner, project director of the Peconic Housing Initiative, the few area shelters that exist are filled to capacity and the numbers of homeless on the streets continue to increase.[48] Robert Barbaro, Southampton town housing administrator,

said, "We want to create more shelter space so we don't have to use motels, but it hasn't come close to handling the number who have become
homeless in the past two years."[49]

Meanwhile, controversies over shelter motels have reached a
pitched level in the Southampton communities of Hampton Bays and
East Quogue. Beginning in August 2000, the East Quogue Civic Association complained that recently housed people at the Best Eastern Motel
were responsible for increases in local crime. Al Algieri, the Association
president, explained to the Southampton Town Board that "senior citizens are afraid to go to the 7-Eleven because of aggressive panhandling
outside." For more than a year and a half, residents continued to raise
issues of safety, crime, and overcrowding at the motels. Algieri and his
group feared that children residing in the motels might end up attending local schools and drive up taxes. Although the Southampton school
board president, Wolfgang Lerch, explained that the board has a policy
of accepting any student who "comes to the door seeking an education," Algieri countered, "I'd like to leave the children out of this. . . .
This isn't about them. It's about the politicians shoving this down our
throats. We'd be happy to pay for any homeless child that came from
this district, but not the ones that are shipped here and shoved down
our throats."[50] Steven Tallides, a motel owner, claimed that this sense of
who belongs and who doesn't is steeped in racism. He said, "All [the
Association] is worried about is their own damn kids and their money.
They have to wake up and see the world how it really is."[51]

Similar sentiments surround the housing situation for Latino workers, many of whom now stay in the East End year-round. Almost all of
the families evicted from the Hampton Frontiers Cottages late in 2001
were Salvadoran immigrants who worked as local landscapers,
painters, housekeepers, and low-wage service employees. The Town of
Southampton had purchased the land in order to preserve open spaces
and restore wetlands. To accomplish this, the town planned to demol-
ish the cottages and therefore evicted the residents. Although town officials promised to find "alternative housing" for the families, Katherine Hartnett, director of the Latin American Solidarity Outreach Center,
knew they would have trouble relocating the group, even temporarily,
explaining that "unless the town is going to develop low-income housing, there will never be enough units available for the growing population of low-wage workers and their families."[52] All of the Frontier residents were documented with "temporary protective status" and had

jobs, and many had been residents for three years or more and had children attending local schools. One resident, Maria Billafrico, had lived in a trailer on the property with her husband and three children for almost three years. They had established roots in the community, and Mrs. Billafrico had even successfully organized the Frontier residents, explaining to a *Southampton Press* reporter, "When we first moved here, there were a lot of fights, but I started talking to people, telling them to get along and they listened to me. I don't want to move from here. . . . Nobody knows where to move to, there are no rentals anyone can afford."[53]

Peconic County may not represent any particular set of class interests per se, but the demographic changes of the past decade make it difficult to see how the "scaled-down" social services of a new county could address the needs of a growing working-class and poor population increasingly priced out of the housing market. Some Peconic County supporters, such as Hal Ross, contend that a more local, accountable government would be more responsive to social issues and would have to consider affordable housing, among other social programs.[54] Other Peconic County advocates, such as Liz Granitz, are more cautious about issues such as affordable housing, calling Thiele's transfer-tax proposal a "well-intentioned but bankrupt idea." She explains that subsidized housing merely encourages tax increases, because decisions on affordable housing inevitably impact other budgets, such as school budgets, which will also require increases. She concludes, "while you might argue that people are entitled to a place to live, it's not clear that you are entitled to a single-family house in the Hamptons." Deluca, an early participant in the Peconic County feasibility study, perceived a kind of "antigovernment" sentiment among some of its supporters. He expressed concern over "some mutterings" about cutting social programs, explaining that, "within the Peconic Movement is another movement towards less government-subsidized anything except maybe open spaces. . . . There is an undercurrent of the movement against what they perceive as a bottomless pit of government programs from public works to health services to welfare."[55] Thiele himself admits that some of the resistance to his affordable housing proposals is a "not so veiled anti-immigration, anti-Hispanic, anti-Black sentiment."[56]

In one of the final public forums before the Peconic County referendum of November 1996, Mary Killoran, former president of the East End chapter of the NAACP, asked Fred Thiele, "When it comes to

Peconic County, what's in it for ethnic minorities?" Thiele responded that "forming a structure of government doesn't eliminate racism, doesn't eliminate poverty—there is nothing inherently good about creating a political structure . . . but home rule will give you greater access." He explained that a smaller county could be more innovative in dealing with issues of prejudice and could improve the delivery of services but added that there was nothing inherent in the entity of Peconic County that would deal with issues of racism or discrimination. In discussing her reservations, Killoran explained that she wanted some assurances that qualified "minorities of all types" would be "part of the governing structure." She had experienced a history of inequities in Southampton, where "qualified minorities are overlooked for important positions of power."[57] The current NAACP president, Lou Ware, has similar reservations about Peconic County. Although he also sees potential benefits and doesn't have a definitive position, he wonders whether such a government structure could "marshal the forces necessary" to address issues of racial discrimination and inequality.[58] One community activist and Shinnecock resident, Melissa Arch Walton, puts it more clearly: "I would support Peconic County if I knew whose Peconic County it would be."[59]

THE FUTURE OF AN ILLUSION

In the foreword to his homage to the region's natural beauty, the former *East Hampton Star* publisher Everett Rattray explained that the South Fork "is an island of an island, separated by the Shinnecock Canal from the rest of Long Island, a 30-mile strip of hills, dunes, and woods with a population of perhaps 30,000 souls, fiercely proud of a heritage largely neglected in the history textbooks, and quick to bristle at the condescension of the summer visitor . . . its extraordinary physical nature usually impresses them merely as pleasant place with fine beaches."[60] Rattray and his paper (eventually passed on to his wife, Helen) often offered a corrective to the glitzy summer tourist view of the "Hamptons," arguing that the term itself belonged to gossip columnists, not to the area's natives. For decades, the *Star* also played a crucial role in developing an environmental consciousness that advocated land conservation, not just to protect economic resources but as integral to maintaining the human identity inherently intertwined with the history of the land. Environmental preservation was, indeed, connected to the East End's quality of life and to the collective identity of its people.

Hal Ross credited the Rattray family and its newspaper with laying the ideological groundwork for the Democrats' victory in 1973 in East Hampton and for the environmental and land-use awareness that buttressed early support for the Group for the South Fork and renewed support for the Peconic County movement. Widespread sentiments about the importance of limiting growth, protecting natural resources, and preserving open spaces converged with desires for more local control and nostalgic ideas about particular kinds of indigenous or authentic identities to create overwhelming support for the creation of Peconic County. Not one of the five East End towns voted against secession in the 1996 referendum, with Riverhead being the most conservative with a two-to-one vote in favor. Despite the overwhelming victory, however, Peconic County has been dead in the state legislature for nearly a decade, primarily a victim of circumstance. Staten Island's attempt to secede from New York City has been linked to the Peconic County issue by Sheldon Silver, the Speaker of the state Assembly, who fears that granting independence to Peconic County would set a dangerous precedent. If Peconic County seceded, the legislature would have to allow Staten Island independence, and Silver opposes such a move.[61] So Peconic County waits.

In the years since the referendum, Thiele, Ross, and others have tried a host of different strategies to force the Assembly to permit a binding resolution on Peconic County. In the spring of 1998, Peconic County Now! filed a lawsuit together with four of the five East End towns (all except Southold), the eight East End villages, Hal Ross, the former Shelter Island supervisor Hudson (Hoot) Sherman, United Southold, and the East End Supervisors and Mayors Association. The groups charged the state legislature with negligence for not allowing a vote on Thiele's bill to create a legal process for forming new counties. They lost that suit, appealed in early 1999, and then lost the appeal. In the summer of 1999, Peconic County supporters joined forces with Staten Island secessionists to introduce a new bill that would allow the areas self-determination. A "Memorandum in Support of Legislation" attached to the bill explained the bill's rationale: "This legislation responds to the clear intention of the people of two areas of the state to govern themselves in a more cost-effective, efficient manner, and one that reflects their unique historical and personal values and needs."[62] This bill was also defeated. In 2001, Thiele introduced a state constitutional amendment that would permit a statewide vote on Peconic County and Staten Island, but it was never voted on.

Throughout this postreferendum period, Peconic County advocates have demonstrated in Albany and on the East End and lobbied legislators and opinion makers, and they continue to come up with increasingly innovative strategies for winning secession rights. Most speak of the movement with great resignation, frustrated by the legislative limbo that now surrounds Peconic County. Some are still optimistic and, like Griffing almost forty years before them, believe that eventually things will change: Silver will retire, New York State politics will shift, and so on. Thiele included a question about support for Peconic County on his 2002 Legislative Survey, and he insists that most surveys demonstrate continued support for secession. Many still seem to think that the battle for Peconic County is not over. But it may be too late.

Peconic County was born at a time when major postwar economic, political, social, and environmental shifts had begun to affect the historical and geographical landscape. The rise of dense, suburban areas, first in Nassau County and then in western Suffolk, appeared to have almost unstoppable momentum. The continued flow of investment dollars and the subsequent subdivisions and malls threatened to bring urban life to the suburbs and suburban life to the country. Griffing and his cohort feared the loss of independence and political power, but more notable was their fear of losing "themselves" and their way of life. As we have noted, in Breen's words, amid massive social transformations, the people of the Hamptons have always been "obsessed with change," in part because what is at stake is always "a distinctive historical identity." In the 1960s, Peconic County was antidevelopment—a direct attempt to stop growth and to preserve Yankee, "native white" control over the region. The politics of Peconic County reflected very particular conceptions of local cultural identity.

In the forty years since that time, however, the suburbs (or at least the exurbs) have arrived on the East End. Environmental awareness, education, and effective organizing have limited the sprawling encroachment of commercial development that engulfed the western parts of Long Island. Similarly, the upscale nature of the area's affluent history and new bourgeois tastes have shaped growth in ways sensitive to open-space preservation and "natural" aesthetics. Continued economic development and threats to the environment inspire persistent desires to control growth. But the images of "the country," of "agricultural settings" or a "rural quality of life," seem more nostalgic than current or possible. These visions emanate from the movement's origins in the 1960s, not from the reality of the twenty-first century. In fact, current calls for the creation of Peconic County are now linked to plans for development, not its elimination, and are strongly supported and led by the same people that Griffing hoped a Peconic County might keep out. It is as if the Peconic County movement is reliving Marx's predictions about history and revolution—first time tragedy, second time farce.

This is not to say that the issues involved in the proposals for Peconic County are irrelevant or that an actual Peconic County would serve no purpose. If nothing else, the general earnestness and good will of its most vocal advocates promise a certain level of integrity. Ross is an old Roosevelt Democrat who believes in the social responsibility of government. Thiele is adamant that issues such as affordable housing not be only about middle-class homeowners but also include the working class and people of color. And the many environmentalists, such as Goell, who support Peconic County have principled stands on the necessity of protecting natural resources and ecological systems. It is possible that a Peconic County could do a better legislative job because it provides for more local, sustainable participation. But, as Mary Killoran has pointed out, there are no guarantees as to who will "make up" the governmental structure of such an entity. Whose Peconic County would it be?

And it may end up that Peconic County is itself, in fact, irrelevant to the physical and cultural future of the East End's landscape. Economically, the savings predicted by the feasibility study were based predominately on a large second-home industry that paid taxes but didn't require much in services. But, as Thiele concludes, "We're going to become more of a year-round community, and that gap will diminish." He continues:

> What is more likely is that the very reason for Peconic County—to protect open space and quality of life [will diminish] as more and more of the area gets developed. It will develop at a slower rate and at a different pattern than western Suffolk—we will protect large areas of our

open spaces, not as much as we like; we will focus development around our hamlet areas, not as completely as we would like. But as the cement begins to harden—we have one-third [land] developed, one-third [land] protected, and one-third is up for grabs, basically. And as that one-third begins to fall on one side of the ledger, as the development pattern is set and the cement hardens, it will be harder to argue to people that we need Peconic County to protect the area. I still think Peconic County will always be there as an emotional issue . . . but as more land-use decisions are made and the pattern is set, some of the reasons for Peconic County will become less than they are today and less than they were ten years ago.[63]

Just what is that emotion, then, that will continue to make Peconic County appealing even after the cement has dried? What is the historic image of land and identity that Peconic County evokes? Is it Yankee independence or arrogance? Is it environmental awareness or an upscale marketing plan? Is it a three-hundred-year sensitivity to survival in nature or a thirty-year history of an urban bourgeoisie claiming (and then protecting) an identity as landed gentry? Perhaps Peconic County's success has been its ability to be all of these things and then again, sometimes, none of these things. It is an identity malleable enough to attract many followers but fixed enough in a particular set of natural images to give everyone something to hold onto.

William Mulvihill, an East End historian, wrote extensively about the place names of the South Fork. Of the term "Peconic," he says, "there appears to be no agreement by the early scholars as to the precise Indian word and its meaning. Tooker concludes an exhaustive discourse on linguistic variants by saying that it might be translated as a 'small field.' There is also no precise knowledge of where the field or the locality or Indian village was originally located."[64] Perhaps there has never been a more appropriate name.

4

Polo Ponies and Penalty Kicks

Sports on the East End

Many of the second-homeowners are now year-round. Technology enables professionals to live here and telecommute to Manhattan or elsewhere. Retirees are making their second home their retirement home. The year-round population is growing. That includes laborers, many of them immigrants working in the construction and landscaping trades who enjoy increasing buying power. For the first time, the Hamptons now has a Mexican restaurant with Mexican customers. I don't mean Tex-Mex, I mean rice and beans.

—Herb Sherman, LIU–Southampton Professor of
Professional Studies

The new and hottest houses on the market are the almost exact reproductions of older houses. Builders in fact use old materials like barn siding and antique floors from old buildings that have been reclaimed. They even stain the shingles so that they look instantly old.

—Frank Newbold, Sotheby's International Realty

A white man pulled up in a big white truck. He was new to the corner and had never hired *esquineros* (Latino day laborers) before. Messrs. Jimenez, Antonio, and Cervantes piled in. The patron spoke loudly as if the sheer volume of his voice would increase their understanding of English. "Boy, that's a zoo, huh? A free-for-all. You do that every day?"

—Charlie LeDuff, *New York Times*,
September 24, 2000

Well gang it was opening day and the [polo] tent was filled to capacity. It looked like Sat. nite at Jet East [a Hamptons night club]. And everyone brought their dogs. Actress Juli Hayek had the cutest mini-spaniel. —"Sudsy Says," *The Morning Line*

The Walentas family estate and horse farm in Bridgehampton is home to the Bridgehampton Polo Club and the new Mercedes-Benz Polo Challenge, a professional polo tournament that now stands, according to one former professional, as "the best polo played in America." As exciting as polo may be, however, most press and spectator attention is paid to the special celebrity guests who congregate under a large tent off to one side of the field. Here, famous entertainers, models, designers, CEOs, and politicos sip champagne and nosh on gourmet snacks before they mix with the hoi polloi during half-time, when the whole audience is asked to stomp down divots on the field.

Well off to another side of the farm is a soccer field that the Manhattan real estate magnate David Walentas had built for his landscapers and stable workers, many of whom come from Mexico or Central or South America. While this field hosts informal "pick-up" games for employees and friends, some of the players also participate in a variety of competitive soccer leagues that have sprung up on the East End. Teams with names such as Team Mexico, Team Colombia, Team Costa Rica, and Team Ecuador wear brightly colored uniforms sponsored by a variety of the area's landscaping firms and building contractors. League games are often played on small, poorly manicured fields surrounded by families with children kicking soccer balls and radios blasting banda music.

The Hamptons have experienced rapid economic, political, and demographic changes over the past three decades. Once regarded as one of the world's best-known summer resort areas for the rich and famous, the area has become an increasingly primary residence for some of Manhattan's newly "ultra-rich." Much of this ascendant class (whom I will call the "hyper-bourgeoisie") has made its fortunes in the 1990s stock market boom and dot.com explosion, as well as in Madison Avenue's advertising firms, the media, the film industry and from the cult of celebrity that surrounds them. They bring to the East End an insatiable and now year-round demand, not for inconspicuous peace and quiet but for publicity and conspicuous consumption. Heliports, expanded jet service, luxury bus lines, cell phones, and "telecommuting" have facilitated this transformation to what one Newsweek reporter dubbed the "Hollywood–Wall Street Hamptons."

The burgeoning economy of wealthy homeowners in the Hamptons has created a huge labor demand in construction and landscaping, as well as in retail and other services. While some businesses have gone so far as to recruit workers directly from Colombia and Ecuador, others have run morning bus services to poorer communities in western Suffolk County to facilitate the commuting of lower-wage, predominately Hispanic labor that works in the Hamptons but cannot afford to live there. Informal "labor halls" have sprung up on busy street corners, vacant lots, outside delicatessens, 7-Elevens, and building supply stores throughout the eastern region of Suffolk County. Also notable are the ways in which more permanent populations of Latino workers have established their own informal networks of job placement, transportation, van services, carpooling, and child care.

In this chapter, I examine the social and cultural impact of these major economic and demographic changes through the lens of sports. Although I'm concerned with specific population shifts, real estate patterns, land use, and labor markets, I focus on how these phenomena are both reflected and rearticulated through cultural activities and events. In particular, I argue that the cultural politics of sports in the Hamptons represents the struggles of both groups—an ascendant hyper-bourgeoisie and a burgeoning Latino working class—as they adapt, jostle, and thrive amid the area's rapid changes. For polo enthusiasts, the sport represents a new elite's attempt to legitimize and propagate its wealth and power by resurrecting historical images of "old" money within a contemporary setting of new wealth and celebrity. For soccer players and fans, sport and leisure activities reflect efforts to preserve and promote traditional social practices and identities within the political borders and cultural contexts of their new homes.

THE GLOBAL TO LOCAL SETTING

From the boom period of the colonial whaling industry to the late-nineteenth- and early-twentieth-century waves of immigrant workers, the political economy and cultural landscape of Long Island's East End has always been linked to the dynamics of international capital and labor markets. Recent economic and social trends, such as the influx of investment capital in home buying and building, as well as the boom in the number of "new immigrants," continue this relationship. The most significant international dynamics that currently dominate the New York metropolitan region in general and the Hamptons in particular include the following: the explosive growth of the financial markets and New York City's pre-eminent position in the global finance industry;[1] the rapid development of telecommunications technology that both facilitates the globalization of media and financial markets and allows for the mobility of a growing corporate elite that can produce for, and manage, these markets from anywhere;[2] the ascendancy of a new "hyper-bourgeoisie" whose upscale tastes and hunger for public legitimacy have fueled new consumer markets and cultural industries;[3] deindustrialization and the dominance of a service-sector economy in "first-world" nations;[4] the massive northward immigration of workers from all over Latin America directly to suburban and exurban areas in search of jobs;[5] and the startling intensification of an economic, cultural, and political bifurcation between rich and poor.[6] These trends have acquired monikers ranging from "postindustrialism" and "post-Fordism" to "globalization." Regardless of the name attached, however, the impact of these forces on both local and regional cultures is indisputable.

The sudden boom in wealth among a growing number of New York's corporate and celebrity elite demanded a second-circuit outlet for investment capital.[7] In the late nineteenth century, the city's first aristocracy converted economic fortunes into cultural capital by erecting glorious estates along Long Island's beachfronts. By the early twentieth century, "new" money had followed old by erecting Gatsbyesque palaces in pursuit of the "orgiastic green light" of social power, prestige, and legitimacy. Similar dynamics led the 1980s' "freshly minted millionaires" described by Steven Gaines to pour their financial windfalls into McMansion status symbols where they could compete socially not only with their Wall Street and Madison Avenue cronies but, more important, with an older aristocracy of the Hamptons' elite.[8] This trend persisted as the prolonged stock market boom of the 1990s continued to feed the financial umbilical cord that nurtured economic expansion on the East End.

Although Gaines is right about the contests over cultural capital involved in buying into the Hamptons (which is part of the "polo story"), he missed the dominant trend that has changed the very nature of the area's economic and social value. The most salient aspect of this new elite's migration is a shift from desiring the symbolic cultural capital of "having a place to go to" in the Hamptons to desiring the use value of "living year-round" on the East End. This transformation has created an additional tangible cultural capital or prestige that emanates from becoming a "local citizen" or to be "in and of the Hamptons."

Competition among the social elite is now less about summer glitz and more about day-to-day lifestyles. As *Town and Country* reported in 1998, only East End insiders stay for the significant and "heavenly" times of fall and winter. The magazine argued that, once the summer "tourists, renters, [and] overnighters [who] clog the roads, restaurants, shops, farm stands, and beaches" leave, "the land is restored to its rightful (in their view) inhabitants." Or, as one realtor described the new homes built during the 1980s and 1990s, "these may be second homes, but they aren't just summer houses anymore."[9]

According to local real estate brokers, this migration of New York City's elite is based on one dominant force, a desire to improve their "quality of life." Despite former Mayor Giuliani's image as an urban leader who cleared city streets of homelessness, pornography, and crime, the images and fear of decline still permeate New York.

Even some wealthy New Yorkers who could afford to consume the protected, upscale environments of Manhattan's "renaissance" have chosen to establish primary residences far from the signs of New York's poor. Thus, the Hamptons now host a convergence of this hyper-bourgeoisie's sense of intraclass struggles and anti-urban consumer tastes. Yet, the region has also resonated with larger economic trends that view real estate investment as a dominant element of economic growth. By the 1970s, midwestern mega-agribusinesses, international competition, skyrocketing property and inheritance taxes, and government policies to tax vacant lands for their "highest and best use" all combined to make most of the East End's farm land more valuable for housing than for farming. Led by a local real estate innovator, Allan Schneider, a post-1960 New York City migrant himself, the East End went from having fewer than ten real estate brokers in 1970 to having hundreds of licensed brokers and almost two dozen agencies by the end of the 1990s. Not since the boom days of the whaling industry had so much investment money flowed into the East End from New York City and elsewhere. Farmers became realtors, landscapers became developers, and, eventually, local building interests helped elect one of their own, Vince Cannuscio, as supervisor of the Town of Southampton in 1995. Without

the structural arrangements and agents of growth interested in capital-
izing on potential development, the East End might still be more of a
summer resort than a year-round residence for New York's rich and
powerful.[10]

But the region has also experienced another new migratory trend:
the immigration of international workers—primarily Latino—directly
to suburban and exurban areas. And the evolving niche for year-round,
low-wage agricultural, landscaping, construction, and service work has
inspired a growing population of permanent migration as the Latino
population in the Hamptons increased more than 350 percent between
1990 and 2000. In Southampton, those of "Hispanic origin" rose from
1,201 (2.6 percent) in 1990 to 4,700 (8.6 percent) in 2000, while in East
Hampton the same group rose from 812 (5 percent) to 2,914 (14.8 percent).[11] Even more noticeable is the evolution of an extensive informal
economy of "off-the-books" house cleaners, groundskeepers, dish-
washers, and both skilled and nonskilled day laborers, many of whom
never appear in official census counts.[12] More than a decade ago, a local
newspaper editorial explained, "The Hispanic community has, for the
most part, come here to fill in the gaps of our service economy . . . [and]
represents a crucial part of the workforce."[13] This trend has intensified
exponentially since then.

Latino workers, however, have been met by a growing animosity
from communities where, as one New York Times report explained, "Immigrant laborers are handy, but not always wanted." Such conflicts and
struggles are often played out in the Hamptons through growing debates over the lack of affordable housing, the need for bigger schools
and more programs in bilingual and "special" education, and unfair
labor practices and illegal immigration. In East Hampton, petitions and
editorials have complained about the impact of a growing Latino presence. While some have worried about "illegal workers" or "loitering
day laborers" who might "ruin East Hampton," others are concerned
about the increasing costs of supporting bilingual education and the
continuing problem of overcrowding in the few affordable housing
units available to Latinos. In Southampton, heated debates have occurred over the availability of Spanish-speaking staff at the area's major
hospital, among the local police force, and in the court system. Meanwhile, the mounting complaints by Latino workers over nonpayment of
wages and other injustices has inspired the Workplace Project of Nas-

sau County, an immigrant workers rights organization, to consider opening a new office in the Hamptons.

Jay Schneiderman, the former East Hampton town supervisor and now Suffolk County legislator, believes that much of this discourse contains "coded language" that betrays a certain amount of racism. He explains,

> You hear things like, "they're dating our daughters" at the high school. Or you hear that "you've got to crack down on code enforcement." This is true in the sense that you don't want overcrowding to adversely impact the neighborhoods. But I think that it sometimes becomes code language for "these are supposed to be white neighborhoods."

In particular, Schneiderman points out that attempts to build soccer fields in East Hampton were met with strong, outspoken resistance as neighbors worried about "drugs, urinating, pollution, noise." Baseball fields and basketball courts bring no opposition, but soccer fields seemed to raise the fears of local residents regardless of where town officials proposed to place them. Schneiderman remarks that, despite some proclamations that residents aren't prejudiced and are concerned only about "what's going to happen to their neighborhood," he can't recall any other public recreation project that has created such vociferous opposition.[14]

In many ways, the "informalization" of the area's low-wage Latino workforce, the settlement of an increasingly ultra-rich capitalist class, and the conflicts that have arisen around both populations' growth represent what Portes and Castells call a global "realignment of class structure."[15] But the Hamptons are also place to observe how the groups that represent the two extremes of this class restructuring (a rising, new hyper-bourgeoisie and a growing Latino working class) have begun the process of stabilizing and solidifying new footholds on the playing fields of global capitalism. In other words, these populations are not temporary and seasonal but part of the permanent geographical relocation of the area's class structure and cultural identity. Nowhere is this struggle for a sense of new local identity and social legitimacy more evident than in the cultural politics of sports and leisure activities.

A BRIEF HISTORY OF THE CULTURAL POLITICS
OF SPORTS ON THE EAST END

Sports and leisure activities on Long Island have historically been sources of conflict between new populations and old. They often reflected many signs of, and struggles over, power—in some cases the assertion of a dominant culture, in some cases the resistance of traditional cultures, and in some cases a complex mix of different economic, political, and historical dynamics. In the early period of colonial expansion, historical records suggest that during times of "unrest" with the original Montaukett residents, the Puritan officials of East Hampton's church and government outlawed native cultural and leisure events, including sporting activities and powwow celebrations.[16] Later, in the mid-1800s, Sunday battles over working-class baseball games and the blue laws of Puritan patricians characterized the early industrial and residential development of Brooklyn and Queens Counties on western Long Island.[17] Throughout the 1900s, first independent baseball clubs and, later, public school athletic teams would be the places where Polish, German, Italian, and other European immigrant men would prove their merits and contribute to community pride. Such achievements gave them and the ethnic groups they represented prestige as "locals" and, eventually, as "natives."

In the late nineteenth century, Manhattan's bourgeoisie first made its way out to the East End and began to impact the physical and cultural landscape by building their own tennis and golf clubs for upper-class leisure activities. In 1879 they founded the East Hampton Lawn Tennis Club and, in 1891, they built the larger Maidstone Club. A year later, under the design and supervision of the famous architect and summer resident Stanford White, a similar group developed the Shinnecock Hills Golf Club in Southampton. These athletic and social clubs soon became the center for much of the summer colony's social life, as well as the source of this seasonal elite's imprimatur on the villages of East Hampton and Southampton. Fearing conflicts with the community's conservative "native" residents (the descendants of Lyman Beecher's Puritan congregation), members of the Maidstone Club felt compelled to reassure the town that "one of the fundamental rules [of the club] is that no intoxicating liquors will at any time be allowed upon the premises." They also agreed that "no games may be played at the club on Sundays."[18]

The second Maidstone Clubhouse, in East Hampton, where sports represented both the conquest and fitness to rule of America's first bourgeoisie. (Photo courtesy of East Hampton Library)

Conflicts, however, did arise among the elite themselves over the "functions" of summering in the Hamptons. A "nightlife" began to develop within the summer colony during the 1890s. For some, the disciplined, wholesome elixir of leisurely athletics and peaceful retreat was now interrupted by evening dances held at the Maidstone, the Clinton Academy, and the new village hall. One summer resident complained:

> This year, tennis is not the chief end of man! Perhaps the new village hall is responsible for the inauguration of something unheard-of in East Hampton—i.e. late hours. One cannot battle the surf all morning, play tennis all afternoon and dance all night. . . . Tennis has suffered. The long and short of it is that East Hampton isn't what it used to be.[19]

In fact, as the twentieth century approached and the Long Island Rail Road reached East Hampton, more and more of the early summer colonists decried the "changing" Hamptons. Over the next few decades, some "summer people" would try to keep the East End "peaceful, pristine, and authentic." But, by 1906, the Maidstone Club sanctioned Sunday golf. In 1907, the town sanctioned the sale of some liquor. And, in 1908, a group of investors calling themselves the Gardiner's Bay Company planned an exclusive summer colony complete with hotels, stables, wine and liquor dealers, barbers, theaters, and numerous other services and amenities. The turn-of-the-century arrivistes and their upscale leisure culture had come east to stay.

But one consistent form of distinction among the early summer colony was the vacationers' economic and social contributions to the community's "uplifting." They helped pay for "sprinkling carts" to keep summer dust from rising over Main Street and for numerous beautification projects advocated by the Ladies Village Improvement Society. Many Maidstone Club members also paid for the building of a local theater (the Guild Hall), the public library, sidewalks, street lamps, and early relief agencies. Samuel Parrish, a wealthy New York City lawyer and among the original Shinnecock Golf Club organizers, also founded the Parrish Art Museum, was a major supporter of the Rogers Memorial Library, and became president of Southampton Village.[20] These kinds of community activities represented a cultural tradition among older elites—a noblesse oblige that the sociologist Pierre Bourdieu argued was symbolic of the old bourgeoisie's sense of distinction. This period's wealthy believed in the essentialism of their social positions; status and power came from lineage and breeding. Responsible citizenship and charitable contributions (especially for civic-focused "civilizing" institutions such as libraries and theaters) were important signs of one's rightful station.[21]

Sports, too, represented and reproduced crucial aspects of social class ranking. While the simple cost of participating in certain sports might signify a participant's economic status, Bourdieu argued that golf, tennis, and riding also have "hidden entry requirements." Such elite sports demand "family tradition, early training, or obligatory manner of dress and behavior" that keep them closed to those of other classes and maintain the activities as "the surest indicators of bourgeois pedigree." In fact, the cultural features of these sports appeal to many dominant tastes:

> Practiced in exclusive places (private clubs), at the same time one chooses, alone or with chosen partners (features which contrast with the collective discipline, obligatory rhythms and imposed efforts of team sports), demanding relatively low physical exertion that is in any case freely determined, but a relatively high investment . . . of

time and learning (so that they are relatively independent of variations in bodily capital and its decline through age), [these sports]
only give rise to highly ritualized competitions, governed, beyond
the rules, by unwritten laws of fair play. The sporting exchange takes
on the air of a highly controlled social exchange, excluding all physical or verbal violence, all anomic use of the body (shouting, wild
gestures, etc.) and all forms of direct contact between the opponents.[22]

In the Hamptons, the turn-of-the-century bourgeoisie sought escape from the hot summers of metropolitan New York, but their social
activities, cultural styles, and, eventually, the Hamptons themselves
symbolized who they were and where they came from. The sports they
played required the wealth they had gained and promoted the distinctions they sought. As a site of cultural and class contests, the Hamptons
became a "playing field" where a particular class played out its ascendancy to power.

In the early post–World War II period, sport fishing became the
most politicized of "sporting" activities as conflicts between local commercial fishermen and promoters of the summer tourist industry
fought over a variety of laws, including fishing quotas and environmental regulations. Initially, the New York State Legislature found in
favor of the baymen who, the officials stated, "like their forbears, have
engaged in commercial fishing [and] are entitled to consideration."
Eventually, however, legislators sided with a sports fishing industry
that generated ten to twenty times the gross income that local fishermen
could. While pollution and rising taxes contributed to the destruction of
commercial fishing on the East End, the baymen's battle mostly reflected primarily the changing economy, culture, and demographics
that were defining the region's new identity.

By the late 1950s and early 1960s, the Hamptons was no longer a
small web of quiet villages or simply a summer colony for Manhattan
elites. While the East End of the 1950s and 1960s was relatively devoid
of Levitt subdivisions and strip malls, the region did rapidly become a
booming summer vacation mecca for those pursuing what still seemed
pristine, peaceful, and authentic. As Peter Matthiessen explains:

With the sudden rise in the value of land, the peaceful atmosphere
of the South Fork [of the East End] began to change. . . . Within a

few years the old Hildreth [general store] expanded its services to accommodate the swelling tide of tourists, and the old village's quiet days were over. A new rash of real estate speculators, entreating others to "share our heritage," discovered Sagaponack, where the smaller local farms, unable to compete with huge agribusiness in the West, or survive the growing tax on land inheritance, had begun to die.[23]

By that time it was hard to identify exactly what or whose "heritage" would or should be "shared," anyway. The Shinnecock reservation and its revived cultural influence, the centuries-old Presbyterian and Congregational churches, the museums dedicated to whaling history, the African American Eastville community's mid-nineteenth-century AME Zion Church with its links to the underground railroad, the saltbox storefronts and rapidly sprouting antique shops, the bountifully stocked farm stands and sprawling potato fields all offered at best a contested historical narrative. The battles between sport and commercial fishing not only symbolized a new stage of conquest and resistance but also reflected the continuity and complexity of all evolving historical identities.

This is the very complexity that Matthiessen's lament obscures. His presentation of the bayman's story (and his own positioning within the narrative as "native" anthropologist) misses the multidimensional history of migrations and conquests. For example, in documenting the rise and fall of haul-seining, Matthiessen does *mention* the Shinnecock Indian influence on contemporary fishing and whaling practices. Yet, the issues of European conquest and racial oppression disappear quickly in the first pages of the book as the author recounts the bayman Milt Miller's family history of multiracial friendships and an intermarriage. While Miller himself might be justified in claiming, "It's a hell of a good feelin' to know that you come from a family that never had no discrimination against nobody," Matthiessen's omissions cannot be so easily forgiven.

The history of bay fishing is an important part of the European conquest narrative in particular and the overall history of the East End's economic and cultural class struggles in general. As Breen observed, "Just as the Bonackers now find themselves driven off the land by rising real estate prices, so too were the Montauket Indians once pushed aside by colonial entrepreneurs who bore the same surnames as the surviving twentieth-century Bonackers."[24] For Matthiessen to lament the passing of one culture without paying much attention to that culture's own role in conquering previous cultures only obscures the cultural politics of both past and present.

Matthiessen also misses his own position within the complicated history of struggle and change in the Hamptons. The writer started coming to the Hamptons regularly in the early 1950s and worked as a charter fisherman for three years. But this came after his co-founding of the *Paris Review* and during his time as fiction editor for the literary magazine. The historian Helen Harrison wrote that when the "triumvirate" of Matthiessen and his co-editors Patsy Southgate (his wife) and George Plimpton "returned to the United States [from Paris] they put down roots in the area that seemed most congenial for their Europeanized imaginations—the inexpensive communities of the East End."[25] Like the artists and writers of a previous generation, they sought an "untouched and idealized" setting for their work. And, like the postwar bohemian artists who cleared the urban brush for the middle-class pioneers who eventually gentrified ethnic neighborhoods in cities across the country, the de Koonings, Lichtensteins, Pollocks, and Steinbecks (and Matthiessens and Plimptons) would lead a stampede of the rising professional middle class and its new money out to the Hamptons for summer respites in the 1950s and 1960s.[26] As one critic described it, Matthiessen's "blurring of history, nature and primitive community" created a "magic" that offered urban Americans "the notion that even as close as one hundred miles out of central New York . . . you can rediscover the American frontier."[27] Ironically, Matthiessen's work entices and elicits the very same movement of curious, cash-flush urban seekers that he criticizes. As the 1960s and 1970s progressed, sport fishing's boom would represent a new class of adventure-seeking vacationers who journeyed to the Hamptons in part to capture the distinction that the old Maidstone bourgeoisie had created and in part to surround themselves with the sense of nature and authenticity that Matthiessen both constructed and celebrated. These were New York City's middle class—both white-collar professionals and, eventually, civil-sector servants like police and fire fighters—who also wanted to experience "men's lives." Although demographic, economic, cultural, and environmental changes during the postwar era signaled the demise of the baymen and local commercial fishing, these trends also hinted at another passing—the end of the exclusive "old" bourgeoisie that had somewhat peacefully coexisted with the bonackers whose boarding houses they rented, whose fish and produce they ate, and whose crafts and services they paid for extravagantly. During the 1960s and 1970s, the Hamptons experienced a frenzy of cultural and economic shifts as the once-exclusive summer retreat became a trendy seasonal resort where even the middle class could afford to vacation (in Montauk, Hampton Bays, and in parts of East Hampton and Southampton). In 1969, the *East Hampton Star* declared the end of the "summer colony" and stopped publishing a weekly section that went by the same name.

But the Reagan-era Wall Street booms of the 1980s triggered yet another discovery of the Hamptons by a new rising class of financial and media industry elite. And the 1990s dot.com explosions again impacted the economic and demographic composition of the region. And once again, the cultural politics of these forces can be observed in the arena of sports.

One obvious result of the changes in the Hamptons' demographics has been the re-creation or reincarnation of the Hamptons Classic. The area's first official equestrian events were sponsored by the Southampton Riding and Hunt Club in the 1920s. Fox hunts, horse shows, and polo matches were popular during the decade and continued throughout the Depression as many of the Hamptons wealthy weathered the economic crisis quite well. The Club, however, disappeared during World War II, and horse shows did not become trendy in the Hamptons again until the late 1970s. Unlike the shows of the past, though, the Classic moved beyond a quiet, local amateur affair. In 1986, it became one of the country's largest equestrian contests, complete with big corporate sponsorships, national magazine and television coverage, and status as a qualifying event for the World Cup. As the Hamptons Classic historian Bryan Carpenter has written, "the rise of the local scene has paralleled the rise of the Classic. What was once a home to a handful of small stables running small lessons and small unrecognized shows has broadened into a veritable universe that features more than a dozen stables and a galaxy of A-rated shows."[28]

Carpenter's hyperbole bespeaks the way in which the Classic really does represent a new local *scene*. While horse shows remain a sport of wealthy patrons, these people are no longer the folks of an early-twentieth-century aristocracy content with a peaceful summer Sunday in the country. In the late 1970s, only two horse farms existed in Southampton;

in August 1998, there were twenty-eight, and almost a dozen applications pending. Five percent of the more than 8,000 acres dedicated to agricultural conservation is occupied by horse farms. And, while some criticize the "newly rich" for building horse farms more for "prestige than a true love for horses," one equestrian homesteader countered that it is not prestige, but "lifestyle. . . . I think you can build something aesthetically nice. It's nice to have a fountain even if you don't [need] to have a fountain."[29]

The identity and dominance of the new hyper-bourgeoisie are both reflected and reproduced through their sports and, by extrapolation, their appropriation and reshaping of the land. Their athletic events and land-use practices are supported by both upscale sponsors and the aristocratic celebrity status these products symbolize. As one journalist wrote, "The presence of a deep-pocketed audience [at the Classic] has not been lost on sponsors like American Express, Crown Royal/Seagram Americas, Hermès, Holland & Holland, Jaguar, Calvin Klein, Land Rover, Manhattan Mortgage, Rolex and Steinway. Support has grown to such an extent that a special Corporate Chalet Tent was added in 1995." The area's finest chefs prepare the food, fancy boutiques display their goods, and the world-renowned jewelry designer David Yurman now furnishes a specially designed championship belt buckle made of eighteen-karat gold and silver. Guests who once paid $400 for "ringside tables" under the "Grand Prix" tent have been priced out of attending, according to Linda Bird Francke. She explained, "We had a table for years, but things escalated out of control and got unattractive. . . . It went to $2,000 per table, and then in the fine print it said that you were expected to make a $5,000 contribution besides. . . . it's all about money and power now."[30]

Although the convergence of a new bourgeoisie with a cult of celebrity and an obsessive upscale consumerism marks part of the cultural climate of the Hamptons, this class's ascendancy is also marked by a territorial triumph that offers still further distinction at the same time that it demands a sense of democratic or populist legitimacy. Along with conquering the land comes the responsibility of governing—if not explicitly through municipal office, then at least symbolically through moral leadership. Thus, the politics of this hyper-bourgeoisie's triumph is complex and its symbolic manifestations intricate. And it all comes together at polo.

POLO AND THE CULTURAL POLITICS
OF A NEW BOURGEOISIE

Polo is a sport for rich people. The game itself requires huge plots of land—a regulation field is at least 160 by 300 yards. To prepare for the game requires even larger tracts; most Hamptons horse farms that train the "ponies" cover between twenty and fifty square acres of the most expensive real estate in the region. The Walentas's farm spreads out over one hundred acres and costs almost $1.5 million a year just to operate. To compete in "high goal" polo (the top level of international play) costs each player anywhere between $300,000 and $1 million for horses and maintenance, equipment, travel, and other expenses. Often referred to as the "game of kings," polo has always been closely associated with colonial power and great wealth ever since the British appropriated it from southern Asia in the mid-1800s. Therefore, the sport also possesses a kind of cultural capital whose regal history of empire bestows legitimacy to newly arrived social achievers. To play polo is both a sign of one's actual wealth and an indication of one's class position.

But sports are not only reflective of class relations; they are also constitutive. Playing exclusive sports such as polo once helped reproduce an aristocratic class by serving as what the sociologists H. E. Chehabi and A. Guttmann described as the means of socialization by which rulers can "develop those traits of character and leadership necessary for dominion at home and abroad."[31] Some of these characteristics are obvious. For example, riding on a stately horse in front of a high-society viewing stand reinforces one's command over troops while simultaneously reaffirming in the popular imagination one's fitness to rule. Yet, the performance of class, both reflected and reproduced by sports, is also temporal. At the dawn of the twenty-first century, on the East End of Long Island, the old aristocracies of nineteenth-century Britain and early-twentieth-century America are being supplanted by a new bourgeoisie. While playing polo carries with it a historical element of prestige and power, the dominant characteristics that must be acquired by this new class of polo players and, perhaps even more important, packaged for a new public's consumption, require a new narrative of changing symbols and values.

Each weekend during the polo season, *The Morning Line* is published to update spectators on the previous weeks' scores and tournament standings, acquaint them with the rules, and present a roster and

Bridgehampton Polo magazine advertisement from David Rubin's RR&A insurance firm represents the new bourgeoisie's ability to conquer and its fitness to rule. (Courtesy of PCI Publishing, 1998)

scorecard for the day's event. *The Morning Line* assumes that few in the polo audience know much about the game itself, let alone the actual teams and their success. While each issue is dominated by advertisements and includes a "Sudsy Sez" gossip column that tracks the "who's who" of celebrity spectators (both of which I discuss later), the feature piece is usually a lengthy profile of one of the players. Similarly, the Bridgehampton Polo Club distributes an annual "guide" at each match that offers another full player profile. A few characteristics appear common to all of these biographies: the players highlighted are white, U.S.-born men (despite the fact that the best polo players are South American); they are of first- or second-generation wealth; and most are newly arrived to the Hamptons as year-round residents.

But more interesting are the similarities in the ways in which these publications present the polo player's narrative. Each player has an athletic history that often includes high-level competition in a more popular organized sport (often college basketball or football). And, while each player's "passion" or "excitement" for polo is declared in numerous places throughout the piece, his conversion to being "hooked on the game" of polo has followed a similar progression: from overcoming fear, to "accepting the challenge," and then to "taking a plunge." For Mike Caruso, whose upscale Country Imports auto dealership sponsors his team, polo is a "dangerous sport." But, as the *Bridgehampton Polo Guide* tells us, "then his natural competitiveness took over. Polo became a challenge, and he seldom walks away from any challenge." In fact, Caruso declared that his life philosophy (passed on from his father) is "You can do anything you want if you really want to do it. There is no luck and there are no coincidences."[32]

David Rubin, a partner at the insurance firm of Rickel, Rubin & Associates, which sponsored his team, had "three guys holding me on the horse. I was literally shaking." Despite an earlier fall from a horse, Rubin said to himself, "I was always good in sports, college basketball at Michigan State University, etc. . . . I can do this."[33] For Rubin, polo was also at first more a challenge that had to be met than an athletic endeavor to be enjoyed. In a later interview, he explained, "I had enough confidence in myself and I wanted to compete. But once I started playing, I developed a real passion for the sport. The feeling is indescribable."[34]

All profiles reveal a similar evolutionary process for "the Hamptons" polo player, whose passion for the game derives from a combination of "natural competitiveness," emotional fortitude, physical fitness, and a sense of adventure. But the transformation reveals two interesting dynamics: the passion follows the desire to "play" the game, and the passion itself emanates from the physical and emotional satisfaction of *performing* polo. For, even during moments of what one polo enthusiast called "pure sport," the experience "of striking the ball twenty or thirty yards" is only part of the pleasure. Not only do the players overcome risk and attain skill; they do so in front of an audience, dressed in full gear and guided through their adventures by professional officials, public announcers, and hundreds of spectators. Thus, while success in polo seems to reflect what is necessary for success in capitalism—the tenacity to compete, the courage to risk, and the ability to win—playing professional "high goal" polo in the Hamptons is also a performance that seems to legitimize and naturalize one's social position of wealth and power at a historical moment when adventure, risk, and tenacity are highly valued in the marketplace.

This triumphal image of status should not be seen as grossly exclusive. Despite polo's expression of bourgeois distinction, the events themselves do integrate the players with their spectators. In particular, Bridgehampton polo unites players with three groups: their hyperbourgeois peers under the "Members and Special Guest Tent"; the upper-middle-class summer tourists and local professionals who pay $10 per ticket to sit in the spectator stands across the field from the celebrity tent; and the general regional and metropolitan audience that reads stories about the events in glossy magazines like *Dan's Papers*, *Hamptons* magazine, *The Hamptons Sheet*, and *Montauk Life*. While this relationship is, in part, generated by pre- and postgame mingling, players also demonstrate their good will toward the general population through their sponsorship of the sport itself. As southeast Indian polo-playing royalty sought to achieve popular legitimacy through sport, players not only participate to show their physical prowess but also express their social grace by "giving back" to their communities (according to the sociologist Peter Parkes, "Sponsorship of new polo grounds, together with the hosting of communal feasts at sporting festivals, were essential policies of populist legitimation for tyrannous princes" in India).[35] Bridgehampton players make up more than a third of the largest individual contributors to the Club, and their own companies often sponsor the tournaments, the teams, and even the publications.[36]

In Bridgehampton, each tournament game is accompanied by a charity auction or drawing that usually benefits a local organization such as Southampton Hospital or Long Island Cares, a group that helps feed homeless people. The charity events, however, were late additions to the polo club's schedule. In early 1996, residents of homes adjacent to the Walentas farm complained to Town Board members that the previous year's polo tournaments had created a "carnival-like" atmosphere, "ruining their entire summer." When the board refused to halt the permit for the 1996 tournament, the residents took the matter to court, filing first with the State Supreme Court (where the suit was dismissed) and then with the Supreme Court's Appellate Division, where they lost as well. Despite their success in the courts, polo enthusiasts recognized that "special events permits" granted by the town were much more flexible if the planned activities were charitable fund-raisers rather than simple amusements or commercial events. The organizers of Bridgehampton Polo established charity events, in part as a response to local opposition and the possibility of losing their permits. But the players' profiles also mention their favorite charities, confirming that the "civic face" promoted by these "benefit" events is also symbolic of the players' (and by extension their class's) generosity and public spirit—their overall fitness to rule.

Perhaps the most important form of populism and legitimacy acquired by the polo elite emanates from the family image portrayed in their profiles. Each piece highlights the players' "commitment" to family, usually picturing the rider with his wife and/or children. Many players emphasize how important it is to have their families present at the games. David Rubin says that "it's hard to explain what it means to have my boys at the matches. They've started picking up the sport and it makes the whole experience more enjoyable, more fulfilling."[37] One article exclaimed that a particular player felt "great joy" at having the whole family attend matches: "It is healthy that everybody has fun around polo . . . the fact that [my son] wants to go to polo and spend time with me is the best." Caruso expressly states that polo is not just an elite sport. "It's full of fun and excitement for both the players and the spectators. . . . It's a magnificent day for the entire family." In an interview, one of his friends describes this player as "a wonderful father and a terrific barbecuer."[38]

In part, this use of family echoes Barthes's understanding of French culture's hegemonic pressure to overlay social distinction with evidence of the common touch, as in the case of French women novelists who must be celebrated equally for their production of books *and* of children, for their roles as authors *and* as mothers.[39] In the case of the Hamptons, the captains of the new bourgeoisie must also be fathers and husbands in order to be elite, yet American. For a post-Depression and post–World War II United States, national values became inextricably linked with promoting the home, valuing togetherness, and privileging the family—family-size cartons, family rooms, family cars, family films, family restaurants, and family vacations.[40] Outdoor activities or controlled adventures beyond the home demonstrated the "unity," "strength," and "fitness" of families in general, and parents (or leaders) in particular. Soon, all members of the power elite, from politicians to corporate executives, from movie moguls to military brass, had to demonstrate their ability to picnic and barbecue, to attend sporting events and other nature outings. Within an American context, family imagery entails a democratic sentiment that allows this new bourgeoisie to achieve certain distinction while at the same time demonstrating the set of values it holds in common with its Hamptons neighbors and its media public.[41]

Nowhere is the democratic sentiment more evident at polo matches than when spectators from both sides of the field are asked to enter the field of play between the third and fourth chukkers and stamp down the divots of turf pulled up by horses during the game. Despite the effort of many club professionals and their publications, however, few spectators come primarily to watch the riders swat a ball across an open field. As the journalist Peter Fearon writes, most attendees are engaged "in a less arcane spectator sport: watching each other. . . . Most of the 'Tent People' are so involved in their own spectacle that the chukker in progress, between [the magazine publisher] Peter Brant's White Birch, ranked fourth in the world, and Revlon, owned by [Wall Street brokerage firm] Bear Stearns partner Mickey Tarnopol, ranked sixth, seems almost an afterthought."[42] Many of the polo enthusiasts speak begrudgingly about the "tent mentality" of the audience.[43] Even the Club's own guide admits that the spectators are as impressive as the polo matches themselves. And, as the stadium announcer periodically reminds the crowd about the day's sponsor, *Town and Country* magazine, the event, too, is "for and about the affluent."

In many ways, the economic and cultural elite that fills today's "society pages" has not changed all that much from the first Manhattanites who "discovered" the Hamptons more than a hundred years ago. While many of Gaines's "arrivistes" who are now battling for acceptance—the wealthiest and keenest of whom might become members or at least regular guests of the Bridgehampton Club—playing polo is still a signal that one has already attained wealth and power.

Playing polo is about confirming contemporary legitimacy, not just about seeking "status." But today's bourgeoisie *is* different from the earlier arrivals in key cultural and economic ways, and the sports they play, even if they resemble the sports of a century ago, have also changed. I want to discuss three integral characteristics that distinguish this bourgeoisie from its predecessors in the early twentieth century: its obsession with celebrity and image; the new saturation of upscale consumer values and corporate hegemony; and its desire to identify the Hamptons as a home, not just a summer respite.

In part, the chaotic speed and spatial dynamics of the global market place have made all images temporal and fleeting. John Berger contends that the abundance of technological images has displaced the physical as appearances are registered and transmitted with lightening speed. The result is that no physical or tangible experience is communicated: "All that is left to share is the spectacle, the game that nobody plays and everybody can watch."[44] A Bridgehampton polo match certainly exemplifies this idea; it is more important to be seen than to do anything. The patience and subtlety of the old aristocracy have been supplanted by the need to reaffirm one's social distinction on a moment-to-moment basis. And if the old aristocracy's distinction was based on a belief in an essentialist, divine, or natural right of birth, the new, hyper-bourgeoisie's power derives from its ability to constantly create, re-create, and publicize its lifestyle. The story of polo in the Hamptons—for both players and spectators—is about the perpetual telling of the story.

Before the Bridgehampton Polo Club had any official members, its founders-to-be first employed a publicist, as if to admit that the Club itself could not exist before an expert propagandist promoted it. Peggy Siegel, hired by the Club's executives Neil Hirsch and Peter Brant, has likened Hamptons polo matches to a "cocktail party."[45] Although *The Morning Line* boasts "all the Polo News that's Fit to Run," one of its longest pieces is the "Sudsy Sez" gossip column. Each week, beginning on the magazine's front page, Sudsy announces new restaurant openings, art gallery exhibits, and Hamptons charity functions. Clearly this is a kind of news that informs the elite communities about its own happenings. But most of Sudsy's columns comprise a list of who's in "and of" the Hamptons. For example:

> We hear the Divine Kelly Klein (nee Rector) has retired to Middleburgh and her horses. Quelle horrible for us. Reaching Divine status this summer is Goddess/writer/best dressed, the one and only JAMEE GREGORY. . . . Mrs. Sudsy says she is so chic that she wants to hang herself. Did you know if you can't get a table from Glen at Red Bar or Roberto at Savannah on Sat. Night you might as well go to Burger King?[46]
>
> Well, gang it was opening day and the tent was filled to capacity. . . . In the crowd we saw Howard Oxenberg, Jonathan Farkas, famous photog Francesco Scavullo, Charles Evans, Alan Beeber, and on and on. Did not see any of my "Divine" ladies, maybe they were all helping Pat DeBary pack to move into her new home at "Whitefields." Did not see the brothers Wilzig either and the tailgate area was sort of empty. Where is Dr. Joe DeBellis and his crew? Off in Speonk at a B-B-Q?[47]

Sex and the City's Kim Cattrell poses in front of both a Mercedes-Benz and the VIP tent. Somewhere, polo is being played. (Photo © Patrick McMullan)

This is pure, unadulterated gossip. But this is exactly the point—the real news at polo matches *is* the gossip. Polo is predominately about which of New York City's rich and famous have made it to the Hamptons. And since so many now make it out to the Hamptons, the distinctions must be made by who is actually reported to have been *seen* at polo matches. To be under the tent is to be embraced by the new hyper-bourgeoisie.

The reportage, however, also goes out to nonelites, represented by those few hundred general admission spectators and the dozens of magazines and newspapers that pick up on the events as material for "society page" stories. The gossip column, like the event itself, is part of this hyper-bourgeoisie's public demonstration of class ascendancy —a cultural event in the class struggle of a new elite with a new set of values and meanings. While polo represents this ascendant class's effort to grasp a sense of historical legitimacy and aristocratic tradition by association with the "sport of kings," the need to constantly create public and publicized spectacle remains the event's raison d'être.

Most of the space within every polo publication, however, is given over to advertising. In fact, corporate logos and slogans appear everywhere around the stadium grounds, on the players' jerseys, throughout the guest tent, and especially in the adjacent merchandise booths. As has happened in both amateur and professional sports around the world, corporations have grabbed the opportunity to market their products and to celebrate their icons by associating themselves with popular teams or events.[48] Bridgehampton polo matches attract a wealthy crowd with great sums of disposable income, and it makes some marketing sense to advertise upscale products at such events. As one New York magazine reporter declared, "What does Mercedes Benz get out of [picking up the sponsorship tab]? Prestige by association. Car sales."[49] But, as Quentin Dante, a polo team patron, coach, and enthusiast, contends, it has not made *very* good marketing sense. He explained, in 1999, that "the corporate sponsorship has decreased over the last two years . . . the tournament needs sponsorship, but not so much that players are willing to make a significant marketing plan or strategy. The corporate sponsorship is developed here [at Bridgehampton] by saying to prospective sponsors, 'Hey, you want to be hot, you want to be visible, throw a two-hour party in the Hamptons for $50,000.'"[50] But the return on the investment hasn't been there for most sponsors.

In fact, Dante wants to "professionalize" polo by bringing in more corporate sponsorship, media coverage, and contracts and by raising the overall level of play. "Even in terms of corporate sponsorship," according to Dante, "it has been difficult to procure it because there has been resistance from the tournament to be willing to offer reciprocal opportunities to sponsors." He concludes that the tournament and its American patrons don't really want to professionalize or commercialize polo, because the sports' growth might reduce its cachet among the elite. As a result, the sport becomes, as Dante puts it, "all about whether some of these patrons get their picture in Hamptons magazine—that's what they're concerned about. They don't care about losing money in the tournament. They don't care about running it like an organization." Dante has suggested that increased corporate sponsorship of teams and individual player endorsements would allow polo to prove to merchants that there is a return on investment because fans would associate the sport and its best players, "like Pete Sampras or Tiger Woods," with certain merchandise.[51]

Yet, Bridgehampton spectators have little, if any, interest in team loyalties; polo's popularity is based predominately on the cultural capital of the spectacle itself. Therefore, the appearance of upscale merchandisers suggests a parallel strategy that has more to do with the players' and organizers' own social sophistication than with corporate marketing plans. To be connected with cars such as Mercedes-Benz and BMW, jewelers such as Cartier and Tiffany, or designers such as Calvin Klein, Ralph Lauren, or Giorgio Armani is an important sign of social superiority. In other words, it is the major corporations whose long history of serving a bourgeois clientele offers the tournament players and their entourage "prestige by association." The appearance of these corporate names is a major part of the total spectacle of the event itself, and polo players and guests reap the distinction associated with such icons of upscale lifestyles as much as (if not more than) the corporations themselves benefit from their act of sponsorship.

And whether players or spectators actually do much purchasing at the matches, the matches provide a place where cultural capital is acquired as images, if not physical or tangible commodities, are bought and sold. In a sense, then, the polo club puts on an event of distinction characterized by what Sharon Zukin has called a "shopping culture," where places of consumption are "not simply . . . central spaces for being-in-society, but the forms and sites and the very experiences of shopping they engender are part and parcel of what makes groups different." She continues:

> Shopping cultures are not important simply on the level of individual preferences or even consumption practices. They are an important part of building the spaces of cities, and by virtue of the importance of seeing and being seen, they build public cultures. They offer opportunities for the representation of group identities, and for the inclusion of those identities in a larger, urban public culture.[52]

While the Hamptons are still far from urban, their inherent link to New York City's upscale metropolitan culture is fundamental to this wealthy migrant group's worldview. The spectacle of polo, and its emphasis on publicity and marketing, makes it an important public site for displaying commercial power and prestige. Cultural capital itself is being shopped, and its production and distribution are vital to the creation of the Hamptons as an upscale exurban landscape.

The level of economic and social status derived from being part of the Bridgehampton polo scene is inextricably connected to the global marketplace, both explicitly (in the types of upscale "foreign" companies and commodities represented) and implicitly (in the underlying knowledge that most of the wealth on display is a direct or indirect result of Wall Street fortunes and corporate globalization and was accumulated after the early 1980s). In fact, the arrivistes' reliance on advertising and publicity for legitimacy seems linked to two important factors. First, the economic foundation for the new bourgeoisie's ascendancy comes from the wealth that these industries have produced. Second, in a society that has no tradition of assigning status in accordance with grand narratives about natural order, bloodlines, and breeding, the hyper-bourgeoisie is left with a postmodern angst about what legitimizes their distinction and rely on a publicized association with acknowledged material luxury to cement their claim to superior status. As Berger once wrote about images of advertising and publicity:

> Publicity is, in essence, nostalgic. It has to sell the past to the future.
> . . . All publicity works upon anxiety. The sum of everything is money,
> to get money is to overcome anxiety. Alternatively the anxiety on
> which publicity plays is the fear that having nothing you will become
> nothing. . . . According to the legends of publicity, those who lack the
> power to spend money become literally faceless. Those who have the
> power become lovable. . . . For publicity, the present is by definition
> insufficient . . . [it] speaks in the future tense and yet the achievement
> is endlessly deferred. . . . It recognizes nothing except the power to
> acquire.[53]

The wealth of contemporary elites rides the frenetic pace of financial speculation and dot.com globalization. The distinction of the hyper-bourgeoisie must also rest on constant images of its own perpetual acquisitiveness. Whether "shopping" takes place at all during polo matches is less important than the event's existence as a place where commercial hegemony and the worship of material luxury can be displayed. Polo produces distinction for its players and spectators, and part of that power emanates from the increasing saturation of corporate images and commercial values. As Berger concluded, "Publicity is the life of this culture—in so far as without publicity capitalism could not survive—and at the same time publicity is its dream."[54] To be at polo is to enter a perpetual dream world that requires the perpetual narrative provided by publicity and advertising.

The most important point about this hyper-bourgeoisie's new life in the East End is that the Hamptons are *not* urban. The changing venue for the kind of cultural practices that will demonstrate the dominance of this hyper-bourgeois is part of what is at stake in its struggle to impose its image on the physical and cultural, *nonurban* landscape. New stories must be told to reaffirm its ascendancy and to rationalize this change in the way class and power are displayed.

When *Town and Country* magazine sponsored the second polo match of the 1998 season at Bridgehampton, its summer issue featured a cover story on the Hamptons. The piece that declared summer to be the "wrong season" for those who are the area's "rightful inhabitants." In other words, the "tens of thousands of people" who flood the East End for summer respite are the interlopers who infringe on the true "locals" who have used their recently acquired wealth to establish residency in the area. In the piece, readers are exposed to more than a dozen photos featuring children with their horses, young students at one of the Hamptons' several new private "day schools," and couples on front porches or playing with their pets in the yard. Each picture reinforces the message that, for this group of newly rich, year-round residents, "it's no longer a question of trying to pack enjoyment into a summer's brief span. The whole year is theirs now . . . as they contemplate what eleven years of Alan Greenspan have wrought."[55]

The polo players' narratives, which focus on family, must also be seen within this framework of establishing a dominant claim to the land. The storytellers of the new bourgeoisie's conquest in the Hamptons legitimize their settlement by focusing on family and nature. The aesthetic link between young parents and children with animals set in beautiful bucolic scenes naturalizes this class as part of the scenery— they belong. Even Sudsy noticed that everyone seems to bring dogs to polo. It is no coincidence that the emphasis is on attractive parents and their young children, for these are new families that have reinvigorated the region with their success and innovation—new money, new families. Even change itself, according to *Town and Country,* is both natural and benevolent:

[Bridgehampton] is not without its share of problems and dislocation which modern life and the global economy have assaulted rural com-

munities the world over—exacerbated here by the fact that the fiercely
self-sufficient vocations of farming and fishing have had the land sold
out from under them. Fifteen years ago, the tensions were palpable,
but today the pace of the upmarket development is regarded as both
inevitable and crucial to the local economy. Landscaping, plant husbandry, carpentry, and other ways of taking the second-home owners'
shillings are now accepted as respectable forms of employment, and
peaceful coexistence is the rule rather than the exception.[56]

Conflicts over land use and class politics disappear as the new hyper-
bourgeoisie declares its local identity and reshapes the physical and cultural landscape. And by conquering the seasonal nature of the Hamptons original bourgeoisie, and by keeping the publicity that documents
its ascendancy in perpetual production, this class seems to have conquered both time and space.

But vigorous public debates over development projects such as
new horse farms and the nationally publicized building of Ira Rennert's
compound demonstrate that the hyper-bourgeoisie's dominance is still
hotly contested. Despite the imagery and the cash, not everyone is com-
fortable with the elite's land-use and cultural practices, as the Peconic
County Now! movement demonstrates. These efforts often reflect other
demographic changes and the variety of cultural politics in the Hamptons. As we have noted, the other group that has, in large numbers,
taken up residence year-round on the East End of Long Island consists
of Latino immigrants from Central and South America. Their struggle
to establish a sense of cultural identity and physical residence in the region can be seen at play on the soccer field.

SOCCER AND THE CULTURAL POLITICS
OF A NEW WORKING CLASS

On most mornings, outside Sal's Country Deli on North Sea Road in
Southampton, you can find dozens of parked pickup trucks, utility
vans, station wagons, and other large vehicles. On their way to paint
houses, cut lawns, install swimming pools and tennis courts, or perform any one of a hundred jobs that the upscale housing boom has created, workers stop at Sal's to get coffee, juice, and bacon and eggs with
cheese on hard rolls. Many of the Latino workers are already part of

work crews and come and go in groups. Some, however, linger in the parking lot, hoping to find work with a team of builders or painters or landscapers in need of some extra hands. Sal's is known as one of many places on the East End where contractors—large and small—can pick up a few extra workers for short jobs and relatively low wages. There are other locations throughout the Hamptons and its environs where *patrones* pick up organized groups of Latino men and bring them to a variety of work sites.

For many years, Latino migrants made their way from New York City or directly from Mexico to the East End to participate in the seasonal summer economy. Since the early 1980s, however, many Latin American families from Mexico or Central or South America have taken advantage of the area's booming year-round economy to relocate permanently. This change is partially a regional trend of burgeoning northward migration from all over Latin America to the United States. New York City's Latino population and Long Island's own Hispanic population have almost tripled since 1980. But the proportion of Latinos on the East End has experienced an even more significant increase in total numbers with some villages such as Montauk experiencing a tenfold change.

Even this local figure is somewhat distorted as the price of housing in the East End remains prohibitive for most low-wage service employees. As one Latino worker told a *New York Times* reporter, $8 an hour was "just about enough" to allow him and seven other adults to pay a $1,300-a-month rent and to feed themselves and the eight children who shared the second floor of a house in Southampton. He explained, "Out here [in the Hamptons] everything is more expensive, but the salaries aren't higher."[57] In Southampton, the median cost of homes rose from $57,600 in 1980 to $245,400 in 2000, an increase of more than 400 percent, and median contract rent increased from $241 per month to $938 per month, a rise of almost 400 percent. In East Hampton, in 2000, homes averaged almost $300,000 and median rents were $1,061. Recognizing the lack of affordable housing for the growing low-wage Latino workforce, the Southampton Planning Board explained that, while "moderate and middle income families and individuals find it difficult to find affordable and year-round rental housing, migrant and seasonal workers employed by the local farm and tourism/service industries are often housed in crowded and substandard conditions. By some accounts, these problems appear to be worsening."[58]

Many of the Latinos who work on the East End live "up-island" (west of the Hamptons), in the towns of Riverhead and Brookhaven. Many Hamptons large-chain retailers such as Caldor (now T.J. Maxx) department stores and King Kullen food markets cannot find enough local low-wage workers and run morning buses to up-island neighborhoods.[59] Similarly, an entire informal economy has risen around transportation as many Latino entrepreneurs have saved money and invested in large passenger vans. These vehicles provide transportation for workers who cannot afford automobiles and who find that the few public buses and trains that do service the area don't stop anywhere near regular job sites. While workers pay between $20 and $30 a week for rides, one driver explained, "I pick them up at home and I pick them up at work, and if I have to take their children to the babysitter I do it, too. All for the same price. . . . We have to help each other because it's tough to survive earning less than minimum wage."[60] But, even with help from one another, Latino workers can find the East End of Long Island an inhospitable place.

On July 24, 1998, health officials and sheriff's deputies in Brookhaven forced forty-four Latino men out of the two houses they were sharing. The Town Council had received numerous complaints from neighbors who had formed the Farmingville Civic Association (eventually known as Sachem Quality of Life) in an attempt to pressure legislators to rid "their neighborhood" of an increasing number of multifamily rental units occupied by Latinos. While some homeowners claimed they were just as concerned about the workers, who "may have been exploited" by landlords, white neighbors began circulating flyers asking, "Tired of seeing hundreds of people hanging around? Afraid to walk down the streets?" The Association president betrayed this convergence of racism and compassion as she told one *Newsday* reporter, "If you had twenty-two dogs in one small area, people would be concerned on a humane level." But, as one Latino worker explained, "If you close the houses where ten, fifteen, twenty people live, where are you going to find other houses to redistribute them? . . . We wait here in the morning because this is a zone the *patrones* know we'll be. If they don't want us on the street they have to help us find a place where we don't bother them."[61]

This dynamic of being welcomed as part of a necessary low-wage workforce but not being accepted as local residents is a dominant feature of East End life for Latino workers and their families. In March

1990, an eviction similar to the one in Brookhaven occurred in Montauk when a landlord locked a Colombian family out of its apartment after disconnecting the gas, heat, and water. Town and county officials were pressuring the landlord to clean up and renovate the complex and to adhere to maximum-occupancy requirements. The pressure from the Montauk legislators began in 1990, when a large number of previously seasonal Colombian workers decided to remain in that town permanently because they feared that their work visas would not be renewed. Area hotel owners and small landlords filled vacancies by allowing large groups of workers to occupy previously unrentable units. At the Montauk site, in the absence of adequate maintenance and infrastructure, garbage piled up and the building exteriors began to crumble. Neighbors complained of the "eyesore," as well as about the large groups of people who would just "hang around" playing loud music and drinking.

In the summer of 1996, Southampton town officials condemned a small cul de sac of six houses shared by a dozen Latino families. Garbage pile-ups, poor plumbing, and decrepit structures had combined with heavy rains to create quagmires of raw sewage and trash. The evictions left all the residents homeless and at the mercy of the local Catholic church. While there is ongoing pressure to provide adequate housing for the burgeoning Latino population, few communities want to risk the profits of upscale real estate development by legitimizing low-income housing or a visible, relatively poor immigrant community. As the Southampton Planning Commission intimated, the lack of affordable housing is not so much a problem of a very large low-income population as it is the result of the rapid expansion of the high-end real estate markets. The Commission continued: "Southampton is one of the most select second-home communities in the United States. Both its year-round and seasonal occupants are drawn by its considerable amenities and ambiance. The high quality of life is, unfortunately, reflected in the high price of housing in the town."[62]

Even the Planning Commission's own studies show that the low-wage population in the area is increasing to service the expanding year-round economy of the area's wealthier residents. Thus, the very success of high-end real estate development has intensified the demand for affordable housing and low-income rental units.

Many Latino workers and families *have* found housing in trailer parks, hotels, group housing, and the few public housing sites that exist in the Hamptons area. Older immigrants who came to the region in the 1970s and early 1980s have even earned enough to buy homes in hamlets and villages like Springs, Montauk, and parts of Hampton Bays. These new residents have had a significant impact on a variety of public institutions, most notably the school districts; almost 15 percent of Southampton students and more than 20 percent of East Hampton students speak a second language at home, and almost half live with families that speak English "less than 'very well.'" School boards have hired more teachers trained in English as a second language (ESL), instituted more free-lunch and after-school programs, and implemented building expansions to facilitate the growing student body.

The Latino community has also organized a number of self-help groups that have created English-language tutoring programs and pressured government officials to make institutions accessible for Spanish-speaking residents. In response, local police in both Southampton and East Hampton have instituted cultural-awareness and sensitivity-training programs, and the local courts have appointed special translators and liaisons for non-English-speaking citizens. The local anti-bias task forces in both towns have been active in pressuring local governments to improve bilingual services. Some local attorneys and other businesses now advertise in Spanish, especially in *El Mensajero*, a Spanish-language newspaper that has been actively supported since 1991. Even mainstream newspapers now include periodic articles written in Spanish. In 1998, a small group of local Latino residents formed Latinos Unidos. Although the group soon disbanded, it held fund-raisers to support English classes offered in Southampton.[63] In 2002, the group OLA (Organizacion Latino Americana) formed; it has since been a driving force behind efforts to achieve action on a number of issues, including bilingual education and discrimination in schools, workers' rights, and affordable housing, that are of concern to Latinos.

Like many immigrants past, the growing Latino community has also established solidarity networks through local churches. While the Catholic Diocese of Rockville Centre has sponsored Spanish-language masses for more than a decade, other denominations, like the Community Bible Church (CBC), in Sag Harbor, and the Methodist Church in Bridgehampton also offer Spanish-language services and try to cater to the growing needs of the Latino Population. Katherine Hartnett, director of Southampton's Latin American Outreach Center, explains that "the church serves the recently arrived immigrant in basic orientation and survival needs. . . . They know to go there to get the basic immediate needs." She adds, however, that "once you get a little deeper, I think you'll find they're looking for a spiritual home. They are displaced and lonely. They miss the familiarities of home."[64] Even the traditional confines of church basements are converted by the Latino congregations as the customary postservice coffee and donuts are replaced by chips, salsa, empanadas, and Colombian sweet rolls.

Even more noticeable to the area's majority population has been the new Latinos' impact on various aspects of social and cultural life. Many clubs throughout the Hamptons have instituted meringue and salsa nights, attracting an almost exclusively Latino population. Large grocery market chains such as King Kullen and IGA have set aside large sections for Spanish and Mexican foods. Small markets and take-out eateries specializing in Mexican and South and Central American cuisine have appeared around the Hamptons. Almost ten years ago, Tom Desmond opened the Embassy Market, a Latino deli in the center of Montauk's business district. As he told a reporter from *Dan's Papers*, "If you asked me twenty years ago if I'd have a Latino deli in Montauk, I'd say, 'What, are you kidding me? There aren't enough Latinos around.'" But, when Desmond wanted to start a business, he explained, "I was looking for a sign. It was Sunday, and I drove past the baseball field where I used to play little league, and there it was—the field packed with Latinos playing soccer. So I looked up and said, 'Gracias a Dios!' and decided to go ahead and open a deli."[65] Now, Latinos themselves own restaurant-markets such as Chiquita Latina, in Amagansett, and El Mundo Latino, in Southampton, as well as the Azuca nightclub in Bridgehampton. Throughout the East End, Latino workers, entrepreneurs, and their families are changing the permanent character and cultural landscape of the area. And nowhere has this impact been felt as much as on the region's soccer fields and the resulting conflicts over their use.

Since the mid-1980s, many of the Latino workers who settled on the East End have created soccer teams to compete in the official East Hampton summer soccer leagues. In recent years, these leagues have expanded to service the growing interest among predominantly Latino players, resulting in the creation of a Latino League. This popular league has its games on a small field just outside the Montauk central business district. From just about noon until well after 8:00 p.m. on Sundays, the field is filled with two opposing teams and at least three or four dozen spectators cheering them on. Each team is composed primarily of players who share a particular national origin; there is Team Mexico, and Team Costa Rica, and Team Ecuador. The referees speak Spanish, the crowd speaks Spanish, and the sound of Latin music and sometimes the smells of Spanish foods fill the air.

Many of the soccer players say they play the game because it is fun. While soccer has been played in the United States for many years, some players claim it is a "Spanish" sport, imbuing its performance with an ethnic quality or a sense of national or regional pride. Other players openly admit that playing the game reminds them of home and, like other special celebrations or festive occasions, gives them a sense of "who they are." For the spectators, the soccer games are an integral part of the community's activities and represent an intergenerational family event where older men can be seen kicking soccer balls with young boys and girls while women sit in the stands or on picnic blankets and talk. Some watch the players intently, but, not unlike polo, the games share a kind of status as community events, not just as sporting competitions.

While polo's fundamental purpose emanates from its public spectacle, soccer games offer the Latino communities of Colombian, Mexican, Guatemalan, and Ecuadorian people a chance to see and converse with one another, reaffirming both their common heritage and their evolving immigrant identities and communities. Although the players often say that they "play to win," both participants and nonparticipants use the games as a place to create a solidarity based on their shared experiences in a new land and a shared sense of cultural history and origin. There are no major corporate sponsors, no player profiles, no paparazzi, only seventy-five to a hundred primarily Latino immigrants celebrating their struggle to negotiate new lives in a new place.

These games, and by extension the Latino communities, are not without cultural and economic stratification. Teams do require some financial support to pay for uniforms, referees, and so on. Often players look to their local employers—the owners of landscaping and construction companies—or to local merchants that cater to Latino clientele —for example, the Embassy Deli—for sponsorship. More recently, though, players who have been in the area long enough to establish their own businesses have become sponsors, too. Carlos Vargas, a former local star player and currently the owner of his own contracting business, has several sets of uniforms at his house in East Hampton. He

Team Mexico celebrates both a soccer league championship and its own cultural identity (*East Hampton Star,* 1998; photo by Jack Graves)

explains, "New teams often call me for uniforms and pick them up before the game." He also holds celebrations for winning teams and hosts parties for important occasions in the Costa Rican community. More important, Vargas says, "players who get injured rarely have insurance or any other support. . . . We have fund-raisers and barbeques to raise money for guys who get hurt to pay medical bills, food for kids, and other things."[66]

Similarly, David Rodriguez, a Mexican-born player, has his own building company and often acts as a source of economic support for soccer teams, as well as for family and friends who are recent immigrants to the area. He states: "All of us have to help each other. Some friends of mine got me my first job; I got my brother his job, and we all played soccer together when I started Team Mexico a few years ago." In many ways, soccer not only represents the place where Latino men come to perform their ethnic identities, but it also helps solidify new networks that allow players to enhance their employment opportunities.[67]

Some players also achieve significant individual acclaim. Some players, like Vargas and Rodriguez, gained a kind of star status in the Latino communities. Joel Gomez, the top goal scorer for Team Mexico, was heavily recruited by soccer coaches from local colleges. While he never accepted any offers, he explains that everybody in the Latin community "knows about him," and it means a lot to "walk into a night club and be congratulated for winning a game." In the summer of 1998, a high school star, John Villaplana, was murdered outside a Montauk night club. His death hit the Latino community hard. Carlos Vargas held a huge fund-raiser to help the family pay for funeral expenses and helped organize a charity game to both raise money and honor Villaplana's memory. Vargas explained that "John was important to the non-Hispanic community, too. He bridged both worlds and was an important symbol of our acceptance and achievement in the Hamptons."[68]

Most of these community dynamics remain highly gendered. While young single women, girlfriends, wives, and mothers do attend games, more often they are too busy on weekday evenings and weekends during the spring, summer, and fall to make up much of the audience. As the former director of the regional Hispanic Apostolic, Sister Cathy Kugler explained that soccer is just one of many events that brings Latinos together. According to Kugler, soccer games are almost always followed by parties organized by women. But, she says, "most of the networks and activities that women participate in are informal—no uniforms, no spectators, and no local newspaper reporters. Women in the Latino community are usually working two or three jobs, have primary-care responsibilities for children, and are the links between families and available social services."[69] Still, the Sunday soccer league in Montauk seems to bring out women, as well as older men and children. It remains one of the few outdoor *public* sites where the community openly perpetuates its own relatively autonomous cultural traditions.

These efforts, however, are under attack from a variety of local merchants and homeowners, who, for the past five years, have complained to Montauk Village and East Hampton town officials about the soccer games. Some local retailers worry about increased traffic and parking problems, while neighbors have protested the noise that comes from the field. Members of the Montauk Fire Department have argued that the field was originally built for baseball and that when their Department team goes to play ball, members first have to "bring tools and shovel in the earth because there are holes in the field from soccer."[70] But, as Jay Schneiderman explained, solving these problems is complicated by resentment toward "undocumented laborers: First people complained that the baseball fields were being torn up by soccer players. Then, when we proposed building more soccer fields, people complained that we were spending tax dollars on illegal immigrants."[71]

Chiquita Latina, in Amagansett, is one of the growing number of Latino-owned businesses on the East End. (Photo by author, 2004)

According to one Colombian player, the merchants in Montauk are happy to have Latinos work for them washing dishes in their kitchens and cleaning rooms in their hotels. Yet, the same employers don't like to see these same workers have fun in town. He asked, "Why do they want us here when we are workers but not when we are soccer players?" A player from Mexico stated that some of the business people are "O.K., and others don't want to look at you." And even in their small communities, white neighbors are always complaining to the police about noise. But he continued, "we always eat and talk and relax outside whenever we can. That is how we do it at home [in Mexico]. Here, people don't like to see so many people hanging around, especially Latinos."[72]

Local media coverage of the games is scanty at best, and when pictures of the game do appear, they rarely have names below the photos of the players. One local sportswriter, Jack Graves, covers the Latino League with regularity and does a meticulous job of keeping track of goal scorers and other stars of the game. In his columns, he has argued that the level of play is excellent and that the League itself should be able to stay in Montauk, despite the local protests. He wrote, "[The

League] should remain right where it is, and the powers that be should see to it that the grass is cut regularly."[73] In gratitude for Graves's support, the League organizers put together a special game after the season a few years ago to honor him. The group presented Graves with a trophy that called him a "friend to soccer." More important, though, Graves's reportage treats the Latino players with respect and gives their presence a kind of legitimacy; he has been a friend to them as well as their game.

As soccer leagues on the East End continue to grow as the Latino population grows, government officials will be faced with increasing conflicts over land use. Some contests will be fought over which sports are permitted in which locations. Other battles will occur because many white residents are unfamiliar with or intolerant of the kinds of cultural practices that Latino immigrants bring with them. And struggles will take place because some image-conscious merchants and racist homeowners would prefer that Latinos be as invisible in their leisure time as they are at work. As the recent economic slowdown wreaks havoc on the kind of second-circuit economic investment represented by some of the Hamptons exurban development, tensions over jobs and wages may fuel struggles that will play themselves out in social and cultural conflicts over sports and leisure activities.

Polo and soccer represent a complex set of cultural practices and politics for the fastest-growing populations on Long Island's East End. The permanent migration of the hyper-bourgeoisie and of Latinos to the region has already resulted in a variety of changes in both the physical and the cultural landscape as large-scale economic and social transformations and regional and local dynamics converge. The ways in which the people of the Hamptons face these changes will determine future government policies, as well as the use and design of public space. Part of the process will reflect the struggles of new populations to establish their own sense of identity and place. For polo players, armed with public relations experts and the economic resources to conquer huge tracts of land, the image of the Hamptons will continue to reflect and reinforce their elite identity of celebrity and privilege as they claim their historical ascendancy and a postmodern sense of natural right. The soccer players whose hands work the land, clean the mansions, and serve the wealthy, however, will continue to struggle to shape the region's everyday physical environment in a way that reflects their own experience, culture, pride, and dignity.

5

The Other Hamptons

Race and Class in America's Paradise

When I first came to the Hamptons I looked around and thought to myself, well, this is just another nice, quiet Southern town.

Lou Ware, president of the East End chapter
of the NAACP

Mockler motioned toward the large window in the living room, which overlooked an almost unbroken sweep of landscape and sky. One of his neighbors, he said, was the vice-president of a large soft drink corporation. During the summer he often commuted to the city by helicopter, landing on the lawn behind his house. "And just a mile up the road are those shacks on Sunrise Avenue," Mockler said. "Sometimes I wonder why there hasn't been a revolution. Upward mobility is just not for the Black people out here."

—Calvin Tomkins and Judy Tomkins,
The Other Hampton

The racism at Southampton College is unbelievable. It's amazing that in 1997 people have become so institutionalized in their thinking that they don't even see it. And it's the same outside the College. Take a look at your LILCO trucks or the telephone company; I do a double take if I see a person of color driving those trucks because it's so rare. Even at the stores in town, if I go to a car dealership or P.C. Richards, I've had other people walk in the door after me and get waited on first. But white people don't even see it.

—Tony Smith, Shinnecock resident and former
custodian at Southampton College

For those of you who have been in this situation and treated this way, you understand. For those that don't understand, I would hope you will never be put in this situation. We are protesting now for our job security and we feel (as a team) we have been treated with no respect.

As I told Provost Bishop, we want to be part of the family again; we want our green uniforms back.

—Percy Hughes, former custodian
at Southampton College

On February 14, 1997, custodial services at Southampton College of Long Island University (LIU) were contracted out to LARO Service Systems, a company that specializes in providing maintenance to large corporate facilities such as the Port Authority Terminal, in New York City, and John F. Kennedy International Airport, in Queens. Custodians suddenly found themselves forced to fill out new job applications for positions some had held for almost thirty years. LARO supervisors told custodians that no one's job would be guaranteed and that changes in the workforce, schedules, and procedures would soon follow. Although the custodians' union, United Industrial Workers Local 424, immediately negotiated a contract addendum that protected jobs for the last year and a half of the existing contract, the custodians were forced to trade in their green LIU uniforms for blue LARO overalls and an uncertain future. As one custodian told the local press, "we felt like dogs kicked onto the sidewalk."[1]

At a faculty meeting a few days later, the college provost, Tim Bishop, announced the outsourcing and explained that the decision was "budget-neutral" and had been based solely on a desire to improve the campus's appearance. The history professor John Strong complained that custodians had never been consulted either about persistent maintenance problems or about the LARO contract. He expressed concerns about the ramifications of inviting "sleazy" companies onto the campus to exploit workers who had been a part of the College community for so long. He reminded the faculty that the College's own brochures described the campus as a "caring and compassionate community." Bishop scolded Strong for commenting on the character of the College's new partner without any background knowledge. Although he admitted that workers had not been consulted, the provost assured the faculty that the conditions of custodial employment would not change.

By the next week, however, Bishop's comments proved curious at best. Background research by the custodians showed that LARO had a history of violating policies set by the National Labor Relations Board and had tried to bust union locals throughout the New York metropolitan area. Meanwhile, the custodians' work conditions and compensation changed significantly: they lost eligibility for TIAA-CREF retirement benefits, tuition remission, and access to emergency loans and other "perks" offered to College employees, and they experienced immediate shifts in work, pay, overtime, and vacation schedules. LARO threatened and intimidated the custodians, asserting that the company "knew" that some of them were "lazy workers and thieves." LARO warned custodians that "fraternizing" with students, faculty, and other staff would not be permitted. It became clear that the custodians' conditions of employment had not only changed but had been radically transformed.

One week after the outsourcing, a group of students, faculty, staff, local residents and custodians met to discuss the situation. The author of this book, a professor in the Friends World Program (a global studies program at the College), and Melissa Arch Walton, a student and community activist, presented evidence of a national movement toward corporatization in higher education. We compared the situation to outsourcing efforts at Tufts College, the University of Pennsylvania, and elsewhere. While the custodians agreed that economics had influenced the College's decision, they felt confident that racial dynamics had also played a crucial role in the LARO contract. Their unit was the only one on campus made up predominately of people of color—twelve of the nineteen members were either African American or Native American. In thirty years, only two people had ever been promoted from custodian to the next level within the Physical Plant Department, and neither had been a person of color. The unit's shop steward, Michael Knight, had recently started pressuring the College to create a formalized "promotional pipeline." The custodians believed that the College wanted to avoid addressing long-standing inequalities and explained to the group present that the director of the Physical Plant Department had punctuated the LARO announcement by saying, "and now I wash my hands of all of you."

Over the next year and a half, the group that gathered that night continued a fight to terminate the LARO contract. Eventually identifying itself as the Southampton Coalition for Justice (CFJ), the group persisted in a struggle that reflected many of the racial and class dynamics in the Hamptons. This chapter documents how the CFJ organized an effective campaign by building a coalition that challenged historically rigid and hierarchical racial and ethnic identities. It also examines the CFJ's ability to build a community-based labor organization that succeeded in supporting workers' rights despite contemporary trends toward privatization and weakened unions. The CFJ struggle not only reflects the convergence of historical and contemporary racial and economic conditions on the East End but also represents a model for democratic social movements fighting to change those conditions. The Coalition's efforts to expose the tensions and conflicts of race and class that lay beneath the surface of everyday life in the Hamptons demonstrated that political organizing and activism could alter the social and political landscape of a campus and its surrounding community.

THE MAKING OF THE HAMPTONS WORKING CLASS

Much of the scholarly debate around American "exceptionalism" relates in one way or another to the historian Louis Hartz's argument that the United States has no feudal past and, therefore, never developed a serious radical tradition to respond to feudal conditions.[2] Most discussions of how the working class of a nation "born equal" (in de Tocqueville's words) failed to develop a radical socialist legacy begin from a similar premise. Many writers claim that because most Americans had access to the ballot box, a shared sense of republicanism developed among workers that allowed them, although sometimes quite militant individually, to be either co-opted by or blended into existing political structures, thus neutralizing independent, radical political movements.[3] Others suggest that economics served to mitigate bourgeois liberalism, that so-called middle-class mobility itself (or at least the ideological illusions of it) undercut workers' more radical tendencies.[4] Recent scholarship, however, has broken somewhat from this mold, emphasizing the role that race and ethnicity played in the formation of U.S. class structure, and particularly the ways that working-class Americans' identities were fragmented because of the role of racial as well as economic factors in assigning class.[5] For these scholars, white identity infused class consciousness with a sense of racial privilege that not only resulted in a lack of radical solidarity among workers of different races but also inspired white workers to distinguish themselves as white in an effort to advance their own economic and social status.

The history of working-class life in the Hamptons, given the lack of any significant radical legacy, requires an analysis that integrates all of these economic, political, and cultural perspectives. Racial identities themselves developed within a context of changing economic conditions—conditions that were different from those that prevailed elsewhere.

As I've explained earlier, regional Native American societies had their own hierarchies, but little of this stratification could be considered class-based by any traditional definition.[6] Even after the earliest Europeans came to the East End, there was little sense of an entrenched class structure among either Native Americans or whites (with the exception of a small number of indentured servants) or between the groups.

The first significant evidence of a class structure occurred as continued land disposition forced the Shinnecock and Montaukett Indians to look to the European community for their economic survival. And, while Native Americans were no strangers to a money economy, it was the European-controlled capitalist cash economy that eventually pressured Native Americans into becoming an embryonic proletariat. According to the historian John Strong, in the late seventeenth and early eighteenth centuries, "as more and more of their ancient hunting grounds were cleared for agricultural production, and their dependency on manufactured tools and other trade goods increased, the Indians were drawn into the European economic system."[7] For many years, local Native Americans built and watched fences, tended and rescued livestock, acted as guides for hunters and fisherman, and provided a host of other services, most often as day or seasonal laborers.

The rise of the local whaling industry in the late 1600s changed these relations forever. The earliest companies were owned by European settlers but employed almost exclusively Native American crews because of their skills and experience. This dynamic gave Indian whalers great leverage in negotiating compensation: not only wages, but usually trade goods, such as coats and clothing, gun powder, and alcohol, as well as shares of whale blubber and bone. The labor market for Native American whalers was so good, in fact, that company owners had to devise mechanisms to control wages. After years of lobbying, New York governor Francis Lovelace finally consented to limit worker

Pyrrhus Concer, African American whaler, 1814–1897. (Photo courtesy of
Southampton Historical Museum)

compensation to "one-half share of the season's hunt to be divided
among the crew, and a cloth coat for each whaler for every whale
killed."

Even more significant was the implementation of a credit or "lay"
system that created a kind of debt peonage very similar to the "lien"
system of sharecropping used in the South after slavery. In the beginning of each season, as Strong describes it:

> The owner would enter the value of goods he gave each whaler in his
> account book. When the season ended, the total value of the whale oil
> and baleen from the whales killed . . . would be determined by the
> company owner. The value of the goods taken on credit was also set
> by the owner, who would then calculate the cash value of the individ-
> ual share for each crew member and deduct the amount owed him.
> This system enabled the owners to have the total income from the sea-
> son's hunt less only the cost of the goods, which they sold at a profit,
> to the Indians.[8]

By the 1680s, Native American whalers had practically bound themselves to the companies, as was made clear in a 1681 contract between five Montaukett Indians and Benjamin Conckling, a company owner. The contract states that the Montauks agreed, "if any of us shall be indebted unto the said Conckling or his assigns, then we do oblige ourselves to go to sea for him again the season that shall follow upon the same terms and so from year to year until we shall have wholly paid what we are indebted to him."[9]

The whaling industry also shaped the history of African Americans and slavery in the region. It is known that Lyon Gardiner and other early settlers purchased African slaves in the 1630s and 1640s; by 1687, almost 5 percent of East Hampton's population was African. While the earliest slaves performed primarily agricultural work, the whaling industry's success created a growing demand not only for sailing crews but for laborers who could perform a variety of skilled and unskilled tasks—coopers, carpenters, clerks, shipbuilders, and myriad other workers. Between the late seventeenth and the mid-eighteenth centuries, the African population of Suffolk County grew extensively; by 1700, more than 20 percent of Suffolk County's residents were Black, and by 1750, about 25 percent were Black, with almost all people of African descent living in slavery. Almost 20 percent of all white households in Suffolk County had at least one African slave, and almost 25 percent had at least one Black worker, slave or free. As the historian Grania Bolton Marcus has concluded, "the growth of slavery on Long Island occurred for the same reason it did in the South: an acute shortage of labor."[10]

But the offshore whaling boom died eventually on the East End, as ecological changes and technological advances transformed the industry. By the 1730s, offshore whales were scarce, and industrial investment favored deep-water fleets that pursue large sperm whales far from the sandy shores. Although Sag Harbor became a key Atlantic port for this part of the industry, it too boomed and busted quickly as the sperm whale population diminished rapidly. By the early nineteenth century, whaling was surpassed by haul-seining and agriculture as the area's most important industries, and by the end of the Civil War, whaling had all but disappeared. Native Americans and African Americans remained crucial elements of the workforce in fishing and farming, but the area no longer suffered from a labor shortage. In consequence, the

African American population on the East End remained unchanged for the more than fifty years from 1810 to the end of the Civil War.

Meanwhile, various manumission laws continuously changed the institution of slavery during the late 1700s and early 1800s; in 1827, New York State permanently abolished the practice. According to Marcus, this evolving period of emancipation, and continued discrimination against freed Blacks, "produced a society in which the distinction between slave and free was not always clear." She continues:

> Many slaves continued to work for their masters, either under a form of indenture or tied to their former owners by their indebtedness for basic goods and services. For example, John Lyon Gardiner's workforce consisted of eight slaves and nine free African-Americans, some of whom were regularly in debt to him. The society provided relatively few opportunities for advancement through property ownership or skilled work. Ex-slaves were rarely given the credit they would have needed to buy property or start a business of their own.[11]

Thus, despite an end to slavery, Blacks continued to make up the lowest echelons of the area's workforce. While some Black families did become property owners, usually through gifts of land from former owners or thanks to small savings earned from wages in the whaling industry and elsewhere, these men and women generally lived in segregated areas such as Three Mile Harbor, Eastville, and Greenport. These towns developed their own Black churches, local Black businesses, and a semblance of a "middle class" within the stabilizing African American community, but Blacks' class position remained characterized largely by their geographic segregation and their economic relegation to the lowest-paid, most physically difficult work.

While the whaling industry's demise diminished the labor demand for African and Native American workers, increased European immigration had an even larger impact on regional labor markets during the late 1800s. As stated in chapter 1, the period between 1890 and 1910 brought the largest influx of European immigrants to the East End since the early decades of settlement. By 1910, 45 percent of Suffolk's population was either immigrant or the children of immigrants. Most of these immigrants worked in agriculture or at the few growing industrial sites, such as Fahys Bulova Watch Case Factory, in Sag Harbor, or for small manufacturers of silverware and textiles. Immigrant workers in the Hamptons had experiences very different from the sweatshop labor that greeted many of their urban brethren. According to the Brooklyn *Eagle*, Fahys "brought large numbers of Poles and Russian Jews to the village [Sag Harbor] to seek employment in that manufactory. . . . In business, the Jews have pushed rapidly to the fore . . . [controlling] the clothing and fruit trade, and upon the main business thoroughfares 15 large stores testify to their industry." These families formed the Jewish Association United Brethren, bought land for a Jewish cemetery, and sponsored other local programs both for themselves and for the larger secular community.[12] Similarly, other groups quickly formed ethnic associations, often through churches such as the Poles' St. Isadore's Church, in Riverhead, or St. Mary's Roman Catholic Church, in Southampton, which was Italian; there were also a variety of social clubs and ethnic mutual benefit societies. Three major dynamics converged to shape these immigrants' experience, making their class trajectory very different from that of the African and Native American workers who had preceded them. First, while much has been made of the historical discrimination against many Europeans, especially Irish, Italian, Jewish, and Polish workers, these immigrants' arrival on the East End coincided with both the emergence of an expansive civil sector and a rapidly changing economy. In the late nineteenth and early twentieth centuries, cities and towns around the nation developed service-oriented local governments and expanded public institutions such as schools, hospitals, and recreation facilities. Similarly, they helped sponsor holidays, festivals, and a host of other programs aimed, at least in part, at constructing a national identity that would connect local experiences to national expressions of patriotism and Americanism.[13]

During this period, Southampton, East Hampton and the Town of Riverhead expanded their school districts, created social service programs to help assimilate newcomers to the area, and initiated civic-sponsored events such as Fourth of July parades and Founder's Day celebrations. These liberal and patriotic efforts to assimilate immigrant populations did not capture everyone's imagination, and the East End witnessed a rise in anti-immigrant and Klan activity very similar to that which occurred in other areas in the Northeast and in the Midwest after World War I. Klan strategies tended to mirror the more liberal assimilationist efforts; the Klan used popular holidays, festivals, and civic occasions to create a sense of national identity and patriotism linked to white supremacy. While the defeat of Klan candidates in Sag Harbor and resistance to Klan rallies in Hampton Bays and Speonk expressed the area's general tolerance for immigrants (or at least an intolerance for blatant racism), these events also tended to reinforce the importance of assimilation and Americanization. The messages were sometimes mixed, but always clear: immigrants would be welcomed but were expected to fit in quickly, in part by adopting a white identity.[14]

The second dynamic in the late nineteenth and early twentieth centuries was the economic forces that changed the region. The Manhattan summer colony's increased financial investments in the area and its cultural tastes eventually changed the area's economy, turning the economy of "the Hamptons" into one that was primarily seasonal and service based. The region's growing immigrant population during this same time period found fairly lucrative seasonal work both in the service of the already established aristocracy and in construction and other trades necessary to accommodate the rapidly expanding summer colony in the 1910s and 1920s; the new, wealthy population required more services, and many immigrants skilled in tailoring, cooking, carpentry, and similar trades found good work. The years between 1880 and 1920, in the Hamptons, therefore, held out great opportunities for the newly arrived immigrant population.

But perhaps the most powerful phenomenon (in part because of its invisibility) was the third dynamic—the ability of these new immigrants to adopt a white identity over time. Despite their obvious language and cultural differences, European immigrants did not face racial segregation in schools or housing or, most importantly, land purchases. Their hard work quickly enabled them to buy property more rapidly and without restrictions. The more property they acquired, the less the seasonal nature of the economy threatened continued economic success and increased social status. This stable base gave these immigrants even more opportunities to develop cottage industries and self-sustaining practices during hard times, too. Such conditions also meant that European immigrants could not be played against each other very successfully—especially as ethnic differences blended into white identities.[15] Thus, a number of factors—economic, social, and political—combined to facilitate the assimilation of European immigrants as they acquired both an American and a *white* identity. These new identities significantly distinguished their life and class experiences from those of the Native and African American workers who had preceded them.

While these race-conscious class conditions continued through World War II, they were further influenced by the migration of southern Black farm workers, which began slowly in the 1930s and 1940s. By 1960, the Black population of Suffolk County had increased almost 400 percent, from 8,701 in 1940 to almost 34,000 in 1960. In the five towns of the East End, the increase of African Americans came from North Carolina and Virginia to work in the potato and vegetable fields. Initially, they stayed in labor camps on the fringes of town or on the farms themselves; but many eventually settled in the historically Black neighborhoods in Southampton (the Hillcrest area), Bridgehampton (on Sunrise Avenue and along the turnpike), Riverhead, and Greenport. These workers found a very different set of circumstances, in the fields and migrant bungalows on the North and South Forks, from those that had greeted the earlier European arrivals. Agricultural work had always been hard, but the treatment that southern Black migrants received clearly differentiated their experiences.

Predominately Black labor camps usually consisted of dilapidated barracks where several dozen workers (mostly men, but sometimes women and children, as well) shared one latrine and one shower. While some camps were better than others, most were terribly overcrowded, offered substandard food and sanitation facilities, and, in the words of one Bridgehampton farm worker, "existed strictly for exploitation."[16] Eddie Clark, a migrant who arrived in the mid-1960s, described a labor camp on Cox's Lane, in Cutchogue, as a "hellhole" with "a bunch of shabby cabins up next to each other. . . . Too much booze, too much fighting."[17] Added to the horrible physical conditions migrants experienced were strict, yet often informal, racial codes. George Harney, a Southampton custodian who first came to pick potatoes in the mid-1950s, remembers that "we always knew our place" as Black laborers; "there were things we could and couldn't do and places we could and couldn't go." Few stores in either Bridgehampton or Southampton would hire Black men or women, and some would pass over Black patrons in order to serve whites first. Those migrants who decided to stay in the Hamptons and who saved enough money to consider their own home found few local banks that would finance construction or mortgages, forcing them to use more expensive construction companies' financing arrangements.[18]

Despite the racial segregation and indignities, workers did build small, successful Black communities. Like previous ethnic groups, workers pooled their funds to build churches (such as the Cutchogue, Bridgehampton, and Southampton Baptist churches and the St. David AME Zion Church) and started small businesses and social establishments such as the Pinckney Inn, in Bridgehampton. Mae Anderson, a Southampton College custodian who came with her husband and two children from Virginia to Bridgehampton in the early 1960s, saved enough to buy a new house in a new development near Huntington Crossway. She remembers a stable, but highly segregated, community of Black families in the 1960s and 1970s. And where these stable pockets evolved, so did community leaders who participated formally in public meetings, such as school board and town board meetings, and in commercial enterprises, church groups, and official civic activities.

Even more important was the substantive history of informal support networks that empowered segregated Black American communities in both the North and the South. Mary Killoran remembers her mother, a seamstress, using material left over from dresses she made for wealthy women or repairing secondhand coats to make clothes for other families in the area. And Sharon Saunders, from Hillcrest, recalls her mom's reputation in the neighborhood for her hot bread and biscuits on Tuesday night. Children might be playing or visiting friends, "but when they smelled that bread wafting from our house they knew that Mother Saunders was gonna pass out bread to everybody." While she hesitates to romanticize the past, Saunders says that children were raised by everyone in the community. She explains:

> We grew up in this neighborhood [Hillcrest] almost self-sufficient. Neighbors were like aunts and uncles. We cared and shared everything together. We laughed together as a neighborhood. We cried together as a neighborhood. If we were out of eyesight of our parents but in the eyesight of other parents, we were being parented. We respected that. It made a neighborhood a neighborhood, a community a community.[19]

Racism, however, continued to limit opportunities. Unlike the ethnic "white" immigrants who had preceded them, Black workers on the East End never fully gained entrance into white social and political spheres and often had to settle for "separate and unequal." Yet, until the 1960s, according to Calvin Tomkins and Judy Tomkins, "black people in Bridgehampton had done very little demanding of any kind. They bore the small daily humiliations with dignity—not protesting, for example, when white check-out cashiers at the grocery store chose to wait on white shoppers behind them in line. They seemed scarcely to have heard of the civil rights movement's more militant successors in the urban communities . . . and to this day show no visible resentment of their year-round white neighbors or of the vast influx of summer residents."[20] Inspired by the beginnings of a formal civil rights movement in Bridgehampton, Calvin Tomkins and Judy Tomkins, in their 1970 book *The Other Hampton,* chronicled both the local Black community and the community's race relations. Many African American residents disagreed with the Tomkinses' portrayal of their community; they point out that many Black people had been working hard to survive for generations and had resisted both formal discrimination and informal daily indignities for years. Killoran explains, "Many people did not shrink to white domination . . . did well despite unfair treatment and helped to support other Black people in the community who may have been struggling to make ends meet."[21]

The Tomkinses do portray a Black community proud of its hard work and success. In the book, James Robinson boasts that "black people have really pulled themselves up and around here . . . broken away from farm work, they've built themselves homes, really nice places." Nellie Parker also claims that "You got to work. You got to have some of that greenback power before you're going anywhere, that's what I tell my kids."[22] Mae Anderson, whose photo in the book shows her and her family standing in front of their new house, remembers how proud she was to own her own home and to raise her kids in a good neighborhood with decent schools. But *The Other Hampton* also demonstrates that even whites who "took an interest in the Black community" remained heavily prejudiced and ignorant of the specific differences in the historical experiences of white European immigrants and Black and Native American groups.

In part, the Tomkinses depict a white community afraid of even the most tentative assertions of civil rights and Black Power protests. As African American parents demanded more control over local schools that had disproportionately Black enrollments in the 1960s, white parents withdrew their kids and white officials "threw up their hands" in frustration. One white official exclaimed, "The colored have taken over at the [Bridgehampton Child Care] Center, and they've taken over at the school, too. It's a mess." Sons of Polish and Italian immigrants such as

Migrant worker camp in Cutchogue, New York, 1947. Eddie Clark called these places "hellholes." (Photo courtesy of Charles Meredith Collection, Southold Historical Society)

Anthony Tiska recalled their own parents who had had to work hard to get ahead and didn't understand why Blacks couldn't do the same thing: "I had to come up all the way myself. I always figured that the opportunity is there, and if you don't learn, what can we do about it? There are some that learn—why don't the others?" Similarly, Thomas Halsey, a descendant of one of Southampton's founding families, claimed that poor conditions for Black migrant workers were the result of poor educational standards in their home states, where living conditions were so bad that "you can't expect them to be any different . . . they live the way they want to live is what I think." He added, "if [people on welfare rolls] would just buckle down and be dependable, I think they could replace the entire migrant workforce."[23]

Although the Black population stabilized in the late 1960s and 1970s, the continued development of agricultural land left more and more African Americans unemployed. Limited by prejudices and informal codes as well as by a changing economy that made land too expensive to buy and less profitable to work, people like Anderson and Harney considered themselves lucky to get custodial jobs at Southampton College. Some Black workers found similar jobs in the public school system, at Southampton Hospital, and at other public institutions. Others catered to the increasing number of seasonal tourists and the growing permanent population of wealthy former New Yorkers. While some African American women continued in traditional roles as domestic servants and cooks, other women (and some men) opened their own cleaning and catering businesses. But the realities of segregation, both in the labor markets and in residential neighborhoods, had not changed. Black workers generally found themselves employed in the lowest-paid, most physically demanding and degrading jobs; housed in the poorest communities, in dilapidated buildings; and served by unsympathetic white police, sanitation workers, and other public employees. At the end of the twentieth century, the Hamptons' working class remained divided between nonwhites and whites in much the way it was in the early eighteenth century.[24]

Migrant Latino workers began to make their way north and east during the same period of the 1960s, but they did not become dominant in the labor force until the late 1980s and 1990s. While I have discussed this demographic group in greater depth in previous chapters, it is important to note here that this group has had a significant impact on the nature of today's working class in the Hamptons. Although the growing demand for services from an increasingly year-round wealthy population has bolstered the job market for all workers, wages have not kept up with the cost of living (especially for housing). Unemployment in the Hamptons has stayed exceptionally low compared to elsewhere in the nation, but working long hours even for decent wages is no longer a guarantee that workers can equal the success of earlier white ethnic immigrants. And while most Latinos are meeting the area's unfilled labor demands, they have sometimes been used to help drive down wages and even break unions in the service industry and elsewhere. According to Katherine Hartnett, many Latino families, despite working full-time, overtime, and at more than one job, need to supplement their income with food pantries and charity clothing to make ends meet.[25] And while local schools, hospitals, and courts have implemented a variety of language programs to address primarily Spanish-speaking consumers, some residents complain that "too much" is being done to treat recent immigrants "special." (In 2001, for example, Darryl Glennon collected more than one hundred petition signatures in East

Hampton complaining that the "uncontrolled influx of illegals in the last five years has caused an increase in litter, crime, taxes, insurance, and health-care costs, as well as a decline in property values and the excessive need for affordable housing.") Those Latinos who have been in the area the longest and who have worked hard to earn enough money to buy their own homes and to start their own businesses make up a fledgling middle class that buttresses informal networks of support, leisure, and recreational activities (such as soccer) and that often acts as an intermediary between newer immigrants and public institutions.

Latinos occupy a complex place on the working-class trajectory in the Hamptons. Although they face discrimination, the economic boom of the 1980s and especially of the 1990s gave those who arrived earlier an opportunity to achieve certain levels of success. Some who settled permanently and established connections prior to 1990 are seen by other area residents as different from the migrant day laborers and "illegals"—a term often used inaccurately to refer to class and race, rather than immigration status. The future of the economy and the commitment of the town to programs that embrace primarily Spanish-speaking laborers and their children will set the parameters within which Latinos negotiate their own local identities as workers and residents.[26]

While Latinos' place within the working class is somewhat in flux, the position of African Americans and Native Americans remains relatively fixed. Melissa Arch Walton explains that most people of color are still encouraged to "know their place" in the Hamptons. She says: We know that there are these secluded enclaves and we know what Black people and native Americans and Latinos are there for. They are there to either pick your vegetables or clean your houses or do custodial work or retails sales—but only in large places like Bridgehampton Caldor or King Kullen or the A&P because they're not in the stores on Jobs Lane or Main Street. It's very hard to find people of color in the posh boutiques. . . . I have spent most of my life knowing that when white people came into a place that I worked and said that I was so wonderful or smart or attractive, that the next thing in the conversation would be requests to baby sit their children or clean their house. "You seem polite and cooperative, why don't you clean my house?" The assumption is that here is a bright, attractive, young Black woman, she would be wonderful to clean my house—she won't steal anything or hurt my children.[27]

These are the realities of race and class dynamics on the East End that have evolved over three hundred years. While few East End whites (or people of color, for that matter) would claim that local businesses or industries use overtly racist policies to discriminate, segregation and segmentation of labor markets are still the norm. These race-conscious class dynamics continue to evolve as the global economy transforms the local social landscape and people organize to resist both racism and class exploitation.

THE GLOBAL BECOMES LOCAL

In June 1998, Tim Bishop, the provost of Southampton College, pleaded guilty to violating zoning regulations by hosting two major factory outlet sales sponsored by the Maslow Group (sellers of home furnishings) and J. Crew (the clothing and accessories company). It was the third year in a row that the College had raised money by holding such events. Local retailers were concerned that these College enterprises would threaten their businesses, but Provost Bishop explained that "we are an enormously powerful economic force, bringing in at least $30 million to the East End. . . . The broader perspective is that we are decidedly pro-business."[28] Bob Fischer, of Fischer's Home Furnishings, in Sag Harbor, told a local reporter that Bishop's statement was "the lamest excuse I have ever heard." After all, retailers did not care about the College's ideological position; they were worried about increased competition. And they had reason to be concerned. Like many educational institutions around the country, Southampton College was intensifying its economic plan to increase revenues and cut costs, and its own financial goals undoubtedly conflicted with those of other local businesses. As Fischer explained, "The College is contributing to the same trend as Donna Karan, Banana Republic, and other upscale chain retailers in East Hampton—big-volume sellers are moving in and pushing out the local mom-and-pop stores."[29]

According to many critics of contemporary higher education, corporatization and privatization are now commonplace at colleges and universities. While some have argued that stronger links between higher education and private industries have evolved steadily since the early twentieth century, the infusion—if not saturation—of educational practices and policies with corporate, bottom-line mentalities is now widespread. University administrators currently engage in a variety of revenue-seeking ventures that range from outright sales of research to corporations, to exclusive contracts with food service and bookstore conglomerates, to the marketing of "educational products" by forcing teachers to transform their courses into "cyber-friendly" packages that can be sold to private educational companies or directly to consumers.[30]

At Southampton College, the 1990s ushered in an era of increased corporate sponsorship and revenue creation. Nothing symbolized these trends better than the institution's new chancellor, Robert F. X. Sillerman. Sillerman, a communications industry mogul, became chancellor in 1993, promising to build an endowment that could help the declining liberal arts institution address ongoing financial crises and meet the physical improvements mandated by its regional accrediting agency, the Middle States Association of Colleges and Schools.

Sillerman was a symbol of the post-Reagan economy, having made his most recent fortune first by engineering a series of mergers and acquisitions in the television and radio industry and then by taking the merged companies public under the banner of SFX Broadcasting. After the passage of the 1996 Telecommunications Act, SFX quickly gobbled up small stations around the country, eventually becoming the seventh largest radio broadcasting company in the United States. Simultaneously, Sillerman started buying up concert venues, music promotion companies, and celebrity management groups. Thus, SFX could sign artists, promote their tours on radio and television, and control the concert venues and ticket sales. In 1997, Sillerman sold SFX's radio holdings to a Dallas firm for $2.1 billion, netting him a personal take of $250 million. Three years later, Clear Channel Communications, the country's largest radio conglomerate, bought SFX (which had become the nation's biggest producer of entertainment events) for $3 billion; Sillerman's take was $474 million.[31]

Sillerman took the chancellor's job for the symbolic salary of one dollar per year, explaining to a *Newsday* reporter that "the benefits [of being chancellor] far exceed the salary. . . . [It's] almost a sense of rebirth. . . . I don't benefit materially from this job. But there's something thrilling and exciting about approaching intellectual discourse for its own sake."[32] Of course, participating in such "discourse" serves serious tax write-off purposes (Sillerman and his wife, Laura, had donated more than $20 million to the College as of 2000, much of it through the Tomorrow Foundation, which they established to funnel contributions to various charities, but primarily to the College). But Sillerman's association with an institution of higher learning also provides the kind of cultural and social capital craved by the new bourgeoisie. Like playing polo, becoming the chancellor of a college infuses a member of the newly wealthy with the mystique of traditional intellectual status and authentic leadership. Robert Danziger, a Southampton physics professor, explained, "We see Sillerman only a few times a year at various ceremonies: graduation, the Steinbeck awards, or a major fund-raising event. . . . he [sic] and his wife's image is really one of owning a boutique college." Although Sillerman has donated directly and helped raise millions of dollars for the College, he has also gained much in prestige and improved his image by becoming chancellor. And, given his lack of educational experience and academic credentials, his ability to raise money seems to have been his only qualification for the job.[33]

But the College also represents Sillerman's efforts to acquire his own sense of identity as a "local" or "native." In an interview with the Hamptons journalist and publisher Dan Rattiner, Sillerman revealed the secret of "Road D." On one of his many trips out to Southampton as a college student, he discovered Road D, "a 100-yard-long dead-end road in Southampton that is right off Meadow Lane and ends at the beach." He soon found out that Road D was a "favorite spot" for some of Southampton College's administrators who had grown up in Southampton and knew all about Road D, where one could park without a town sticker. According to Rattiner, "he met Tim Bishop, the Provost, Alice Flynn, the head of Freshman activities, Jane Finalbargo, the Director of Public Relations, Carol Lynch, the Director of Admissions . . . and has been coming to Road D for the better part of fifteen years." In fact, his house on Meadow Lane was built adjacent to Road D, where, Sillerman says, "I am known as Road D Annex. When Road D is full, you can park here and walk down."[34] For Sillerman, Southampton College has given him not only cultural cachet as the head of an elite institution but also a cultural identity as native.

Although Sillerman rarely involved himself with the day-to-day management of the campus, his presence was certainly emblematic of the ways in which Southampton College infused its academic mission with a new zeal for fund-raising and corporate-driven policy making. In 1996, administrators initiated regular breakfast meetings with regional corporate executives to determine ways in which the institution's curriculum and policies could address the "educational and training needs of area businesses." Throughout the 1990s, the College also expanded its internship and cooperative education programs to link students with local businesses. At the same time, it replaced most faculty-level super-visors with administrators who possessed few, if any, serious academic or teaching credentials. The College Web site's section "Facts about Coops" boasts that 80 percent of all students gain "continued or perma-nent employment from their coop employers" and that coop "students earned an average hourly salary of $7.95 in 1998–99." But the informa-tion says little about the academic or intellectual quality of these experi-ences. In 1998, the president of the Happauge Industrial Association honored Southampton College's coop programs, raving that "Long Is-land businesses could not survive without well-trained employees, and this education must start early. Programs like the Southampton College program should be encouraged to continue to expand."[35]

And while the decision to contract out the custodial unit may have been the most blatant act of corporate banditry, it, too, fit into the chang-ing dynamics of the regional economy and demography. LARO's own executives admitted that they were in the business of driving down wages by taking advantage of the area's growing surplus of immigrant labor.[36] In June 1998, *New York Times Magazine* writer Michael Winerip did a piece on Robert Bertuglia Jr., LARO president and founder, enti-tled "The Blue-Collar Millionaire." Winerip recounted the middle-class-to-riches story of a Nassau County kid who started with a landscaping business in high school and parlayed it into a multimillion-dollar clean-ing business when one of his corporate landscaping clients "was having trouble with their cleaner." Winerip explains:

> The year 1981 was a golden time to start a cleaning company. The Rea-gan revolution was fresh under way; the air-traffic controllers' union had just been broken. Businesses and municipalities were looking to cut costs by laying off in-house union crews and outsourcing work to companies like Bertuglia's that paid cleaners pennies above minimum wage. One of his first big contracts was the Nassau County court com-plex. "They wanted to get rid of—I don't want to use 'get rid of'—*phase out* the union cleaners," says Bertuglia.[37]

According to Winerip, "if ever there was a metaphor for America's booming economy, it is LARO Service Systems."

Of course, the boom was born on the backs of busted unions and a new immigrant labor force prepared to work for the lowest wages.

LARO vice president Lou Vacca Jr. explained to Winerip, "How do you do it cheaper? . . . You take it out of labor." One of LARO's specialties was breaking unions, and Bertuglia boasted about how the company had been "tipped off" to a surprise walkout by union workers at the Port Authority Bus Terminal; LARO managed to have four hundred replacement workers ready to move in and take over the contract the moment the union went on strike. Given LARO's record on cost cutting and union busting, Provost Bishop's claim that the outsourcing of custodial services was "budget-neutral" seemed disingenuous at best. In fact, the burgeoning East End service sector in the 1990s had demonstrated that a continued surplus of largely Latino workers was available to provide an increasingly low-paid labor force on a year-round basis. LARO was just the company to provide the College with the tools to make a transition to nonunion custodians. And, because the custodians would become LARO employees, the College could avoid any negative press for breaking the union and evade the mounting pressure to address charges of racial discrimination against members of the custodial unit. From the perspective of the College, outsourcing its custodians was a logical business strategy and a particularly effective political strategy—it was just a local example of the global "race to the bottom."[38]

For College custodians, most of them working-class men and women of color, these economic and political trends meant an intensification of a highly bottom-line-oriented service economy that featured declining wages and benefits, decreasing job autonomy and dignity, and increasing financial insecurity. Although new economic and demographic dynamics would shift some labor market parameters, the basic conditions of a racialized and exploited working class disproportionately made up of people of color remained much the same. The implications of the new economy, booming though that economy might be, promised men and women of color in the Hamptons the worst working conditions on the shop floor and the least political power and social status in the community. Such a result was implicit in the language and images of the Peconic County movement; more explicit in local conflicts over soccer fields and labor halls; and perhaps most blatant in the decision by Southampton College administrators to, in the words of one custodian, "sell us off like we were on the auction block."[39]

BUILDING A COALITION—THE CUSTODIANS

The Coalition for Justice began meeting every Monday night in a dormitory basement that held the offices and classrooms of the Friends World Program. The Coalition initiated a campaign of letter writing, postering, leafletting, and speeches to educate the campus and the community about the outsourcing issue and immediately attracted more students, staff, and a variety of community activists. Each weekly meeting began with one of the senior custodians recounting the history of the conflict and explaining the Coalition's strategy in initiating a public campaign to pressure the College. In part, the opening narrative served as a ritual activity that both indoctrinated new visitors and solidified the evolving collective identity of returning members. In addition, with each repetition of the story, new voices and new subtexts would arise. One of the most significant of these was the long-standing nature of the custodians' complaints and the tensions among custodians over how to handle them.[40]

Although the outsourcing was the "trigger event," workers, especially workers of color, were angry about the way that they had been treated over the years. Although administrators spoke of "great labor relations" and a "family environment" among workers on campus, custodians of color had long employed traditional forms of resistance to conditions they found exploitative, oppressive, and degrading.[41] As one explained, "we were used to being ignored by white employers or even talked down to and mostly just let things roll off our backs. We had some of the best jobs around and there wasn't any need to make a big deal about it."[42] Still, not all custodians of color reacted in the same way. Mae Anderson, an African American woman who had worked at the College since its inception, had a reputation for "speaking her mind" and admitted to more than once telling students, colleagues, and supervisors how she felt about "being disrespected." Other custodians, such as Percy Hughes, an African American from Riverhead, and Tony Smith, who lived on the Shinnecock reservation, had unsuccessfully pursued legal action for racial discrimination and civil rights violations.

Senior custodians possessed a great deal of control over their work schedules, which gave them opportunities to employ informal and covert methods of resistance. This power sometimes resulted in a reluctance to make waves about what they perceived of as either inevitable, or at least relatively minor, acts of racial discrimination. Some custodians felt lucky to have good union jobs where they had a modicum of control over their work days and avoided the kinds of persistent surveillance and insecurity that most low-paid, working-class people of color in the region faced. Many were willing to put up with both institutional discrimination and periodic personal indignations, in part because they were concerned over losing what power they had achieved but also because the power they possessed permitted at least somewhat effective, if not direct, forms of resistance and autonomy. Some custodians did complain about inefficient and discriminatory management policies. Yet, according to union steward Michael Knight, "as soon as I raised issues of bad management or discrimination in promotions, LIU [the College's parent institution] responded with threats and intimidation." Knight explains, "I tried to talk with Bishop numerous times and finally wrote a letter about the physical plant management to LIU administrators. In return, I received a threatening letter from the LIU attorney telling me that I should apologize for negative comments or I would be sued." The College's refusal to address Knight's concerns and its attempts to quiet "troublemakers" exposed new schisms within the custodial unit. Some workers were willing to settle for current conditions and wanted Knight to "calm down." Others, especially those who had convinced Knight to become steward, wanted to press for better treatment and for the establishment of a "promotional pipeline." Knight, himself, was sometimes considered an "outsider," since he had only recently moved to the area from New York City.[43]

While the political differences among custodians were not necessarily racially based, race and ethnicity were at the source of many other internal struggles. Regional and historical tensions between Native Americans from the Shinnecock reservation and African Americans from the Hillcrest neighborhood and Bridgehampton sometimes informed conflicts between workers and tended to produce ethnically based cliques among the unit members. Even before the LARO contract, one custodian claimed that workers "stuck to their own camps." These divisions resulted in a lack of unity among custodians and hindered any serious attempts at formal collective action. As one custodian, Tony Smith, stated, he had tried to organize the unit to "get rid of Local 424 because they never responded to complaints from the members. But we could never get it together to bring in someone new." Persistent racial and ethnic tensions and the lack of solidarity left workers opened to management efforts to further divide them. Administrators often referred to white custodians as "the good workers" who didn't make trouble and often gave them unofficial perks like overtime and use of college vehicles and other resources. Smith explained his experiences with such "labeling":

> I had been at the College a few years when the College hired a few white custodians in 1994 or 1995. All of a sudden these guys became recognized as the best workers. I mean guys who had been here a year or two years were put on a pedestal compared to guys who had been here almost thirty years. . . . We were always being pitted against each other. White workers were called "natural leaders." I never heard that about myself. It caused conflict.[44]

These dynamics of race and power became more salient within the Coalition when conflicts from the workday spilled over into evening meetings. In particular, one of the younger custodians, a Yugoslavian immigrant, Manny, who spoke English well but with a marked accent, was very angry about the outsourcing. He came to the first few CFJ meetings and wanted to protest but was reluctant to agree that racism had played any part in the LARO decision. In fact, Manny thought that by being too militant about racism and discrimination, custodians themselves might have been to blame for the College's actions. On numerous occasions, his supervisors had told him that he was "not like the lazy ones" who did not pull their weight. He was using his tuition remission to take classes at the College and believed that he could get a better job at the College or use his education to improve his position elsewhere. In many ways, he was following a very traditional, European-immigrant path where hard work and obedience would be rewarded with economic advancement and social acceptance, even assimilation. Part of this process included his adopting and fitting into a white identity, one partially identified by his supervisors and, therefore, closely linked to a class position, as well. Manny was uncomfortable accepting racism as an explanation for others' discriminatory acts or for his own hoped-for success.

When the group decided to approach the town's Anti-Bias Task Force, some of the white custodians (including Manny) were apprehensive about making race a significant issue, partly because they disagreed that racism had played a role in the outsourcing but mostly because they did not want to "press buttons, because American society is very sensitive about race." Manny eventually did agree that some workers were discriminated against, but he was concerned about jeopardizing his own status as a "good worker" by supporting statements that his supervisors would balk at. Smith, who had been described to Manny by supervisors as an example of a "bad worker," argued that race had "separated the workers too long" and that custodians of color had always gotten "the short end of the stick." Manny protested that he was often "discriminated against, too," because of his accent and that he had been contracted out just like all the other custodians. Percy Hughes, an African American custodian, countered, "Manny, you *can* be white; you're not white yet, but you can *become* white."[45]

At one meeting in April, Manny and Mae Anderson got into a verbal sparring match over an incident that had occurred earlier in the afternoon. While the actual event was never fully described that evening, it was clear that both had used racial epithets in their fight, and they repeated them at the evening meeting. The other custodians intervened and tried to find out what had really happened, but both Manny and Mae were tight-lipped. Percy Hughes, one of the custodians, looked across the group's circle and said, "Manny, you know I've never said anything bad about you and I've always been with you, but we can't say things like that. We have to be able to disagree and argue without using that language." Mae was still angry over the situation and suggested that Percy just "forget about it." Percy continued, though, exhorting not just Manny but all of his colleagues that "we have to fight like we're family, you know? We can't let arguments break us up . . . if we don't stick together, we'll all be working at K Mart."[46]

Manny eventually stopped attending meetings, although he said he still supported the CFJ's efforts to terminate the LARO contract. But for those who continued to attend, especially for white and nonwhite custodians, the issue of race took on new dimensions as the group openly discussed what it meant to be white and nonwhite. Before he left the group, Manny admitted that all of the members who had been labeled "bad workers" were African or Native American and were often those who complained about working conditions. Eventually, other white custodians, such as Wayne Hudson, remarked how unfair it was that some senior custodians of color, like Mae Anderson and Frank Jones, who had both been at the College for almost thirty years, had never even been considered for promotion, while some white workers who had been there only a fraction of that time had been told by supervisors that they might be considered for promotion if a position opened up. The racial tensions never completely disappeared, but through the process of discussing them openly, CFJ meetings became a place that exposed and challenged previously fixed racial identities, allegiances, and divisions. The commitment of white workers and other CFJ members to accept and, eventually, support race as a crucial issue in the campaign against the outsourcing convinced some custodians of color to trust the group's sincerity. Eventually, a new identity group based on regular CFJ attendance formed within the unit; participating custodians referred to themselves as "Coalition members." This new form of solidarity eventually allowed the custodians to address their lingering complaints about Local 424 and demonstrated the power of the coalition's organizing process.

Custodians often lamented the poor quality of their union representation and wondered aloud about collusion between Local 424 and the College. Noncustodial members of the Coalition participated in these discussions but always made it clear that custodians, as a unit, would need to address problems with their union representation. By the fourth CFJ meeting, Local 424 sent its business agent, Rudy, to attend. Most custodians believed he had come to "keep an eye on them." They challenged Rudy about collusion and questioned his (and the union's) commitment to CFJ. Initially, Rudy was defensive and said that he was only following directives from his superiors. Mostly, he said his "hands were tied" and that he would "change things if he could." Eventually, though, he started contributing substantively to the Coalition's discussions and closed one meeting by comparing the group to his early union experiences; he recalled "roomfuls of workers joining hands and singing *Solidarity Forever.*" Rudy volunteered to talk at the first CFJ campus rally and gave a rousing speech that compared the custodians and their struggle to his boyhood hero, Jackie Robinson. Rudy claimed that Robinson had shown great dignity and humanity while struggling for justice and equality; it was his "integrity that exposed the viciousness and immorality of racism in baseball." According to Rudy, the custodians and the CFJ were simply "speaking truth to power, forcefully, but with dignity." Ultimately, though, the custodians were probably right about Local 424; Rudy was immediately "reassigned" to another district following the rally.

Despite their dissatisfaction with Local 424, the custodians had never achieved the level of solidarity necessary to act on changing their union representation. But the experience of organizing rallies and educational campaigns on campus and in the community changed the internal dynamics of the custodial unit. Even their identity as "the custodians" gained a certain status as they became celebrated civil rights activists. Progressive faculty referred to the custodians as important "educators" on issues of democracy, human rights, and citizenship. Community activists such as Lou Ware, the president of the NAACP's East End chapter, credited the custodial struggle with once more exposing the all-too-often hidden problems of racism and inequality in the area. While some level of animosity and conflict remained among the custodians, a burgeoning unity of purpose and a sense of shared commitment developed among them and empowered them to create a powerful new collective identity, one that challenged the earlier rigid and divisive ones. This cohesion enabled the custodians to finally terminate their affiliation with Local 424, and, in the summer of 1998, they voted 18–0 (with one abstention) to sign on with Teamsters Local 898.

BUILDING A COALITION—THE STUDENTS

Students played a crucial role in organizing the Coalition, because they often made up the majority of those who attended meetings and participated in campaign activities. Melissa Arch Walton, an early organizer, was one of few Southampton College students who lived locally. Melissa's parents were African and Native American, and she had lived on the Shinnecock reservation for many years. She was an older student (in her late twenties), a single parent of three children, and she worked part-time at the College's switchboard and in the College's Center for Racial Diversity. Melissa was already a community activist, having participated in local Democratic Party politics and worked with direct-action groups such as the Suffolk County Welfare Warriors, an advocacy organization formed to fight the 1994 Personal Responsibility Act welfare cuts. Melissa knew most of the custodians personally, was related to some, and was engaged to Michael Knight. Melissa's skills and her stature as a campus figure inspired a lot of student support, and some of this support translated into participation at meetings.

But the bulk of CFJ student members came from the Friends World Program (FWP). The FWP was originally an independent Quaker college, the Friends World College, founded by Morris Mitchell in 1965 and located in western Suffolk County on the shores of Lloyd Harbor. Mitchell's goals were to create an international, interdisciplinary, and experiential curriculum that would allow students to use "the world as their classroom" and "the problems of human society as their curriculum." Although financial difficulties forced the College to affiliate with Long Island University in 1991, faculty and staff fought hard to maintain the program's consensus-based governance structure and its progressive mission statement, which committed the College to programs that enabled students

> to combine first-hand experience of diverse cultural realities with the critical study of academic disciplines and human and ecological problems; to test intellectual theories and skills against the demands of practice and service; to carry out specialized field study under expert guidance that synthesizes cross cultural understanding; and to develop a broad world view and a level of achievement in a chosen field sufficient to prepare for a life of committed action in the interest of the world community.[47]

In particular, FWP students were encouraged to perform community service and to engage in campus and community organizing efforts as part of their course work and through independent internships. According to an FWP faculty member, Kathleen Modrowski, these internship and field experiences differed from most Southampton College internships and coops in two ways:

> First, Friends World students self-select the program for its focus on social change and, therefore, they choose internships with not-for-profits and social change organizations, not private-sector business or industry. We encourage them to work for groups whose primary mission is the betterment of people as defined by the people themselves. Secondly, we emphasize the interconnection between the community and the classroom so that students not only gain and reflect on experiences in the field, but they contextualize these experiences with historical and theoretical readings and discussions.[48]

Since the merger, however, many FWP faculty and students expressed concerns over the University's desires to "depoliticize" the program. Administrators wanted to phase out program-specific courses that trained students in progressive pedagogies based on the philosophy of educators such as John Dewey and Paulo Freire and of community activists such as Francis Moore Lappe and Myles Horton.[49] According to a former FWP faculty member, Hugh McGuiness, these courses provided the crucial intellectual and practical framework for creating a synthesis between education and action. Without the FWP curriculum, the faculty believed, the program would lose both its political and its academic integrity.

Although most Friends World students were away doing internships in other communities during the winter of 1997, many participated in CFJ activities when they returned in April and May. One of the first major impacts of their work with CFJ was that students pressured FWP faculty and administration to offer a course in social activism. This demand resulted in FWP's hiring Bob Zellner, a long-time civil rights activist who had begun his political work as the first white field secretary for the Student Non-Violent Coordinating Committee (SNCC) in the early 1960s. Zellner had moved to Southampton about sixteen months earlier and had already been involved in local political issues, including the CFJ. In putting together an "activism course," Zellner decided to introduce students to a variety of social and political movements and to analyze how they had shaped the contours of American life. But he also included an action component that required students to engage in some form of campus or community activism. Zellner explained that "this element of the course addressed the Friends World emphasis on experiential education and, more importantly, forced students to contemplate the practical and emotional dynamics of political work. . . . They had to understand social action as praxis, or the junction of theory and practice."[50] That fall, Zellner invited students to participate in the CFJ as one of the choices for their action projects, and almost two dozen of them did.

One student who attended the CFJ's first fall meeting thought that the custodians' situation was part of a larger problem with racism and segregation on campus. She explained: "Since my first days at LIU I have been aware of the lack of minorities within the student body and the faculty, and the segregation within the dorms. I have seen rent-a-cops [campus security], and I have yet to see one of them be a minority. On more than one occasion, I have seen them pull aside an African American man from a group to check for ID with no apparent reason." Another student who attended, Meghan White, said that she was "really upset and disgusted" at the way custodians were being treated by the College. But, she explained:

> Coupled with anger toward the college was a growing respect directed at the custodians and an understanding of their situation. The custodians were very grateful toward the students for wanting to be involved and for caring about the situation. I was taken aback by their compassion at first; I considered it my duty and responsibility to become part of the coalition. For it was not "their problem" but our community's problem. Moreover, in fact, the situation on our campus is a microcosm of what has happened and is still happening throughout the country.[51]

From the moment these students encountered the Coalition and its organizing, they began synthesizing their increasing academic knowledge about the history of racism and exploitation, as well as the history of protest and of the struggle for equality and freedom, with their own experiences and their desire for a different kind of world. It was a powerful combination that, Brian Quist, another first-year FWP student, summed up in his journal: "Wow! I can't think of any better words to describe how I'm feeling after today's class. I got a feeling today that I don't ever recall having before. It happened during the Coalition for Justice meeting. . . . I felt a deep emotional excitement mixed with a feeling of power and a new sense of realness and seriousness. It truly can't be explained, but it was a powerful moment which I won't forget for a long time."[52]

The student members also presented important racial and class identities that had to be addressed by the Coalition. Most were white, middle- and upper-class sons and daughters of professional parents from suburban communities around the country. While the FWP curriculum prepared some of them to work with a consensus-based organizing process and to challenge the legitimacy of cultural domination based on class, race, and gender, the students were not necessarily ready to challenge their own deeply ingrained conceptions about race and class. Many were noticeably uncomfortable with some of the more heated discussions about racism on campus and the privileges that white workers and students enjoyed simply because they could, for the most part, ignore issues of race altogether. Still, many FWP students felt strongly about letting the custodians lead the struggle and waited for that leadership to inform strategies and actions.

This dynamic within the group quickly led to student frustrations, in part because of the continuing intransigence of the administration but also because of the CFJ's "slow pace" of organizing early in the fall of 1997. The previous spring and early summer had ended with a partial victory for the group as the administration agreed to significant concessions. The College was in the midst of negotiating a deal with the town of Southampton in which the town would commit $5 million toward the building of an aquatics facility at the College; in return, the College would accept a certain number of local families as members. It was a controversial proposal that was competing with applications from other organizations that also wanted to host a town pool. CFJ decided to oppose the project publicly, explaining that the outsourcing of, and discrimination against, custodians were evidence of the College's poor citizenship and shouldn't be rewarded with taxpayers' money. To keep the CFJ from mounting a publicity campaign against the College's efforts, Provost Bishop agreed to (1) restore the custodians' College tuition remission; (2) revisit the "promotional pipeline" issue; and, (3) incorporate the CFJ as part of the College's overall evaluation of LARO. The Coalition accepted the agreement, even though Bishop refused to terminate the LARO contract immediately. Some CFJ members wanted to hold out for a complete victory, but the custodians themselves argued for accepting the concessions. They explained that the pool proposal was very popular among students and that the group might lose support if it opposed the facility. Ultimately, the College's proposal was rejected, anyway, thus making the CFJ (and especially the custodians) look prescient.[53]

The victory, however, also created a situation that most custodians were used to. With the Coalition as a steady watchdog, LARO ceased most of its efforts at intimidation and allowed the custodians to work in much the same way they always had. Although the custodians were grateful to see so many students interested in organizing more campaign activities in the fall, few were inspired to take much of a lead in these plans. In fact, the Coalition decided to meet monthly instead of weekly. Although CFJ made plans to continue with educational efforts and conducted an informational rally during Parents' Weekend, in October, students grew disappointed and impatient. One student wrote, "Our effort reached very few parents. We were hoping for a constant flow of parents in and out of the building, but we got only a trickle of people every once in a while. Overall, we felt that we had not succeeded in what we set out to do." The Coalition agreed that students should form a separate task force and meet weekly to plan other actions, but by early November, little more had been accomplished. Another student expressed her exasperation: "It drives me crazy because I feel that as students involved in the [CFJ] we do absolutely nothing. Every meeting is talk about the last meeting and about what we could do but there doesn't seem to be any initiative to actually do what we talk about. This drives me crazy and frustrates me. I wish that something would happen and that is before we leave."[54]

The frustration continued as new students joined the student task force who had never attended a full CFJ meeting and had never even met many of the custodians themselves. Students began wondering aloud about the issues and the various positions that CFJ had taken. Some students were especially dubious about the role that racism was alleged to have played in the decision. A few student CFJ representatives met with Provost Bishop and discussed a variety of issues. The meeting had an interesting impact on those who attended. Cassie Watters, a student who had been with the Coalition from the outset and had regularly attended full CFJ meetings, was upset with Bishop's continued intransigence. She felt he had "whined" about the Coalition and its "bias against him." In fact, Bishop refused to even discuss the race issue with students. However, Brian Quist, who was new to the CFJ and who had not attended many of the large meetings, met with Bishop and wrote: "After the meeting I came to the conclusion that I no longer felt appropriate accusing the University of acting with racial bias. I feel that Tim was a good person who is not a racist and who simply made a stupid and unfair decision about switching over to LARO." After a second meeting, Quist wrote: "Tim will not consider discussing the issue if race is involved. He says that he is not a racist, nor does he discriminate against people on the basis of race. He feels the coalition is not practicing what it preaches by creating prejudices against him."[55]

Some of students began to waiver in their support of CFJ positions. While they still thought it unfair to contract out workers because it violated many of their predispositions toward consensus and community, they did not want to blame Bishop himself, who seemed sincere and compassionate. In particular, students were swayed by his argument that race had not played a role in the decision and accepted the provost's premise that for racial discrimination to have played a part would de facto mean that Bishop himself was a racist. It became clear that students who had attended regular meetings with the larger, diverse group of CFJ members were much more likely to see racial discrimination as the basis for the custodians' situation. Participation in those meetings had created a collective identity defined in part by a historical and ethnographical view of conditions that rendered the custodians' point of view both convincing and legitimate; those students who had talked with and worked mostly closely with the custodians were less likely to accept Bishop's explanation that outsourcing was an "administrative" decision. Instead, they accepted what became the CFJ analysis—that administrative decisions had for some time reflected and reproduced the historically race-based dynamics of local class relations. These conditions had become so institutionalized that what seemed to be simple "administrative" decisions could, in fact, also be racist without any one particular administrator actually appearing racist—even to himself.

The practice of looking to the custodians themselves as authoritative sources not just for documenting their own experiences but also for analyzing conditions on campus was reinforced in Zellner's activism class. Zellner's own perspectives on grass-roots organizing had been shaped by his work with SNCC and, in particular, his relationship with SNCC organizers like Ella Baker. According to the historian Charles Payne, Baker, along with Septima Clark and Myles Horton, whom she had met at the Highlander Folk School, developed and propounded a "philosophy of collective leadership" that challenged the limitations placed "on the ability of the oppressed to participate in the reshaping of their own lives."[56] Zellner referred to this approach as an "organic intellectual and political leadership" and discussed the importance of such a dynamic within the civil rights movement. He often compared these experiences to the Coalition's work and style of organizing, thus reinforcing the legitimacy of custodians as both political leaders and teachers.[57] But students who had not spent significant time meeting and discussing issues with the custodians and others in the larger CFJ meetings were more likely to identify with a white, professional man who felt guilty about racism but wanted to ignore it, than with the custodians and experiences of institutional disrespect and discrimination.

For many students who did work with the larger Coalition, their experiences inspired other, larger questions about their own power and about their role in shaping the community's identity. According to Zellner, the outsourcing of the custodial services became representative of a larger issue—the lack of a democratic sensibility in everyday life, both on the campus and in the community. At CFJ meetings, students posed questions such as "Who makes decisions and in whose interests are they made? Who legitimizes knowledge and gets to define what a 'caring and compassionate community' means?" Meghan White explained that one of the most important lessons she learned from CFJ was that "social conformities, barriers, and hierarchies could be broken down." Watters, too, described the process of organizing as different from the status quo of rigid class, racial, and bureaucratic boundaries. She wrote:

> Through meeting with the custodians and those faculty and students who had taken an interest, I was beginning to feel what it was like to be a community. This was a feeling different than any that I had felt here before. We were discussing issues that, according to the usual run of the campus, should not have included us. However, even though the coalition of people came together with a common goal, stopping the custodians' outsourcing, we discussed things in the context of all of our lives.[58]

The students ended the semester by conducting a rally on the streets just outside the campus, and, on December 15, 1997, holding a day-long sit-in in the provost's office. Once again, Bishop defended the decision as purely administrative. However, this time, Meghan White responded by explaining the larger issue of institutionalized racism and noting that even though one did not intend to act in racist ways, one's actions could still be racist in effect if they accepted or reaffirmed institutional conditions and policies that have been historically racist. According to White, unless the provost challenged those traditional practices, he was only reinforcing institutionalized racism. To this, Bishop was silent.[59]

But most students left campus with a renewed sense of having contributed to the struggle and with a belief in their ability to participate in the political life and the diverse cultural identity of a community. As one first-year student, Sarah Zitterman, wrote:

> It is only with hard work in the coalition and further research into the history of people faced with plights like the custodians are faced with today that anyone may ever be able to [answer which solution to the outsourcing] would be best. . . . One could easily be tempted to get discouraged with the idea that one person, or even one group of people

could do anything worth doing to solve the [world's] problems. But it is not true. There is something we can do. . . . We must take action . . . and we must start in our own backyards! That means organizing where there needs to be organizing. . . . When there is something wrong in your school, or in your job, or in your life that is when YOU, the people directly affected by such injustices, must take up arms. The Coalition for Justice and the plight of the custodians of Southampton College is just one example of a group of people taking action and taking control over their own futures. . . . They will continue to take up the arms of organization, as history tells us that self-organization is the only way people ever make a lasting improvement in their own plights. Maybe someday all people will come to realize that once we are united, none of us shall fail.[60]

The Coalition had made a huge impact on the people who participated in meeting and organizing. Building the CFJ had challenged many of the students' and custodians' sense of themselves as individuals and as members of a community. But the group's impact was felt beyond the confines of the campus. By linking institutional racism on campus to the political and social history of the area, and by looking to local governmental agencies such as the Southampton Anti-Bias Task Force for redress, CFJ had forced the larger community to address the issues of race and class that generally lay hidden beneath the official face of the Hamptons.

FROM ANTI-BIAS TO ANTI-RACIST

During the Coalition's second meeting in March 1997, a local community activist suggested some of the custodians go to a meeting of the town's Anti-Bias Task Force (ABTF) and ask for assistance in challenging the College's discriminatory employment practices. Tony Smith attended the group's monthly gathering and explained the situation at the College. The ABTF initially responded with outrage at both the College's past practices and its recent decision to outsource the custodians' jobs. But when pressed to take a public position on the matter, more conservative ABTF members decided to meet with the College's provost, instead. Although the ABTF and the custodians had been told the meeting would be open to all Task Force members, when Bob Zellner, an ABTF member for more than a year, showed up, he was not permitted in. At the meeting that ensued, Bishop and an LIU attorney assured ABTF executive officers that no racism was involved in employment decisions. These ABTF members reported back to the group, and, despite controversy over whether Zellner should have been allowed to participate, the ABTF backed off.

Over time, however, the ABTF shifted back and forth, sometimes taking a conservative and defensive position in which some members claimed a lack of ability or interest in "getting involved with College business," sometimes taking an active role in trying to negotiate some resolution to the issues of promotion and hiring practices. But the Coalition refused to let ABTF off the hook. The author, Smith, Watters, and others continued to attend meetings and demanded that the ABTF take an official, public position on the history of discrimination at the College. The continuing controversy resulted in local newspapers' covering ABTF meetings and activities, thus making the group more visible than ever before. The combined pressure to address the "College problem" and to become more viable and active in general led to the resignation of many conservative ABTF members and ushered in a more progressive and activist group of leaders. Eventually, even the more conservative members of the ABTF admitted that the custodial situation presented a prima facie case for racial discrimination that needed to be addressed. Soon after, during the winter and spring of 1998, the College made two more concessions. First, the College promoted an African American custodian, Frank Jones, to a position as mechanic. The administration also agreed to a provisional policy for future promotions, a policy that had yet to be made permanent in a contract as of 2003.

In the summer of 1998, intimidated by the prospect of another barrage of bad press and concerned about the custodians' new union affiliation with the Teamsters, the College agreed to terminate the LARO contract and to rehire the entire custodial unit under the same terms as before the outsourcing. The new custodial contract, which would come up for renegotiation in late fall 1998, would be bargained over with representatives of the Teamsters. Provost Bishop told the custodians not to think of the LARO contract termination as a "victory," but, as the custodians later told a Coalition meeting, "It felt like a victory to us." This feeling was shared by all of the Coalition members.

CFJ, however, had already gained quite a bit of support from local community groups and activists, and it wanted to build on its success.

During the first meeting in September 1998, CFJ decided to put together a conference to focus on local and regional community organizing. It would pull in a wide range of groups interested in a variety of issues. CFJ also discussed the possibility that without the custodial issue, the group might not be able to focus on some of the broader concerns raised during the struggle, such as the fragmentation and hierarchy of power in campus governance; the lack of minority representation on faculties and staffs; the need for adjunct faculty to organize a union; and the desire to have an environmentally safe and sustainable campus. While all of these issues had been discussed at CFJ meetings and demonstrations, the Coalition itself had rarely done specific work or crafted any particular strategy to deal with them. The group, now led mostly by students and ad hoc gatherings, continued to organize the conference, but it became increasingly clear that CFJ itself would cease to meet once the conference was over.

The conference, held late in the fall of 1998 drew more than one hundred people who attended sessions on youth organizing, environmental sustainability, protests against the School for the Americas (which had been attended by some CFJ students), antibias activism, and a variety of other local issues. Over the ensuing months, a number of local activists would credit the Coalition with raising the community's consciousness about race and class issues and bringing together activists to network and set strategies to deal with a number of different topics. On campus, adjunct faculty continued to organize, and students held a demonstration and sit-in in the provost's office to protest the school's lack of an official policy on sexual harassment. Many of the students who led the protest against sexual harassment had been involved in the Coalition's efforts. As one student explained, "The Coalition still remains with each person who participated in it. The group and the experience is part of us, and we bring it to other places and groups of people."[61] But the CFJ's work remained a part of the community, as well.

On a frigid winter's day in January 2000, more than one hundred people marched through the streets of Southampton to protest the Town Board's violation of affirmative action policies. The demonstrators nailed a three-page list of demands on the door of Town Hall, calling on the local government to diversify its staff positions—only 29 of 345 government workers were African American, and two-thirds of those workers were in the lowest pay grades. The trigger for the march was the Town Board's hiring of five new attorneys, all of them white, despite the application of a highly qualified Black woman, Judith Mitchell. Lou Ware, of the NAACP, chastised the town for its long history of racism and discrimination, while Sherry Blakey-Smith, director of the Shinnecock reservation's Community Learning Center, observed that "People are coming together and waking up. . . . We need to go on, to stand up and say we want a better community. Everyone needs to be a part of this. Let's get those people out of their mansions and into this kind of forum."[62]

This demonstration was organized and cosponsored by the ABTF. It considered the demonstration a follow-up event to its "People's Board" meeting of a few weeks earlier, when it had usurped the seats of town board members during an adjournment in the official meeting. ABTF members then welcomed those in attendance to the "first civil rights sit-in of the twenty-first century" and began a series of speeches that outlined the continuing problems of racial discrimination on the East End. Ware stated, "If we are being civilly disobedient then so be it. . . . This is the people's room, and we are not going anyplace."[63] Bob Zellner, recently elected the ABTF co-chair, contended that "This is the new activism." He explained that issues of discrimination remained rampant throughout the Hamptons—in town government, schools, area businesses, and the local media. Zellner continued, "This is not a flare-up that will die down. We will carry on. The Anti-Bias Task Force initiated this. There is a broad range of people from all walks of life who are with us." A new ABTF member, Sharon Saunders, exhorted the community to "get mad about [racism]. We've got to make a change all over this town."[64]

Over the next two years, the ABTF would challenge local authorities on a variety of issues. The group initiated a campaign to change the town's logo, a Pilgrim symbolizing the town's first European settlers, on the grounds that it omitted the history and culture of Native Americans, celebrated the eventual conquest of Europeans, and, according to Zellner, provided for the continuing "domination of whiteness" in characterizing the town's own identity. The ABTF also intervened in the beating of a local youth by a Southampton village police officer, supported charges by Ware and the NAACP that the district school board's hiring policies were discriminatory, and became involved in ongoing negotiations with Southampton Hospital over staff diversity and the need to hire more Spanish-speaking staff to meet the needs of the growing Latino community. The ABTF also branched out to form coalitions with local environmental groups over contamination in the Peconic River, with local housing groups demanding increased low-income properties, and with local workers calling for bus shelters along major transportation routes. According to Zellner, the "ABTF has become the town's leading antiracist organization, not only advocating for civil rights in general but by making connections among economic, educational, environmental issues and their impact on racial and ethnic discrimination."[65]

CFJ's determination to hold the ABTF accountable for addressing specific race-related issues in the community forced the organization to move from promoting "tolerance" and sponsoring programs that celebrated "boutique multiculturalism" to becoming what Sharon Saunders has called "the only real game in town, the only real forum, for fighting racism and discrimination of all kinds." Saunders believes that as the group became more activist, conservative members dropped out, and the ABTF "grew in its determination to really fight for people who had been discriminated against for so long."[66] ABTF members like Zellner and Ware give credit to CFJ for pushing the organization in an activist direction and, as Zellner puts it, "creating the space for a new kind of civil rights activism that builds on the legacy of the movement that I first participated in during the 1960s."

BUILDING DREAMS NOT DEFERRED

Robin D. G. Kelley, a historian of Black radical politics and social life, has written recently that "social movements generate knowledge, new theories, new questions." At their best, they "do what great poetry always does: transport us to another place, compel us to relive horrors, and, more important, enable us to imagine a new society . . . the conditions and the very existence of social movements enable participants to imagine something different, to realize that things need not always be this way." He concludes, "Revolutionary dreams erupt out of political engagement; collective social movements are incubators of new knowledge."[67]

The history of the working class in the Hamptons is in part the story of how individuals and groups struggled to survive and thrive amid changing economic and social conditions, some more conducive to success than others. Most workers struggled individually or with their families to make a living and to improve the lives of their children. Others worked collectively to build ethnically or racially homogeneous communities where individuals could find the autonomy and power to resist discrimination; achieve success, helped by mutual support networks; and, eventually, assimilate. But there are few examples of social movements in the Hamptons that actually inspired people with a radical vision of a society free of racial discrimination and economic exploitation.

The Coalition for Justice was not a major social movement. But it did represent a type of social movement organization as it picked up the loose and disparate strands of resistance in the Hamptons and built a group that not only successfully challenged a powerful institution to change an unjust policy but also offered a vision of an alternative democratic process that embraced historical, social, and cultural diversity as part of a new collective identity. This identity was never pure or uncontested, just as the vision itself was never crystal clear. But the impact of the group's work continues to resonate throughout the community. In particular, CFJ demonstrated that a historical consciousness informed by diverse histories and cultures could be a powerful force, not just for understanding the complexity of history but for making history as well.

In an article for a book examining labor movements on college campuses, Kelley once claimed that new visions were "sorely lacking" among progressive organizers, "especially when it comes to dealing with the problems of a predominately nonwhite, urban working class relegated to low-wage service work, part-time work, or outright joblessness." While he thought that universities might be a source for new radical visions, he suggested that, to grasp such a vision, "we would do well to pay less attention to the classroom and its attendant culture wars and more attention to the cafeteria and the workers there."[68] CFJ did just that.

Soon after CFJ's work with the custodians, students, faculty, and community representatives from the ABTF joined Native Americans in a land struggle over the Parrish Pond Estates subdivision, located adjacent to both Southampton College and the Shinnecock Indian reservation. These demonstrations began a new chapter that harkens back to the early days of class and race formation in the Hamptons. But, this time, activists bring with them a new understanding of what class and racial identities mean and how they can be transformed.

6

From Clam Beds to Casinos

The Enduring Battle over Native American Land Rights

The 1500 Wampanoag Indians who inhabited Nantucket when it was first charted in 1602 must have eventually evolved their own word for Hamptonization. By the height of the whaling boom, the island had grown to 10,000. The Wampanoag witnessed the arrival of these ill-mannered people with their cobblestone roads, their ships that clogged the harbor. And the houses! Huge!

> —Patrick Cooke, "Hamptonization and
> Its Discontents"

For 363 years we have cleaned your homes, yards, cooked your meals, and raised your most precious gifts, your children. We have watched you take our land, our inheritance, and even our name for your businesses. Shinnecock this, Shinnecock that, and never once have I seen a Shinnecock benefit or even work at most of these establishments. We never asked for anything, and you never offered anything. We were given menial jobs, and with God's help, we did survive.

> —Cheryl Crippen Munoz, *Southampton Press,*
> February 20, 2003

Members of the Shinnecock Indian Nation didn't block the bulldozer this time—they cheered for it.

> —Selim Alger, *Southampton Press,* March 7, 2003

On a cold Thursday morning in February 2000, state troopers arrested the Shinnecock activist Becky Genia for disorderly conduct and resisting arrest. Along with a few dozen other tribal members and supporters, Genia was protesting the development of a sixty-two-acre piece of land adjacent to the Shinnecock reservation in Southampton. The developers, Parrish Pond Associates, had hoped to begin work clearing the wooded parcel and building their thirty-eight-lot McMansion subdivision. But local Native Americans argued that the land contained a sacred burial ground, and environmental groups claimed that a large residential development would result in hazardous groundwater runoff, eventually contaminating the reservation's drinking water. Chanting "not one more acre," demonstrators met bulldozers on Tuckahoe Road, and a standoff ensued.

Genia explained that she and others had made sure they weren't trespassing and that they planned a "peaceful protest" that included possible civil disobedience. Before any formal activities had begun, state police moved in and, according to witnesses, "severely manhandled" some of the demonstrators. Three Shinnecocks were arrested that morning, and a fourth was arrested the next day when, once again, protesters gathered at the site. This time, however, the tribe had won an injunction against the subdivision and called in Bob Zellner, co-chair of the Southampton Anti-Bias Task Force, to help mediate the situation. Zellner had barely introduced himself to the supervising officer when he was "knocked to the ground and brutalized" by police. He, too, was arrested.[1]

Eventually, all four of the Shinnecock protesters and Zellner were either acquitted or had their cases dropped or dismissed. They are all currently suing state police for brutality and false arrest. The Shinnecock did, however, lose their court battle to stop the development, not on the case's merit but on a technicality stemming from a missed deadline. Today, Parrish Pond Associates advertise 4,000+-square-foot luxury homes on one-and-one-half-acre lots "in a unique community of meadows, tall pines, and a magnificent pond." Realtors boast about the subdivision's location, "[o]nly minutes from some of the most spectacular beaches in all the world, the famous Shinnecock Hills Golf Club, mere footsteps from fashionable shopping and the finest dining experiences imaginable, and completely surrounded by the history, culture, ambiance, and world-renowned style of Southampton." Starting at about $1 million apiece, the Parrish Pond Estates homes now stand as the most recent symbol of the Shinnecock Nation's long history of losing land struggles.

On March 5, 2003, just a few weeks after the last protesters had won acquittal, the Shinnecock Indian Tribal Council broke ground on a new development project that would include a casino and resort hotel located on the tribes' Westwoods property, in Hampton Bays. A high-profile ceremony to commemorate the event featured a few Shinnecock speakers, a brief press conference, and a "turtle walk" during which indigenous box turtles were relocated to tribal lands across the street to protect them from the bulldozers. According to Council leaders, the 65,000-square-foot casino would be the lynchpin of the tribe's economic self-sufficiency and empowerment plans and would be constructed to meet the highest standards for environmental protection. Charles Smith, chair of the Shinnecock Trustees, explained that "this is about the preservation of our people. . . . We can no longer live on handouts from the government. We need to work for ourselves."[2] The Council has contracted with the casino developer Ivy Ong to supervise building and operations and has hired a public relations firm to garner support for the project from the surrounding East End community and from others in the region.

However, the opposition to the casino project is large and loud. Hampton Bays residents, especially those near the property, have begun lobbying efforts and have threatened full-scale demonstrations and possible civil disobedience. One resident has started a "Stop the Casino in Hampton Bays" Web site. A larger group that calls itself "Save the East End" has organized, claiming that the Shinnecock project would result in "the East End [becoming] a Casino HELL." It contends:

> If the Shinnecocks claim to be such "good neighbors" and so environmentally sensitive, then why don't they honor the state and local zoning laws and regulations that are in place to protect the local environment and our quality of life? These laws would prevent anyone else from constructing such a huge, environmentally damaging, commercial enterprise on Peconic Bay! A healthy environment IS our economy![3]

While it is true that local zoning laws, strictly speaking, would forbid such a project at the Westwoods site, it may be more than just a tad ironic to ask Shinnecock descendants to abide by the laws of a nation that swindled them out of much of their land and whose agricultural and industrial development has destroyed much of the Indians' native environment and indigenous economy. As always, the Shinnecock wonder just *whose* economy, *whose* environment, and *whose* quality of life are being protected. Yet, politicians ranging from local town super-visors and state assemblymen to U.S. Senators Hillary Clinton and Charles Schumer have registered strong opposition to the casino.

These two recent events represent some of the most controversial elements of contemporary cultural politics in the Hamptons. They demonstrate the volatile nature of political coalitions; while many of the same environmental organizations that supported the Shinnecock's protests against Parrish Pond Estates strongly oppose the casino proj-ect, many developers who have in the past ignored Shinnecock land claims have spoken in favor of the casino. Even former town supervisor Vince Cannuscio, a builder who resisted affirmative-action policies and who strongly opposed changing the town seal that many Native Amer-icans found insulting, has written in support of the casino. Calling them "wise and respectful people" who have more "rigorous" environmen-tal rules for development than government standards, Cannuscio ex-plains, "The Shinnecock people understand better than we do the issues related to developing land. They, the original inhabitants of this land, have been exposed to the consequences of development for more than 363 years."[4]

As different groups of new migrants and old-timers, environmen-talists and developers, antiracist activists and those who believe Native Americans already receive too many "special favors" all side up on the issues, it is impossible to ignore the ways that the Parrish Pond Estates development and the casino project also demonstrate the impact of his-torical conditions and consciousness on contemporary culture and pol-itics. To better understand these two distinct, yet interrelated, struggles, this chapter begins with an overview of Shinnecock and Montaukett land struggles from the early 1700s to the post–World War II era. It ex-amines the variety of methods and the evolution of cultural identities and political strategies that informed these battles over time. The many failures and the few successes of local Native Americans as they sought to remedy a history of European land conquest and political disenfran-chisement still dominate the local political and cultural landscape.

The chapter then focuses on the Parrish Pond Estates protests and on the way that evolving economic and political conditions set the stage for the formation of new coalitions among a variety of East End activist and advocacy groups, even as growing frustration combined with the emergence of a more radical consciousness to inspire what some Shin-necock call a "new militancy" among the tribe. A rising interest in cultural identity and a growing historical consciousness over the past few decades have led to a new commitment to political activism among the Shinnecock. Combined with other recent activism aimed at protecting the environment, opposing racism, and seeking economic justice, the most recent Shinnecock land struggles may be a harbinger of social ideas and political actions once thought of as impossible in the Hamptons.

The chapter concludes by studying the controversy over the Shinnecock's proposed casino. In some ways, this project has fragmented the coalition that had developed in support of stopping the Parrish Pond Estates. In other ways, however, it has enhanced the power of the Shinnecock themselves, promising them at least a modicum of self-determination and autonomy through economic self-sufficiency and political power. The Shinnecock imply that such power will help them restore a more humane and just stewardship over the area; opponents accuse them of simply mimicking the worst aspects of capitalism and development that have caused the ravaging of local landscapes and cultural traditions. One Shinnecock trustee, Lance Gumbs, claims that the tribe will no longer be "good little Indians" or "succumb to their rules and wishes to keep us subservient."[5] But others claim that "two wrongs don't make a right" and sense some hypocrisy in the Shinnecock's "giving the keys to the bulldozers to out-of-town lawyers, investors, and consultants." These dynamics and debates, informed by 350 years of history and struggle, are shaping the future of the Hamptons.

IN THE BEGINNING THERE WAS LAND

There should be no doubt that from the beginning of the European occupation and conquest of what would become North America, the most valuable bounty in the struggle among European powers and Indian peoples was the land itself. While scholars have recently emphasized the "cultural conflicts" that shaped first encounters, by the early 1600s, the contest for land acquisition dominated European policies and practices. Whatever cultural differences may have enabled Dutch and British settlers to appropriate large tracts of land, the fact is that "Europeans found an immense continent inhabited by people who lacked the military technology to defend their lands."[6] By and large, Europeans used whatever means were necessary to conquer the new world.

The signing of treaties and the development of local law, for instance, may have been more a strategy for acquisition than a principled element of European business culture. The Dutch began the practice of signing treaties primarily in response to the intensified efforts of the English to claim ownership over areas in New England and Long Island. Local "aboriginal titles" or agreements made with Native Americans were largely ignored. Once initiated, though, titles and treaties became an integral part of the process of acquiring land. The negotiation process employed by Europeans did take advantage of Native Americans' different "understandings" of property and their culture of communal, rather than individual, use and "ownership." By the 1660s, however, most local tribes had gained some understanding of what land deals with Europeans entailed, and, according to Strong, "it became more and more difficult to find local village headmen [who would] sign away their land."[7]

In response to changing conditions, the English developed other strategies for taking land. The historian Francis Jennings has documented five basic methods of property acquisition. These included creating a "puppet sachem" to sign agreements; plying the Native Americans with alcohol; employing military force; constantly harassing Indians by cutting wood, burning hay, and grazing cattle on their land; and levying fines on various Native American "offenses" and then seizing lands when the fines could not be paid.[8] Again, these practices place the conquest of Long Island's East End within the global process of colonialism; similar strategies were employed by Europeans time and again throughout South Asia and Africa. Ownership of the land guaranteed political and economic control, which enhanced the newcomers' power to make laws, establish courts to rule on those laws, and employ military might to enforce the courts' judgments. By the early eighteenth century, the Shinnecock and the Montaukett Indians found themselves living much like tenants on their own soil, searching for wage labor and with limited political control over their own affairs.

Still, Native Americans on the East End protested the loss of their land. From the inception of land transfers to the English, the Shinnecock and the Montaukett violated agreements (wittingly and unwittingly) by trespassing on English territory. They sometimes responded to the destruction of their crops by settlers' livestock by killing settlers' hogs and horses. In East Hampton, the Montaukett also threatened to burn the hay of English residents who had mowed the meadowlands that were still considered the Indian's territory. In other cases, Native Americans refused to pay fines or fees levied by English settlers and risked imprisonment or other forms of physical punishment, such as public whippings. The early history of European conquest details many ways in which Native Americans, informally, yet openly and constantly, struggled against settlers' increasing land acquisition.[9]

Shinnecock and Montaukett Indians also sought formal and official means of redress. As early as the mid-1660s, a group of thirteen Shinnecock Indians protested to New York governor Richard Nicoll that the Indians who had sold Shinnecock land to Thomas Topping in 1662 did not have the legal right or authority to do so. Over the next 150 years, the Shinnecock and the Montaukett would seek redress from local, state, and even federal officials. Despite having unsuccessfully petitioned New York State leaders in 1764, 1800, and 1808, the Montaukett sought help from Governor Daniel Tompkins in 1818. As in previous complaints, the Indians protested that their lands had been obtained through a variety of fraudulent practices and that East Hampton town officials had severely mistreated them by burning their wigwams, killing their dogs, impounding their livestock, and levying steep restrictions on their fishing rights. Although state-appointed investigators upheld the legitimacy of local land transfers to the East Hampton trustees, for the first time these officials recognized the plight of the Montauketts, suggesting that the state perform some act of benevolence to aid "those poor distressed native Indians of Montauk, who are suffering greatly for many of the conveniences of life."[10]

Little would change, however, over the next half-century as Shinnecock and Montaukett Indians remained politically powerless against Southampton and East Hampton trustees. In the 1870s, though, the Montaukett employed a new strategy of resistance by taking the trustees of Montauk to court over property rights. During the next few decades, local Indians had a modicum of success in the courts, especially regarding tribal recognition. By the late 1700s and 1800s, many Europeans and their descendants fought Native land claims by arguing that few indigenous Indians still existed. But the courts reaffirmed the integrity of the Montaukett's survival and the legitimacy of their leaders, despite a long diaspora and the decline in their actual numbers in the local area. Notable was Judge J. O. Dykeman's opinion that "Montaukett rights to Montauk belonged to the tribe that included other persons not living in Montauk."[11] This recognition would prove a crucial point of contention in future trials, the most significant of which involved Austin Corbin's plans to create summer resorts and major shipping hubs on the East End.

In 1879, Montauk's trustees auctioned off 11,500 acres to Arthur Benson, a shipping magnate and Brooklyn-based real estate developer. While his initial interests in the area appeared limited to hunting and fishing, soon Corbin (who was president of the Long Island Railroad) and other investors seized the opportunity to partner with Benson and to develop Montauk. Much of the project hinged on removing the Montaukett who still resided on a 1,200-acre parcel known as Indian Fields. Benson and Corbin employed an East Hampton resident, Nathaniel Dominy VII, to negotiate with the Montaukett, and Dominy proceeded to defraud them through deceptive practices and false promises. The most glaring of these lies concerned Dominy's claim that selling their "share in the residence rights would not mean that they could never return to Montauk," even though the actual bill of sale states that the Montauks "do hereby further covenant and agree to remain away permanently from the said Montauk."[12] Once again, East End Native people were robbed of their land by economic entrepreneurs willing to employ a variety of disingenuous means.

But this time the Montaukett fought back. Between the late 1890s and the early 1920s, the Montaukett brought Benson and Corbin and their various corporate partners to court time and time again. Although the Indians suffered a series of judicial defeats, the court battles delayed the development projects. Eventually, both Benson and Corbin died, and most of the plans for industrial and recreational expansion in Montauk expired with them. In fact, much of their holdings became public lands and have been preserved as open space or parklands. The Montaukett did not get their land back, but they had proved that they could successfully fight against the worst exploitation of the East End.[13]

There were few open protests over land from the late 1920s through World War II. Still, local Native American populations maintained a keen interest in their cultural heritage. Throughout the nineteenth and twentieth centuries, Montaukett and Shinnecock Indians continued to meet for seasonal celebrations and rituals of all kinds. Traditional crafts such as wood carving, basket making, beadwork, and the production of "scrub brushes" (tools for cleaning large pots) all survived the many years of diaspora and defeat. Similarly, a variety of songs, dances, and other performance arts remained an important form of cultural trans-

Shinnecock Indians at a powwow, circa 1920. They maintained their cultural identity and integrity as a means of resisting complete annihilation. (Photo courtesy of David Martine, personal archives)

mission and survival for East End Indians. But perhaps the most important cultural event that marked both the endurance of native culture and the resurgence of collective identity and empowerment after World War II was the powwow.

In his examination of the Shinnecock powwows the historian Harvey Laudin concluded that the word "powwow" is a "generic term that refers to a genus or a class of related things." He has described a variety of Native American celebrations, political meetings, and other similar events as falling under the category of powwows. Although the activities and cultural significance of the powwow has changed historically, Strong argues that it has always existed as a "rite of intensification," reinforcing "the group bond, provid[ing] a feeling of security, and remind[ing] everyone of the values they share."[14] A contemporary history of Shinnecock ceremonies shows that none were documented between 1915 and 1937. Following World War II, however, powwows were held annually. A former Shinnecock chief, Thunderbird (Henry Bess), explained that he had been participating in powwows throughout New England for years and, in 1946, decided, along with his friends and relatives, to renew the traditional ceremony in Southampton.[15]

The post–World War II period witnessed a resurgence of Native American cultural traditions. Thunderbird described some of this process, explaining that, prior to the reestablishment of the powwows, most "rich people living across the water" had never heard Indian drums or celebrations. He explained:

> The Indians here were used to thinking about making a living and how they were going to sleep and eat and so forth, and didn't bother much with drumming because the white man taught him he should live in homes and houses and do away with old hogans and wigwams that the old people used to live in. It kind of got away from the old culture, but by associating with the other Indians it came back, and really, now the young Indians are all interested in dancing.[16]

Along with renewed interests in traditional forms of agriculture and aquaculture and the development of cottage industries in traditional arts and crafts, the powwow symbolized the revitalization of Native American cultural practices and identity on the East End. This transition also signified a political awakening.

Perhaps the most important case of modern Shinnecock resistance to the conquest of their land came in the early 1950s, when the Cove Realty Company tried to build houses on a small strip of land at the north boundary of the Shinnecock reservation in Southampton. After receiving intimidating mail from attorneys and police visits "with orders to get off their land," the local tribe created the Shinnecock Indian Community Group. Although the organization had no official maps or papers to confirm the northern boundary of the reservation, Harriet Crippen Brown Gumbs, a Shinnecock activist, and David DuVivier, a white attorney and neighbor, believed that residents could argue that "possession and occupancy were sufficient grounds for the Shinnecock case." Gumbs proceeded to collect testimony from older tribe members and from elderly citizens in the area. The data proved convincing enough for Suffolk County Judge J. Hazelton to find in favor of the Shinnecock and for both the New York State Supreme Court and the U.S. Supreme Court to deny appeals.[17]

This successful battle might not have been possible without the local Indians' ability to recover their cultural heritage. The process of cultural awakening not only empowered the Shinnecocks themselves but created a better-informed and supportive local community. Thunderbird believed that "if we hadn't had the powwow going, this land case might not have gone through so well back in 1954. People began to know that there were Indians existing here, that they had a right to live on the land, the land should actually belong to them, and I think that helped the judges and the people who ruled in our favor."[18] In her account of the Cove case, Harriet Crippen Brown Gumbs also cited the powwows as an empowering force that helped the Shinnecock tribe, which had become "almost too lackadaisical for [its] own good," to come together and fight back.[19]

Throughout the 1960s and 1970s, Native Americans around the nation built on similar resurgences of cultural identity and empowerment to organize and to assert their political power. The American Indian movement and other groups helped establish what Nancy Lurie calls an "articulatory movement" in which Native Americans reject assimilation into the dominant culture and assert their power and pride in traditional values and identities; at the same time, they pursue political, social, and economic connections to the outside world.[20] On the East End, the Shinnecock and the Montaukett renewed sweat lodge ceremonies and other traditional rites and rituals, and they also began to seriously research their family and tribal histories. When two corporations attempted to develop an ancient burial ground in Montauk, the Montaukett went to court and blocked the project. Under pressure from Indians, environmentalists, and others, East Hampton's Town Board voted to buy the site and preserve the land. In 1989, local tribes again saved sacred land by holding a protest rally that pressured the Town Board into preserving another burial ground near North Neck.

But their successes have been limited. Montaukett leaders continue to make the reclaiming of Indian Fields their primary objective. Similarly, the Shinnecock have remained vigilant in their attempts to protect reservation land from intrusion. As recently as 1997, the Shinnecock won a case against a Southampton man who held a deed to a small parcel of land adjacent to their reservation. But economic and political conditions for Native Americans on the East End have remained fairly bleak. Despite the resurgence of Indian cultural identity and political engagement, poverty and disenfranchisement remain powerful detriments to political action by local tribe members. The renewal of pride and purpose, combined with a lack of mainstream economic and political opportunities, has led to increased frustration and militancy among the East End's Indians. When Parrish Pond Associates declared its intention to develop a sixty-two-acre parcel of land considered sacred by the Shinnecock and located immediately across from their reservation, many members declared that "we have had enough."

NOT ONE MORE ACRE

Within the context of this long history of land struggles, the handful of Shinnecock members arrested for protesting the Parrish Pond development might not seem like a very significant historical shift. Those who showed up to block bulldozers on the mornings of February 25 and February 26, 2003, were clearly acting out an important part of their cultural and political legacy. Yet, the Parrish Pond protests marked a crucial rupture in the continuity of relations between the Shinnecock and the community; there are few accounts of organized and formal direct action protests by local Native Americans against developers over land issues. The events surrounding the Parrish Pond protest marked a

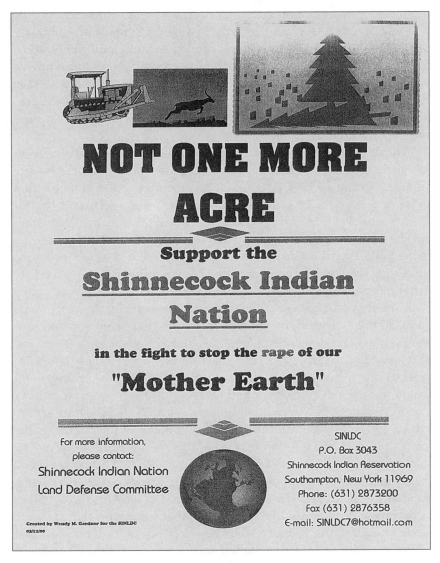

Not One More Acre! poster. (Created by Wendy M. Gardner for the SINLDC, March 12, 2000)

significant transformation in the Shinnecock's political identity over the past few decades, changes that include a new, vigorous, and sophisticated militancy; a willingness and an ability to build multidimensional coalitions; and a motivation to gain real economic and political power, even at the risk of severing some community ties. While this shift in both strategy and identity can be traced to the tribe's own internal evolution and local responses, it must also be placed in a larger historical and national context.

The development site in question at Parrish Pond is part of a larger area for which the Southampton trustees paid the Shinnecocks twenty pounds sterling in 1703. The town, however, gave the Shinnecock a 1,000-year lease on 3,600 acres, land that includes the current Parrish Pond estates. In 1859, Town officials persuaded the state legislature that the Shinnecock were willing to break the lease to facilitate the extension of the Long Island Railroad. Town officials presented a petition to the state, signed by twenty-one purported Native residents who agreed "to surrender their lease." In truth, only a few tribal leaders agreed to the deal, and they had been severely pressured for years by the people who harassed them about rights granted in the original treaty. Recent European settlers and descendents regularly trespassed on, stole from, and developed Shinnecock property. Officials had promised those few Shinnecocks who actually did sign the petition that the new arrangement would solve the disputes once and for all.[21]

Immediately, however, other Shinnecock protested the transaction. Their petition to state officials argued that many of the names on the town's petition "were forgeries, and of this we are ready to offer substantial and conclusive evidence in any court of law." They continued that some "signers were not signed by the parties bearing the name thereon the petition"; that others "who had a right to those names signed were dead and buried for years"; that some who signed "were never known to the tribe, nor did they ever belong to the tribe"; that others who did exist "never signed the petition as claimed"; and that some signers were minors.[22] Not only did the state ignore these protests, but it also ignored the federal Trade and Intercourse Act that required congressional approval of all Indian land deals. The Shinnecock did receive the 750 acres that now make up their reservation across the street from Parrish Pond, but many tribal members argue this is land they already had.[23] The rest was lost.

For many years afterward, the Shinnecock Nation decided against openly protesting these decisions. The local historian and resident Harriet Gumbs, however, has noted a recent change in tribal attitudes:

> Our people have been laid back, and one of the reasons was they were working for the townies. . . . They felt they couldn't say anything . . . because their children's lives and food and bread depended on them being servants of the townies. But as time goes on, our children are becoming educated and more sophisticated, and the majority are not servants dependent on the townies anymore. And, as we are seeing our property dwindle down to nothing, there is a feeling that our town of Southampton does not respect us as Indian people.[24]

Elizabeth Haile-Davis, another Shinnecock elder and spiritual leader, agrees that for many years, the Shinnecock remained quiet, independent, and secretive "because that's been our best defense. We didn't do anything physical." But she claims that younger people have been brought up to believe that "we will get the hills back." Thus, "when the young people saw that the bulldozing was going to happen, they said this is the last piece of property that has been taken inch by inch. They said not one more acre, and I said you're right, not one more acre."[25]

This spirit had been brewing among younger members for many years. Margo Thunderbird, forty-seven years old, remembers chasing trespassers off the reservation as a youth. She explained that those actions were "our political goals as children. We would throw stones at them and tell the non-Indian people to get off our land." Thus, in 1997, when Doreen Dennis-Arrindel, one of the Shinnecock eventually arrested at Parrish Pond, heard a bulldozer behind her house in the woods, her instinctive response reflected an increasing sense of resentment and militancy. Arrindel immediately sat down in front of the earth mover, explaining, "It was just automatic, spontaneous . . . the land, the reservation mean so much to me. It's my heritage. The history here is part of my soul."[26] This historical consciousness, shaped by an increasing post–World War II cultural awareness and empowerment, has led to new political strategies and a commitment to direct action tactics.

Claiming that past leaders were either too complacent or too corrupt, a new generation of tribal members, like Chuck Quinn, declares, "No more selling us out, no more backdoor deals with the whites."[27] At a Town Hall demonstration, one tribal council member, Lance Gumbs, explained, "We have lived in peace for the last 350 years, and we hope to continue that peace. . . . But we will no longer tolerate the desecration and rape of our lands."[28] Becky Genia understands that previous generations sometimes "did what they had to do" just for her people to survive. Still, she argues that white people knew the Shinnecock were a "passive, peaceful, sharing, and compassionate tribe" and through fraud and forced assimilation took advantage of them. Genia says that a lot has changed at the reservation over the past couple of years. She explains that current activists saw the Parrish Pond development and "knew it was time to get together and act. . . . The only way to deal with this here and now was to physically stop this development and physically stop the bulldozers. . . . The Shinnecocks are coming out of a coma."[29]

The convergence of cultural awareness and political militancy has also occurred within a national and historical context of increased militancy among Native Americans. Despite the decline of the American Indian movement in the late 1970s, the legacy of political radicalism and cultural awakening intensified a variety of empowerment efforts among Indian tribes around the country. Like other 1960s social movements that inspired Black studies, women's studies, and Latino studies programs, the "Red Power movement" gave birth to a prolific Native American history and culture curriculum in higher education.[30] Political sophistication, along with newly trained "ethnocentric" scholars fueled new legal claims for long-lost Indian lands and created a growing interest in renewing Native American land struggles through the courts.[31] Meanwhile, economic entrepreneurship, especially in retailing and in the gaming industry, brought financial resources together with burgeoning political and cultural resources. Soon, native groups from around the country were tapping into the newly formed Native American Rights Fund (1971), the Indian Law Resource Center (1978), and more recent groups like the National Tribal Justice Research Center, the Tribal Court Clearinghouse, at UCLA, and the University of Oklahoma Law Center's American Indian Legal Resources.

The Shinnecock have also experienced increased cultural, political, and economic development of their own over the past few decades. The powwows of the postwar period grew into a full-fledged cultural movement as the Shinnecock Indian Development Board and Steering Committee helped organize the Shinnecock Native American Cultural

Coalition in the early 1970s. In the early 1990s, the Shinnecock Community Center hosted a variety of heritage projects and tutoring programs funded through New York State's Title V program.[32] Most recently, the Shinnecock completed a ten-year development project and opened the Shinnecock Nation Cultural Center and Museum on the reservation. Winnonah Warren, a museum spokesperson, emphasizes the importance of culture and education for political empowerment, explaining that "Our people have realized that they have to strengthen their culture, not only for the sake of others, but for their own sake, too."[33]

Economically, the Shinnecock have been gaining experience and sophistication in marketing and entrepreneurship. Throughout the 1970s and 1980s, the powwows became more than just Shinnecock events—they attracted increasing interest from the local community and, especially, from tourists. Soon the Labor Day weekend celebration became the major revenue producer of the Shinnecock Nation. According to Strong, the powwow was bringing in more than 30,000 visitors by 1995. Meanwhile, other tribal entrepreneurs like Lance Gumbs have developed retail businesses both on and off the reservation. His Indian Outpost, located on Montauk Highway, began by selling tobacco (taking advantage of state tax laws that exempt those on reservation land from having to pay cigarette tax); now his inventory includes Native American CDs, food products (especially baked goods), and a delicatessen. In the mid-1990s, Gumbs opened the Trading Post, in the Green Acres Shopping Center, up-island in Valley Stream. Just a stone's throw from the Gumbs place on the Highway is the Thunderbird Coffee Shop, which also sells cigarettes and Native American crafts and merchandise but specializes in organic coffees and teas. Gumbs is a strong advocate of economic self-sufficiency and believes strongly that retail businesses and the tourism industry are "viable prospects" for Shinnecock entrepreneurship and empowerment.[34]

The Parrish Pond protests, therefore, represent a unique historical moment where cultural, political, and economic developments among the Shinnecock converged with regional and national movements to provide both the organizational resources and the rationale for more confrontational politics and direct-action strategies. This combination also allowed the Shinnecock to transcend their previous strategies of isolation and independence and to begin building coalitions that recognized Native American land struggles as integrally linked to other groups' agendas. While environmental issues had in the past brought the Shinnecock and the Montaukett together with organizations like the Group for the South Fork and the Nature Conservancy, the Shinnecock had never *reached out* to build a multi-issue coalition in quite this way. When the Shinnecock activists contacted Bob Zellner, of the Anti-Bias Task Force, they initiated a process of coalition building characteristic of a changing political awareness.

The Anti-Bias Task Force had itself been radicalized, as presented in the previous chapter. Bob Zellner's own civil rights story had become common knowledge in the community, and his support for the janitors at Southampton College and his willingness to upset the racial status quo made him a natural ally. His immediate arrest at the protest site only strengthened the bonds of trust and mutual commitment.

With the Task Force came the local NAACP, another group long nascent and recently stirred back into action by leaders like Lou Ware. Meanwhile, the Shinnecock themselves began discussing how to mobilize the increasing support they were receiving. According to Becky Genia, they decided to create opportunities around the Parrish Pond protests that would both forge alliances and educate new coalition participants. On May 13, the Shinnecock sponsored a "caravan of awareness" in which they invited supporters to join them in touring lands lost under the 1859 petitions. The fifteen-mile trip began in Hampton Bays, near the railroad station, and wound up at the Thunderbird Coffee Shop, on the edge of the Shinnecock reservation in Southampton, where speakers from groups as diverse as Peacesmith House and the National Civil Rights Coordinating Committee spoke in support of Native land claims and environmental protection.[35]

On Memorial Day, a few weeks later, the Shinnecock worked with a variety of local groups and individual residents to hold a "march for Mother earth" in the middle of Southampton Village. Susanna Powell, co-char of the Anti-Bias Task Force, explained that her group understood the Parrish Pond development on sacred Shinnecock grounds "as one form of discrimination against the Shinnecock Indian Nation. . . . If a Christian burial ground was to be built upon, there'd be an uproar."[36] Also present at both events were students from Southampton College, some of whom belonged to the student environmental organization, PEACE, and others who were studying with Scott Carlin, a professor of environmental studies and a member of the Long Island Progressive

Coalition. As one student activist, Valerie Suzdak, wrote, in the *Southampton Press*:

> Our society seems to believe that we are past the days when land is taken from the Native Americans and they are just pushed onto reservations. The truth is—we aren't. And to think any differently is to walk with blinders on. These things do not just happen in other towns, cities or countries, they are happening right under our noses. . . . It is very difficult for me to even look at the Parrish Pond property anymore because I know what it used to be. Unfortunately, the [new] homeowners will not have the same privilege as me. All they will see is their new house and a pond. They will not realize there are people right across Montauk Highway devastated by the building of homes on their sacred land.[37]

Students joined with other community activists in strengthening the growing coalition, not only against the particular Parrish Pond development but in recognizing the Shinnecock's multidimensional political and cultural struggles.

Over the ensuing weeks and months, Shinnecock activists appeared before a host of Town Board meetings and zoning meetings and in a variety of other settings to protest development projects in the Shinnecock Hills. Along with representatives from the Group for the South Fork and other environmentally concerned residents, the Shinnecock spoke adamantly, not only against Parrish Pond Estates but also in opposition to the building of subdivision after subdivision. By the summer of 2002, however, few of these battles had been won. Addressing a Southampton Town Zoning Board meeting in August of that year, Randy King, a Shinnecock resident, listed the names of recent development projects and declared, "Romeo, Belesis, Barone, and now Mahoney . . . we have voiced our displeasure with each one of those projects, and we will continue to do so." Yet, the Shinnecock were also frustrated and growing weary of losing their battles against a variety of development projects on land they had once controlled. While one could argue that much of that land had been lost centuries ago, these most recent conflicts over development on that land merely recreated the historical experience of Shinnecock loss, now at the pace of a few acres at a time. Even Larry Toler, a Zoning Board member, became exasperated, exclaiming, "The laws we pass seem to go nowhere . . . they appease no one. We're doing nothing whatsoever to protect the Shinnecock Nation. They come and complain, but nothing, nothing, ever happens."[38]

Even though the Shinnecock lost their battles against Parrish Pond and other land projects, Becky Genia recognizes that forging alliances and building coalitions was an important form of success. She celebrates the fact that Shinnecock activists "have met so many people who support us [and] people realize that we are fighting for the same thing. So this is not just the Shinnecocks causing trouble." Bob Zellner sees the Shinnecock playing a leading role in radicalizing local antiracism and other social justice groups. He explains that "not only do the Shinnecock bring a long history of struggle and resistance to any issue; they also have a more holistic perspective of social justice. Race, class, gender, and the environment are all linked in their traditional approaches to social relationships and the natural landscape."[39] The Parrish Pond protests brought together a variety of racial, class, and environmental concerns, and many community activists envisioned the possibilities of a powerful grass-roots coalition in the future.

Yet, even with an increased militancy and an ability to link their struggles and issues to the concerns of other local groups interested in environmental preservation, antidiscrimination work, and Native American land rights, nothing seems to be powerful enough to stop the onslaught of residential development on land to which the Shinnecock still claim entitlement. Despite having mobilized various cultural and political resources, the Shinnecock have few tangible rewards for their efforts. In the meantime, life for many on the reservation grows worse: high poverty and cancers rates; high unemployment and low level of school retention; poor sanitation and unclean drinking water; and little access to the kinds of financial services that might help to change the conditions Bob Zellner has called Southampton's "dirty little secret."

THE WONDER OF IT ALL

When Isaac Keeler and Richard Hubbell concluded their 1818 report to Governor Tompkins about the conditions of Native Americans in East Hampton, they suggested that, "unless the Montauketts had some help in developing some form of industry at Montauk, which could provide a source of income, it would be difficult to stop the population decline as the youth left to find employment elsewhere."[40] Almost two hundred years later, little had changed for Native Americans on the East End. According to recent census data, almost 30 percent of households on the Shinnecock reservation have annual incomes under $10,000, and almost two-thirds have incomes under $15,000. In contrast, only 6.3 percent of Southampton's other households make less than $10,000, and only 10 percent make under $15,000. Yet, more than 50 percent of the town's households have annual incomes over $50,000, and almost one-quarter more than $100,000. Without economic power and resources, the East End's Native Americans have had great difficulty in successfully challenging the history of land usurpation, political disenfranchisement, and social marginalization. They have fought, nonetheless.

Suddenly, however, the Shinnecock have an opportunity to exploit federal legislation and policies to their own economic benefit. Over the past few decades, the Red Power movement and a revival of interest in tribal sovereignty led Indians around the country to take advantage of federal ordinances and to establish bingo parlors on reservation lands. In the 1970s, the Penobscot Indians, of Maine, developed high-stakes bingo and became one of the most economically successful tribes in the nation. In the 1980s, as bingo sprouted on other Indian reservations and some moved from bingo to card clubs and larger gambling facilities, some states moved in to try and regulate growth. In a landmark case, the U.S. Supreme Court ruled that California state laws could apply to sovereign Indian land only if Congress passed laws to support such interventions, and it had not. Meanwhile, President Ronald Reagan issued, in 1980, an Indian policy statement that supported gaming as an alternative to dependence on federal funds. The 1988 Indian Gaming Regulatory Act (IGRA) set the stage for Native Americans to pursue a potentially powerful economic resource. The Native American historians Josephy, Nagel, and Johnson write that "by 1989 it was estimated that there were more than one hundred gaming operations on Indian land, and by the early 1990s, some estimates placed aggregate reservation gaming revenues in the billions of dollars."[41]

The Shinnecock did not immediately take to the possibility of following such a lead, and for years the casino question lay dormant on the East End. As Ian Frazier has suggested, not all tribes consider gambling establishments to be a viable source of income, since they require large investments and because the IGRA does allow for increased state and federal interventions in Indian affairs. Still, Frazier admits, "No other tribal enterprise in history has succeeded even remotely as well as tribal casinos . . . the rise of tribal gambling has given some tribes economic power greater than Indians have known since the years when they had the continent to themselves."[42]

Over the past decade, the Shinnecock have watched their Connecticut neighbors, the Pequot and the Mohegan tribes, build the Foxwoods and the Mohegan Sun casinos, respectively, and quickly earn multimillion-dollar profits for their people. The Pequot, in particular, have become one of the leading employers in the state, funding ballets, museums, and a variety of other educational and cultural projects. According to Frazier, "Gambling revenues have enabled some tribes to reduce or eliminate unemployment, pay for schooling, hire tribal historians, build clinics and roads and houses, get tribal members off welfare, and in some cases give members per capita payments ranging from thousands to hundreds of thousands of dollars a year."[43] The Mohegan's profits, for example, have supported a language restoration project, senior housing, documentary film production, and the purchase of ancestral burial grounds.

Despite its earlier misgivings about gaming ventures, the Shinnecock Tribal Council decided, in early 2003, to pursue developing a bingo hall—with future plans for a full casino—on their Westwoods property, in Hampton Bays. The plans for such a venture created immediate political chaos; Southampton town supervisor Skip Heaney exclaimed, "A casino would absolutely destroy the community character not only of Hampton Bays but of all of Southampton Town." Bob Deluca, president of the Group for the South Fork, has gone so far as to call the project an "atomic bomb" that would spur "uncontrollable East End development." State senator Kenneth LaValle has criticized the Shinnecock for "blatantly threatening the quality of life on the East End." Senators Hillary Clinton and Charles Schumer have both registered their opposition; Schumer has even written to the Bureau of Indian Affairs to intervene in the tribe's recognition process, claiming that Southampton residents "do not want their idyllic environment hurt by the added traffic, congestion and noise of a gaming facility."[44]

Many who oppose the project, however, recognize the impact of oppression and land loss experienced by the Shinnecock and have tried to find some alternative to a gambling facility. Hal Ross has suggested that the Town of Southampton use $20 million from the Community Preservation Fund to purchase the seventy-nine acres of Westwoods property. If the Shinnecock then invested the money "in a thirty-year U.S. treasury bond, [it] would give each of the 200 Shinnecock households approximately $5,000 per year, probably forever."[45] Bob Deluca has presented a variety of alternatives ranging from "selling development rights" on the Westwoods property in order to fund a "Shinnecock saving and lending institution," to establishing a foundation for tribal members' education, to building a resort hotel and spa or gas station that would be subject to limited taxation.[46] Assemblyman Thiele has recently stated that "anything is on the table, except for casino gambling," hinting that "an inn or spa could provide the right kind of income." And Congressman Tim Bishop concurred, calling the Shinnecock's options "broad and open to the imagination."[47]

Yet the Shinnecock have been firm in their pursuit of a casino. Claiming that officials' refusal to discuss the project has "forced them" to push forward with the casino development, trustees continue to argue that "the reality is that Indian gaming works." This doggedness has led some to contend that the Shinnecock tribe is refusing alternatives because it is after the multimillions that only a casino offers. And it is true that economic empowerment tops a list of concerns voiced by tribal leaders. Lance Gumbs, a trustee, believes that other economic options "have been exhausted." In an interview with a local newspaper, Gumbs explained that previous efforts to "improve economic conditions on the reservation . . . including oyster hatcheries and a paint factory" all failed.[48] Even a major regional paper like *Newsday* has agreed that "the Shinnecock Indian Nation truly needs the means to achieve self-reliance, a source of development that can bring its members solid jobs, housing, health care and education."[49]

But the casino clearly represents more to the Shinnecock than simply the generation of cash; it represents the potential for significant political power that would enable the tribe to become a key player in local and regional land-use issues for years to come. This is evident in part from the ways that the Shinnecock discuss the casino, venting their frustration. Listen to Harriet Gumbs as she responds to a reporter's question about public officials who oppose the casino: "they have a lot of nerve. . . . We gave them the town to begin with, and they have been taking and taking and taking until we have just our reservation and our little woods. . . . But we no longer feel we have to be the last people on the totem pole. . . . We are embarking on one of the greatest things our nation has ever tried to do: we're creating our own self-reliance."[50] Genia is even more direct, claiming that "you can be poor and passive and invisible all your life, or you can take the opportunities that come your way finally . . . before every inch of our sacred hills are lost, we will fight fire with fire."[51]

A successful casino project would produce enough money to bring the Shinnecock out of poverty, but, if the Pequot and other tribes are examples, the Shinnecock tribe could also become one of the area's largest employers and would have the ability to engage in political battles at the highest level. It could not only fund its own legal battles over land claims, but, like other tribes, it could also aid local groups (like the Montaukett and the Poospatuck) in asserting their claims. Genia explains, "We don't have much left. . . . It seems like our land has been disappearing quietly for so long. We have been poor and passive for too long. . . . But we have grown up a little bit. We can't just take whatever they give us. If we have to sacrifice some land to save the rest, that's what we'll do.[52] Even Gumbs believes that the goal is not completely economic, arguing that self-preservation is also about "the protection of our culture. . . . We call economics . . . our new savior."[53]

Despite major opposition and recent court injunctions, the Shinnecocks continue to press forward in hopes of building the casino project. But their doggedness has damaged aspects of the coalition they forged during the Parrish Pond protests. Environmental groups like the Group for the South Fork have been vocal opponents, despite sympathetic comments from Deluca, who believes that the town's own hypocrisy and discrimination so marginalized the Shinnecock that they saw the casino project as the only logical alternative. He states, "The final straw that drove the tribe to the waiting arms of casino investors can be traced to the Southampton Town Planning Board's pathetic mishandling of the Parrish Pond subdivision." The development project's design, town officials' unwillingness to inform or negotiate with tribal leaders, and the eventual arrests of protestors all combined to enflame the tribe. Deluca concludes,

> From the day of those arrests, it was clear to me that many members of the tribe had reached their breaking point, and there was a new willingness to consider the option of something like casino development. Not only had the tribe endured generations of neglect from its postcolonial neighbors, but now its people had been

shackled, hauled off, and arrested for daring to peacefully protest
the further destruction of Southampton Town by real estate speculators.[54]

Still, the environmental community remains steadfastly in opposition,
and Deluca has recently speculated that the continued pursuit of a
casino has "seriously eroded their credibility on land conservation issues and has made local governments and communities less likely to
extend themselves for the tribe."[55]

But other groups who had joined the Shinnecock in support of the
Parrish Pond demonstrations have voiced strong support for the casino
project. Bob Zellner, the NCRCC, and the NAACP remain advocates for
Shinnecock empowerment and agree with the Shinnecock position that
they should be able to use their property for any kind of development
they deem necessary to achieve economic security and political enfranchisement. While these groups have always appreciated the environmental concerns of organizations like Group for the South Fork and the
Nature Conservancy, NAACP leaders like Mary Killoran have always
wondered "whose environment" we are conserving and "in whose interests" we embark on preservation efforts. Zellner explains this within
a civil rights framework:

> Historically, the environmental movement has been dominated by
> middle- and upper-class, primarily white activists who have ignored
> the racialized elements and impacts of environmental issues. For
> years, environmentalists largely ignored the fact that poor and minor-
> ity communities were the most devastated by toxic contamination, in-
> dustrial pollution, and other forms of environmental devastation.
> There developed a mistrust for environmentalists among many civil
> rights organizations who felt that environmental groups didn't un-
> derstand how race and class were an integral part of how corporations
> polluted urban and rural areas. It's fine to fight for open spaces and
> wildlife protection, but civil rights have to be a part of environmental
> protection, too.[56]

Pursuit of the casino project may produce irrevocable damage to the
larger goal of coalition building, but it may be that the Shinnecock are
willing to risk certain alliances in the hope of attaining a larger share of
political and economic power.

If history has taught the Shinnecock anything, it is that neither subtle resistance nor openly militant protest (even within a large coalition of multiple-issue groups) has stopped encroachment on their land or improved their economic or social status in the community. Nor has their resistance been successful in halting the continued development of the East End as a whole. While environmental groups and other activists have had a modicum of success in preserving open spaces, groups representing the disenfranchised and the marginalized have had much less impact on economic development policies. Even with the support of the rich and famous new migrants to the Hamptons, environmental groups have been able to save only a fraction of the "rural quality of life" that existed before the postwar development booms. And even with the high profile advocacy of Billy Joel and other East End glitterati, the baymen have all but disappeared into the realm of symbolic icon, and farmers now provide more vistas than produce. Many in the Hamptons love the status that comes with having the continent's first residents among them, but they are unlikely to actually do anything to empower Native Americans or any other group of poor people or people of color. After all, the creative options and alternatives to gambling that have been proposed by opponents of the casino project have existed for a long time, but no one took the opportunity to suggest these projects until a gaming facility became a possibility. The continued arrogance of town officials in the face of Shinnecock land claims and protests against development has bred an increased intransigence among the tribe.

The political pitch has reached such heights that neither supporters nor detractors seem able to agree on very much. On the one hand, the tribe refuses to acknowledge that the casino would have a detrimental impact on the local and regional environment. While it would be possible for the gaming facility to be built with state-of-the-art, environmentally friendly materials and practices, there is little that the Shinnecock could do to reduce the inevitable pollution created by increased automobile traffic and greater population density. While the tribe has committed to using its own resources to build an access road that could reduce local traffic jams, the pollution created by millions of new automobile and bus trips to the region can't be avoided. An argument could be made that, given the opportunity to be a major economic and political force, the Shinnecock would do a better job of environmental stewardship than have Europeans and whites for the past three centuries. As

Genia has said, "We tried sitting in front of a bulldozer, but no one will take us seriously until we have the green stuff."[57]

For opponents, the discourse is shaped by a context of political obfuscation and social paranoia. Legislators continue to claim that they have tried to negotiate with Shinnecock, but it is clear that all of their proposals require the tribe to "take gambling off the table" as a starter. The Nation argues that it is willing to negotiate the size, shape, place, and other aspects of building a gaming facility, but it fears losing its most powerful chip if it submits to public officials' terms. Residents involved in organizing against the casino have spread "horror stories" about how "busloads from New York City will be rambling down Hampton Bays side roads, trying to get to the casino." They have even gone so far as to question the real need for Shinnecock economic development, claiming, "They are not as poor as they would like you to think."[58]

Today, the casino remains a hot-button issue that has been relegated to the courts. State laws require the Shinnecock to gain federal recognition before they can open a gaming facility. Although the tribe has applied for such recognition, it contends that it is unnecessary. The Shinnecock argue that neither the Town of Southampton nor the state of New York can enforce local and state zoning laws over a semi-autonomous Indian nation. Meanwhile, local officials and residents continue to organize against the project. Recently, Town Council representatives went to Connecticut to meet with local officials who have consistently opposed Pequot and Mohegan casino development. The www.stopcasino.net Web site now hosts a three-minute video demonstrating the possible impact of the casino, and project opponents now have a weekly cable production, *Stop Casino TV*. The struggles to build and defeat a Shinnecock gaming facility will undoubtedly continue over the next few years and may help to define the future of land-use politics for generations. A casino would undoubtedly have a tremendous effect on the Hamptons' physical and cultural landscape. But the East End landscape has been changing for centuries; this would be the first time since 1600 that Native Americans would have the economic and political power to seriously influence those changes.

Epilogue

Tony Rosalia, one of the many Hamptons residents I interviewed for this project, spoke to me on the phone after he had read the penultimate draft of the book. "I think it's good," he said. "You make some important points about the area's history and recent changes. But, it's too negative. The Hamptons that you write about doesn't feel like the Hamptons I know and see so much of the time." As an example, he related a story from his experience as a court translator and liaison for the Latino community. It seems that two wealthy older women had recently appeared in court on behalf of their Latino chauffeur, who had been arrested for being drunk and disorderly. According to Rosalia, "these women felt very responsible for their driver and genuinely concerned for his welfare." He concluded, "This is the Hamptons that I know."

I think Tony is right about the importance of recognizing the specific ways in which we experience the realities of everyday life. The Hamptons are a place where people with myriad backgrounds relate to one another, often in very intimate ways. Much of my book shows how people have navigated the major social transformations of the Hamptons, from the European conquest, to the rise of an American aristocracy, to the recent changes brought by urban and suburban economic development.

But, what I believe Tony found "too negative" in the book is the unfortunate reality that, despite the noblesse oblige attitude of the wealthy, the best intentions of white politicians, and the sincere efforts of people interested in protecting wildlife and waterways, the structures of economic wealth, social stratification, and political power remain the dominant factors in determining the everyday experience of people in the Hamptons. People may treat each other with great respect and decency, but the frameworks that enable them even to decide what is dignified are powerfully defined by forces that are often out of their control. While recognizing the intersection of structural inequality with

224

individual experiences doesn't always yield a positive picture, let me simply say that no place is "positive" or "negative" in this way. We may applaud the commitment and caring of two women toward their employee, but even their small acts of heroism do little to alter the segregated labor markets, the racially and ethnically insensitive law enforcement, or the larger economic and social conditions that shape daily events.

Karl Marx once wrote that, while "Man makes his own history . . . he does not make it out of whole cloth; he does not make it out of conditions chosen by himself, but out of such as he finds close at hand. The tradition of all past generations weighs like a nightmare upon the brain of the living."[1] For most of this book, I have tried to trace just how such a historical dialectic shaped both the past and the present in the Hamptons. Since the first encounters between Native Americans and Europeans, people in the region have struggled to control the land and its resources, their own cultural identities and integrity, and the richness of their everyday lives. While Europeans cemented their political, economic, and cultural conquest over the territory, the Shinnecock and the Montaukett Indians navigated these changes, sometimes resisting, sometimes accommodating, but always negotiating conditions in an attempt to survive and thrive. Their efforts, in turn, also shaped the course and content of European settlement itself.

Similar dynamics of power and resistance occurred as new demographic groups migrated to the Hamptons and older "local" people were forced to resist or accept, challenge or adapt to the forces of change. From the late nineteenth century, when the nation's first aristocracy began its summer conquest of the area, through the early-twentieth-century arrival of a new wave of European immigrants, to the post–World War II era of professional-managerial-class leisure seekers, the forces of major social transformations have impacted the Hamptons. But each period of rapid change has also witnessed the power of historical traditions and cultural resistance and the struggles of native entrepreneurs and community leaders to meet those large-scale forces with their own stock of local resources through collective action.

Most of the book has been about how these historical struggles set the stage for the recent history of culture and politics in the Hamptons. By examining recent demographic changes, real estate trends, and artistic representations of the region; by documenting the rise and fall of a political movement advocating the secession from Suffolk County of

Peconic County; by looking at the changing local sports scene and how polo and soccer represent the cultural and political, as well as athletic, interests of new migrants; by analyzing recent labor struggles between a traditionally racialized working class and a small local liberal arts college as it attempted to corporatize its policies and practices; and by studying the historical and political evolution of recent Native American land struggles, I have, I hope, offered an effective analytical map of the area's cultural and political landscape. More important, though, I hope that I have provided a guide for those who want to shape the future of the Hamptons.

The real heroes of any age are those who maintain the individual and collective fortitude necessary to fight against the forces that propagate poverty and oppression, racism and ethnic prejudice, environmental devastation and political disenfranchisement. The real heroes of the Hamptons future will emanate from the most recent struggles to improve the lives of those who continue to fight along the margins of the area's great social and economic changes.

Over the past few years, Sharon Saunders has organized children in the mostly African American Hillcrest neighborhood. THANKU (the Hillcrest Avenue Neighborhood Kids Union) has established both formal and informal programs for the community's children who are still marginalized by racism and poverty and who are now victimized by the degradation of what was once a tight-knit village. Saunders's organization has featured an African dance and drum group, sponsored holiday parties and neighborhood clean-ups, produced a play entitled *Back to the Future: Black History in Review,* and organized dozens of other various events. Mostly, though, Saunders's group offers young people between the ages of six and twelve years a place to go after school where they can find help with homework, opportunities to express artistic visions, and activities that challenge their intellect and creativity, a place where they are safe and loved. For Saunders, the roots of the old community can be revived and Hillcrest's sense of pride and identity restored through these children.[2]

But Saunders's work with THANKU has also been part of an overall neighborhood political awakening through which people have begun challenging other aspects of official degradation and neglect. When a young African American man was beaten up and arrested on Miller Avenue in the Hillcrest area, Saunders and others spoke out about the continued harassment of young people by particular officers on the Southampton village police force. With the help of the town's Anti-Bias Task Force, neighborhood residents pressured the police force into providing sensitivity training for all local police. After a young boy was injured on a broken seesaw in the only park in the Hillcrest neighborhood, Saunders and other parents organized a shutdown of the park until it could be fixed up with a combination of public and private funds. According to one parent, "What I don't understand is that the parks crew can go out to Agawam Park every day and clean that up, but our park is in deplorable shape."[3] And THANKU worked along with the Anti-Bias Task Force and the Group for the South Fork in an effort to stop the construction of a 280-bed nursing home facility right in the middle of the Hillcrest neighborhood. Although their protests were eventually defeated, the struggle marked a serious shift in the neighborhood's political presence in Southampton.

Meanwhile, the already difficult situation for Latinos in the Hamptons has been made even more challenging by the recent downturn in the economy. As the number of day laborers looking for work has increased, so has the animosity toward them. In Southampton, calls for the construction of a hiring hall to eliminate the "eyesore" of dozens (sometimes hundreds) of workers waiting outside the 7-Eleven on Montauk Highway have met with protests. While some have argued that tax dollars should not be used to "encourage or legitimize" illegal immigration, others have exploited the opportunity to spew the traditional "anti-immigrant" venom that links foreign-born workers to every malady from leprosy, tuberculosis, and hepatitis to traffic congestion, school overcrowding, and the loss of natural habitats.[4]

In East Hampton, tensions increased again over the location of athletic fields as groups of predominately Latino residents gathered to play volleyball in the backyards of their homes. Neighbors protested that the games encouraged large and noisy crowds, litter, traffic congestion, and even gambling. The town moved quickly to find alternative public space for the games, but the animosity and divisiveness that separate the Latino and the Anglo communities may be growing, and complaints about noise and litter have followed the volleyball games to their new location. Meanwhile, the *East Hampton Star* reminds us that these conflicts are infused with class, as well as ethnic, tensions. The paper reported on the existence of a private residence that doubles as an "unofficial clubhouse" for a private golf course just "up the road" from the backyards that hosted the volleyball games. Noting that little "hand-wringing" took place over parking and traffic congestion at the clubhouse, in contrast to the concern over the volleyball games, the *Star*'s editors cautioned local officials "to avoid the perception that they look the other way when rich and powerful residents are involved in potential violations while at the same time coming down hard on Latino working people having a little fun."[5]

A new group has begun organizing to address the continuing challenges faced by Latino workers and residents in the Hamptons. OLA (the Organizacion Latino Americana) hopes to "unify and integrate the voice of all Latino people on the South Fork . . . [and] develop local leadership and Latino empowerment, be it economic, cultural, political and/or educational, in order to deal with the problems currently affecting our East End Latino community."[6] Since its inception, in 2002, the group has protested the working conditions at local migrant camps, campaigned for increased low-income housing, advocated for literacy and health insurance initiatives, and cosponsored the national AFL-CIO "freedom rides," for workers' rights in the fall of 2003. Along with the Southampton Anti-Bias Task Force and a variety of other groups, OLA has been a strong supporter of the Southampton hiring hall, claiming that a "labor development center" would help protect workers by formalizing and documenting payment procedures, as well as guaranteeing workers' safety and improving the conditions in which they wait for jobs. According to Helena Carratala, a member of the Anti-Bias Task Force, "The main focus would be to take this part of the economy and bring it up from the underground."

Meanwhile, SOLA (the Latin American Solidarity Outreach Center) has shifted its focus in the past year to emphasize community organizing and political enfranchisement. The group's efforts had focused on meeting the emergency needs of the local Latino population for food, medicine, and shelter, as well as offering limited ESL classes. But Katherine Hartnett, the director of SOLA, believes that the organization has to change along with the changing nature of the Latino population itself. She explains:

> I think a lot of immigrants are realizing that they may stay here permanently. . . . For many of them, there is not a whole lot to go back to.

Once they decide that they are going to make a home and raise kids here, empowerment becomes all the more important. They are not just working and sending money home anymore."[7]

Citing the eviction of Latino workers from a hotel in Montauk, Hartnett concludes that Latinos feel powerless. "They need to be able to stick up for themselves without feeling uncomfortable, [and] that's what we want to provide for them."

Both SOLA and OLA have also been working in a coalition with the South Fork Progressive Coalition to improve the availability of affordable housing. SFPC's Kathryn Szoka believes that, despite the group's interest in environmental issues, the key to progressive changes in the region lies in recognizing that one must have both "an environmental point of view" and a "social conscience about poverty and inequality. . . . You just have to look at everything together."[8] In the SFPC 2003 newsletter, the group demonstrates this integrated consciousness by proclaiming that Suffolk County must include "all communities displaced by the housing crisis, like SOLA and OLA, in all levels of planning a response." The SFPC mission statement best articulates the overall sense of synthesis:

> We feel it is particularly important to fight for the hopes and aspirations of the less powerful in our community, including working families, the poor, the displaced and the marginalized. The economic and cultural diversity of our communities is a source of community strength and we want to ensure that the rights of all residents are respected.[9]

The Southampton and the East Hampton Anti-Bias Task Forces and groups like the SFPC, SOLA, OLA, and THANKU promise to remain formidable influences in the shaping of the future of the Hamptons. Their work will provide a site where people can use the tools of the past and knowledge of the present to reshape the future. In coalition, these organizations and their supporters just might use the historical and cultural fabric of the Hamptons to weave a new tapestry free from the nightmares of the past and filled with dreams of better days tomorrow. May such visions result in a new set of raw materials for future generations to inherit.

POSTSCRIPT

As I send the final draft of this book to press, major changes continue to impact the Hamptons. New York City's eastward migration continues unabated, driving up housing prices and upscale commercial markets. But the migration is no longer limited to real estate; it now includes real estate brokerages. In January 2004, Brown Harris Stevens purchased East Hampton–based Dunemere Associates Real Estate. This was the third major takeover or merger in less than a year. According to Arthur W. Zeckendorf, co-chairman of Terra Holdings, which owns Brown Harris Stevens, the acquisition allows his company to expand services for a clientele that owns high-end properties on both Manhattan and the East End. He explains: "Many people who desire high-end properties in Manhattan also reside in the Hamptons."[10] The same clarion call that foretold the passing of baymen and blue bloods, of family grocers and family farms, now signals the end for mom-and-pop realtors. Now it's the "big boys" who will invite New York City's elite nature seekers to "share our traditions."

Meanwhile the Long Island University Board of Trustees voted to close the doors of Southampton College following the 2004–5 academic year. Too many semesters of too much debt, too small an endowment (despite Sillerman's millions), and too much bad management finally caught up with the institution. I am sad to find out that many of my friends and colleagues from the College will lose their jobs. And it is sad to see that a liberal arts college in the heart of America's richest paradise could not raise the necessary capital to succeed. But, as the custodians and their supporters discovered a few years ago, the same institution that proclaimed a commitment to humanistic values and caring communities would forsake its lowest-paid workers at the drop of a dime. The College never escaped the kind of "plantation-style" racism that plagued the rest of the Hamptons, nor could it escape the kind of corporate mentality common in higher education today. When places that might inspire dreams of better days are conquered by those beholden to bureaucratic bottom-lines and cultures of greed, it may be better for everyone that they come to an end.

Notes

NOTES TO THE PREFACE

1. Alexandra Wolfe, "Dune, Where's My Hampton?" *New York Observer*, 25 August 2003.

2. Quoted from ABC Web site.

3. *New York Times*, 29 August 2003.

NOTES TO THE INTRODUCTION

1. The "East End" refers to the five easternmost towns of Suffolk County on Long Island. These towns include Southold and Riverhead on the North Fork, Shelter Island in Peconic Bay, and Southampton and East Hampton on the South Fork. The towns of Southampton and East Hampton are usually referred to as "the Hamptons."

2. Everett Rattray, *The South Fork: The Land and People of Eastern Long Island* (New York: Random House, 1979), p. 211.

3. Corey Dolgon, "Building Community amid the Ruins: Strategies for Struggle from the Coalition for Justice at Southampton College," in *Forging Radical Alliances across Difference: Coalition Politics for the New Millennium*, edited by Jill Bystydzienski and Steven Schacht (New York: Rowman & Littlefield, 2001); Geoff White, *Campus, Inc.: Corporate Power in the Ivory Tower* (New York: Prometheus Books, 2001); and Cary Nelson, *Will Teach for Food: The Crisis in Academic Labor* (Minneapolis: University of Minnesota Press, 1997).

4. Karl Marx, *The German Ideology*, in *The Marx-Engels Reader*, edited by Robert C. Tucker (New York: Norton, 1972), p. 136.

5. A good example of the use of these documents is Nancy Hyden Woodward's selection in her *East Hampton: A Town and Its People—1648–1992* (East Hampton: Fireplace Press, 1995).

6. Jeanette Rattray, *Discovering the Past: Writings of Jeanette Edwards Rattray, 1893–1974, Relating to the History of the Town of East Hampton* (New York: Newmarket Press, 2001), p. 159.

7. Lyman Beecher, "A Sermon, Containing a General History of the Town of East Hampton, L.I. From Its First Settlement to the Present Time" (Sag Harbor, NY: Alden Spooner, 1806).

8. George Rogers Howell, *The Early History of Southampton, L.I., New York with Genealogies* (Albany: Weed, Parsons, 1887), pp. 46–49; Steven Wick, *Heaven and Earth: The Last Farmers of the North Fork* (New York: St. Martin's, 1996).

9. John Strong, *We Are Still Here: The Algonquian Peoples of Long Island Today* (Interlaken, NY: Empire State Books, 1996), p. 9.

10. Gaynell Stone, *The Shinnecock Indians: A Cultural History* (Lexington, MA: Ginn, 1983); Stone, *The History and Archeology of the Montauk Indians* (Lexington, MA: Ginn, 1979); John Strong, *The Algonquian Peoples of Long Island from the Earliest Times to 1700* (Interlaken, NY: Empire State Books, 1997); Strong, *The Montaukett Indians of Eastern Long Island* (Syracuse: Syracuse University Press, 2001).

11. Grania Bolton Marcus, *Discovering the African American Experience in Suffolk County, 1620–1860* (Mattituck, NY: Amereon House, 1988); Natalie Naylor, *Exploring African American History* (Hempstead, NY: Long Island Studies Institute, 1991); Lynda R. Day, *Making a Way to Freedom: A History of African Americans on Long Island* (Interlaken, NY: Empire State Books, 1997).

12. T. H. Breen, *Imagining the Past: East Hampton Histories* (New York: Addison-Wesley, 1989).

13. Rattray, *Discovering the Past*, pp. 136–145; Alastair Gordon, *Weekend Utopia: Modern Living in the Hamptons* (New York: Princeton Architectural Press, 2001), pp. 9–24; Mary Cummings, *Southampton: Images of America* (Dover, NH: Arcadia, 1996); Robert J. Hefner, *East Hampton's Heritage* (New York: Norton, 1982).

14. Bob Deluca, Interview with the Author, Bridgehampton, NY, 25 January 2002.

15. Breen, *Imagining the Past*, p. 71.

16. Tom Twomey, *Awakening the Past: The East Hampton 350th Anniversary Lecture Series, 1998* (New York: New Market Press, 1999).

17. Breen, *Imagining the Past*, p. 12.

NOTES TO CHAPTER I

1. Robert Cushman Murphy, *Fish-shape Paumanok; Nature and Man on Long Island* (Philadelphia: American Philosophical Society, 1964); Mary Parker Buckles, *Margins: A Naturalist Meets Long Island Sound* (New York: North Point Press, 1997); John Hay, *The Atlantic Shore: Human and Natural History from Long Island to Labrador* (New York: HarperCollins, 1969).

2. John Strong, *The Montaukett Indians of Eastern Long Island* (Syracuse: Syracuse University Press, 2001). For more on these cultural differences see William Cronon, *Changes in the Land: Indians, Colonists and the Ecology of New England* (New York: Hill & Wang, 1984).

3. John Strong, *The Algonquian Peoples of Long Island from the Earliest Times to 1700* (Interlaken, NY: Empire State Books, 1997).

4. Strong, *The Algonquian People*, p. 108. Also see Annette Silver, "Comment on Maize Cultivation in Coastal New York," *North American Archeologist* 2, no. 2 (1980); Michael Stewart, "Late Archaic through Late Woodland Exchange in the Middle Atlantic Region," in *Prehistoric Exchange Systems in North America*, edited by Timothy Baugh and Jonathan Ericson (New York: Plenum Press, 1994); Rose Oldfield Hayes, "Shinnecock Land Ownership and Use: Prehistoric and Colonial Influences on Modern Adaptive Modes," in *The Shinnecock Indians: A Cultural History*, edited by Gaynell Stone (Lexington, MA: Ginn, 1983).

5. Neal Salisbury, "The Indians' Old World: Native Americans and the Coming of Europeans," *William & Mary Quarterly* 53, no. 3 (1996); Christopher Miller and George Hamell, "A New Perspective on Indian-White Contact: Cultural Symbols and Colonial Trade," *Journal of American History* 73, no. 2 (1986); George S. Snyderman, "The Functions of Wampum," *Proceedings of the American Philosophical Society* 98 (December 1954); Wilbur Jacobs, "Wampum: The Protocol of Indian Diplomacy," *William & Mary Quarterly* 6, no. 4 (1949).

6. Lynn Ceci, "Reconstructing Indian Culture on Long Island: Fisher's Study of the Montauk," in *The History and Archeology of the Montauk Indians*, edited by Gaynell Stone (Lexington, MA: Ginn, 1979). See also Ceci, *The Effect of European Contact and Trade on the Settlement Pattern of Indians in Coastal New York, 1524–1665* (New York: Garland, 1990).

7. Francis Jennings, *The Ambiguous Empire: The Covenant Chain Confederation of Indian Tribes with English Colonies from its Beginnings to the Lancaster Treaty of 1744* (New York: Norton, 1990); James Axtell, *The European and the Indian: Essays in the Ethnohistory of Colonial North America* (New York: Oxford University Press, 1981).

8. Strong, *The Montaukett Indians*, pp. 11–16.

9. Ibid., p. 17.

10. Kit Wesler, "Trade Politics and Native Peoples in Iroquoia and Asante," *Comparative Studies in Society and History* 25, no. 4 (October 1983); Bruce Johansen, *Native American Political Systems and the Evolution of Democracy: An Annotated Bibliography* (Westport, CT: Greenwood Press, 1995).

11. Jill Lepore, *The Name of War: King Phillips War and the Origins of American Identity* (New York: Vintage, 1998). For more on the use of the term "kings" and its relationship to British Empire see Eric Hinderaker, "The Four Indian Kings and the Imaginative Construction of the First British Empire" *William & Mary Quarterly* 53, no. 3 (1996).

12. Nancy Hyden Woodward, *East Hampton: A Town and Its People, 1648–1992* (East Hampton: Fireplace Press, 1995), p. 19.

13. Henry M. Christman, *Walt Whitman's New York: A Collection of Walt*

Whitman's Journalism Celebrating New York from Manhattan to Montauk (New York: Macmillan, 1963).

14. Helen Harrison and Constance Dyer Denne, *Hamptons Bohemia: Two Centuries of Writers and Artists at the Beach* (San Francisco: Chronicle Books, 2002), p. 43.

15. Ibid., p. 52.

16. Alastair Gordon, *Weekend Utopia: Modern Living in the Hamptons* (New York: Princeton Architectural Press, 2001).

17. Sven Beckert, *The Monied Metropolis: New York City and the Consolidation of the American Bourgeoisie, 1850–1896* (Cambridge: Cambridge University Press, 2001).

18. William Mckay Laffan, *The New Long Island: A Handbook of Summer Travel* (New York: Rogers & Sherwood, 1879). For more on the Tile Club, see Ronald Pisano, *The Tile Club and the Aesthetic Movement in America* (New York: Abrams, 1999); Bob Colacelleo, *Studios by the Sea: Artists of Long Island's East End* (New York: Harry N. Adams, 2002).

19. Christman, *Walt Whitman's New York*, pp. 178–188. For more on the summer resorts and culture of America's post–Civil War elite see Allen Churchill, *The Upper Crust: An Informal History of New York's Highest Society* (Englewood Cliffs, NJ: Prentice Hall, 1970), and David Black, *The King of Fifth Avenue: The Fortunes of August Belmont* (New York: Dial, 1981).

20. Neston Sherrill Foster, "Boarders to Builders: The Beginnings of Resort Architecture in East Hampton, Long Island, 1870–1894," M.A. thesis, State University of New York, Binghamton, 1977; *Southampton* magazine (January 1920).

21. Robert Mackay et al., *Long Island Country Houses and Their Architects* (New York: Norton, 1997), p. 170.

22. Woodward, *East Hampton*; Mary Cummings, *Southampton: Images of America* (Dover, NH: Arcadia, 1996); Jeanette Rattray, *Discovering the Past: Writings of Jeanette Everett Rattray, 1893–1974, Relating to the History of the Town of East Hampton* (New York: Newmarket Press, 2001). Rattray writes that the name "Maidstone" was chosen "because East Hampton's earliest settlers in 1648 were Englishmen from Maidstone in Kent, and they called this New World settlement Maidstone for a year or two" (p. 137).

23. Rattray, *Discovering the Past*, p. 109; see also Helen Penny Walter, "Building Houses and Hotels," *Long Island Forum* (September 1983).

24. Rattray, *Discovering the Past*, p. 109.

25. Everett Rattray, *The South Fork: The Land and People of Eastern Long Island* (New York: Random House, 1979), quoted in Roger Wunderlich, "Go East, Young Man: Nineteenth-Century Farm Life on the South Fork of Long Island" *Long Island Historical Journal* 13, no. 1 (2000): 9. J.. Rattray, *Discovering the Past*, p. 299.

26. Charles DeKay, "Eastern Long Island: Its Architecture and Art Settlements," *American Architect* 1 (April 1908): p. 112.

27. Statistics are taken from the Interuniversity Consortium for Political and Social Research's United States Historical Census Data browser at http://fisher.lib.virginia.edu/census. For an anecdote related to immigrant population growth, Mary Cummings writes that six Polish families lived in Southampton in 1908, while 331 had arrived by 1918, enough to build and support Our Lady of Poland Church. Mary Cummings, *Southampton* (Dover, NH: Arcadia, 1996), p. 58. For more on the role of immigration and its relation to the U.S. census during this period see Donna R. Gabaccia, *Immigration and American Diversity: A Concise Introduction* (London: Blackwell, 2002); Roger Daniels, *Coming to America: A History of Immigration and Ethnicity in American Life* (New York: Harper, 1991). For more on the impact of census changes on ethnic and racial identities, see Susan Cotts Watkins, *After Ellis Island: Newcomers and Natives in the 1910 Census* (New York: Russell Sage Foundation, 1994).

28. *East Hampton Star*, 20 February 1920; 9 April 1920; and 17 December 1920.

29. Salvatore LaGomina, "Fullerton and the Italians: Experiment in Agriculture," *Long Island Forum* (February 1, 1989): 12–20; LaGomina, "Long Island Italians and the Labor Movement," *Long Island Forum* (January 1985): 4–37. See also Vincent Seyfried, *The Long Island Railroad: A Comprehensive History*, Part 6, *The Golden Age, 1881–1900* (Garden City, NY: Newsday, 1968), and Scott Adam Chesin, "Lungs of Brass and Sinews of Steel: The Long Island Rail Road and the Development of Rural Capitalism." B.A. thesis, Harvard University, Cambridge, MA, 1998.

30. Helene Gerard, "And We're Still Here: 100 Years of Small Town Jewish Life," *Long Island Forum* 52 (October 1981): 204–208; Woodward, *East Hampton*, p. 199; Abe Frank, *Together but Apart: The Jewish Experience in the Hamptons* (New York: Shengold, 1966); and Stuart Vincent, "Long Island's Founding Jews," in *Long Island: Our Story*, edited by Newsday Staff (New York: Newsday, 1998), p. 229.

31. Robert Miller, "The Long Island Motor Parkway: Prelude to Robert Moses," in *Robert Moses: Single-Minded Genius*, edited by Joann Krieg (Hempstead, NY: Long Island Studies Institute, 1989), pp. 151–158. See also Louise Carter Smith, "Long Island Motor Parkway," *Nassau County Historical Journal* 23 (spring 1961).

32. Gwendolyn Groocock, "70 years of Polish Politics," *Suffolk Times*, 4 April 2002; Cummings, *Southampton*, p. 58; Drew Featherstone, "Waves of Immigrants," in *Long Island: Our Story* (New York: Newsday, 1998), p. 292.

33. Enez Whipple, "Meet Your Neighbors," *East Hampton Star*, 5 July 1945.

34. Roger Daniels, *Not Like Us: Immigrants and Minorities in America, 1890–1924* (Chicago: Ivan R. Dee, 1992), pp. 90–91.

35. *East Hampton Star*, 25 February 1921.

36. For more on schools and Americanization between 1880 and 1920 see

John W. Meyer, David Tyack, Joane Nagel, and Audri Gordon, "Public Education as Nation-Building in America: Enrollments and Bureaucratization in the
American States, 1870–1930," *American Journal of Sociology* 85, no. 3 (November
1979): 591–613; Cara-Lynn Ungar, "Black and Jewish Working-Class (Im)mi-
grant Women Speak to the Nation: Rhetoric and Pedagogy in Americanization
Practices, 1890–1930," Ph.D. diss., University of Miami, 2000; Joel M. Roitman,
*The Immigrants, the Progressives, and the Schools: Americanization and the Impact of
the New Immigration upon Public Education in the United States, 1890–1920* (Starks,
KS: DeYoung Press, 1997).

37. Joe Gergen, "Three of a Kind: Brown, Erving, Yaz grew up on LI, then
grew into legends," LIHistory.com, available at http://www.lihistory.com/
specspor/stars.htm.

38. Frank Cavioli, "People, Places, and the Ku Klux Klan on Long Island,"
Long Island Forum (August 1986): 166; Cavioli, "The Ku Klux Klan on Long Is-
land," *Long Island Forum* (May 1979): 100–106; David Behrens, "The KKK Flares
Up on LI," *Long Island: Our Story* (New York: Newsday, 1998), p. 293.

39. Frank J. Cavioli, "The KKK Memorial Day Riot," *Long Island Forum*
(winter 1992); Cavioli, "An Incident at Eastport," *Long Island Forum* (November
1984): 211.

40. David Roediger, *Wages of Whiteness: Race and the Making of the American
Working Class* (New York: Verso, 1991). The late nineteenth and early twentieth
centuries witnessed the hegemonic rise of "white identity," not just in the
Hamptons but also nationally. Much has been written about this "construction
of whiteness" as a prevalent cultural and political identity in the United States.
Some of these studies demonstrate how Irish and other immigrant workers promoted the importance of whiteness to compete with freed Black labor. Others
contend that the convergence of racism (in the form of white supremacy and
anti-immigrant nativism) and a burgeoning nationalism created a powerful national identity that fused whiteness with Americanism. While this dynamic
built on pre-existing racism, it was expanded and rationalized by turn-of-the-
century scientific racism, political party opportunism, and the development of
a civic sector that pressed cultural assimilation through education, patriotism,
and antilabor, anti-union rhetoric. Whether it was the conservative and violent
strains of the KKK and the American Protective Association or the more liberal
and assimilationist policies of Native American industrial schools, settlement
houses, and the "Americanization Movement" in general, the construction of a
turn-of-the-century American identity was indisputably constricted by a severely racialized discourse.

41. Robert Caro, *The Power Broker: Robert Moses and the Fall of New York*
(New York: Vintage, 1974); John Black, "Robert Moses and the Ocean Parkway:
An Environmental Retrospective," in *Evoking a Sense of Place*, edited by Joann
Krieg (Interlaken, NY: Heart of the Lakes, 1988); Joann Krieg, *Robert Moses: Sin-*

gle-Minded Genius (Interlaken, NY: Heart of the Lakes, 1989); Robert Moses, "Parks, Parkways, Express Arteries, and Related Plans for New York City after the War" (New York City, 1943).

42. Harrison and Denne, *Hamptons Bohemia*, pp. 76–82.

43. Gordon, *Weekend Utopia*, pp. 110–120.

44. Walter Kuentzel and Thomas Heberlein, "Social Status, Self-Development, and the Process of Sailing Specialization," *Journal of Leisure Research* (Third quarter, 1997): 306.

45. Gordon, *Weekend Utopia*, pp. 120–123.

46. Ibid., 127.

47. Steven Gaines, *Philistines at the Hedgerow: Passion and Property in the Hamptons* (Boston: Little, Brown, 1998); Gordon, *Weekend Utopia*, p. 127.

48. Peter Matthiessen, *Men's Lives* (New York: Vintage, 1986), pp. 157–158.

NOTES TO CHAPTER 2

1. The discourse of urban blight and decay is nothing new and may be integral to the process of urbanization itself. Raymond Williams, in *The Country and the City* (New York: Oxford University Press, 1973), argues that "the city" itself occupies a cultural position whose meaning is defined mostly in opposition to "the country." The city sometimes stands as an image of "worldliness, sophistication, and civilization," in juxtaposition to rural provinciality, ignorance, and "the primitive." Or it may represent "bourgeois corruption, alienation, human degradation and ecological destruction in opposition to the country's innocence and honesty, mutualism, and respect and embrace of nature." As a cultural image, "the city" represents an ideological spectrum that ranges from fears of urban apocalypse to utopian "cities on a hill" or, as the sociologist Geoffrey Pearson has put it, "City of Darkness, City of Light." More recently, however, the discourse of dark seems to be prevailing; Mike Davis, in *City of Quartz* (London: Verso, 1990) and, later, in books like *Ecology of Fear: Los Angeles and the Imagination of Disaster* (New York: Metropolitan Books, 1998) and *Dead Cities and Other Tales* (New York: Norton, 2002), argued for the growing significance of "noire" as a cultural theme for urban life. Within this context, the city becomes synonymous with fear, chaos, and decay, eventually generating a kind of "moral panic" about urban life.

2. Leo Marx, *The Machine in the Garden: Technology and the Pastoral Idea in America* (New York: Oxford University Press, 1964). For more on the history of suburbs see Kenneth Jackson, *Crabgrass Frontier: The Suburbanization of the United States* (London: Oxford University Press, 1987); Robert Fishman, *Bourgeois Utopias: The Rise and Fall of Suburbia* (New York: Basic Books, 1987); and John J. Palen, *The Suburbs* (New York: McGraw-Hill, 1994). For an excellent look at the historical role that garbage played as a symbol of fear and disease in New

York City, see Steven Corey's forthcoming book, *King Garbage!* (Pittsburgh: Pittsburgh University Press, 2004).

3. Rosalyn Baxandall and Elizabeth Ewen, *Picture Windows: How the Suburbs Happened* (New York: Basic Books, 2000), p. 5.

4. For excellent overviews of New York City political economy during this period see William K. Tabb, "The New York City Fiscal Crisis," in *Marxism and the Metropolis: New Urban Perspectives,* edited by William K. Tabb (New York: Oxford University Press, 1978); Robert Fitch, *The Assassination of New York* (New York: Verso, 1993).

5. Martin Shefter, *Political Crisis, Fiscal Crisis: The Collapse and Revival of New York City—The Columbia History of Urban Life Series* (New York: Columbia University Press, 1992); John Mollenkopf, *A Phoenix in the Ashes* (Princeton: Princeton University Press, 1994); William Sites, "The Limits of Urban Regime Theory: New York City under Koch, Dinkins, and Giuliani," *Urban Affairs Review* 33 (March 1997): 88–89.

6. For more on corruption during the Koch period see Arthur Browne et al., *I, Koch: A Decidedly Unauthorized Biography of the Mayor of New York City, Edward I. Koch* (New York: Dodd Mead, 1988); Margot Hornblower, "In the Shadow of the Boom," *Washington Post,* 24 August 1987; Hornblower, "The South Bronx," *Washington Post,* 25 August 1987; and Hornblower, Private Prosperity, Public Corruption," *Washington Post,* 26 August 1987.

7. Jack Newfield and Wayne Barrett, *City for Sale: Ed Koch and the Betrayal of New York* (New York: Harper & Row, 1988), p. 35.

8. Tom Wolfe, *The Bonfire of the Vanities* (New York: Bantam, 1987), p. 247.

9. Frank Conroy, "Sherman's March to Disaster," *New York Times,* 1 November 1987, 1.

10. Mervyn Rothstein, "Tom Wolfe Tries New Role: Novelist," *New York Times,* 13 October 1987.

11. Richard Eder, "Malice toward All, Charity toward Some," *Los Angeles Times,* 25 October 1987.

12. Ewa Zadrzynska, "Nasty? Try New York," *New York Times,* 30 June 1990.

13. *Time* magazine, 16 September 1990.

14. Asher Arian, Arthur S. Goldberg, John H. Mollenkopf, and Eugene Rugowsky, *Changing New York City Politics* (New York: Routledge, 1990), pp. 204–205.

15. Neil Smith, "Giuliani Time," *Social Text* 57 (1998): 3.

16. See William Bratton, *Turnaround: How America's Top Cop Reversed the Crime Epidemic* (New York: Random House, 1998), as well as a great review of Bratton's book by Louis Kontos, *Humanity and Society* 24, no. 4 (2000): 421–425. The "broken windows" theory was first proposed by James Wilson and George Kelling, "Broken Windows: The Police and Neighborhood Safety," *Atlantic*

Monthly (March 1982). For more recent updates see George Kelling and Catherine Coles, *Fixing Broken Windows: Restoring Order and Reducing Crime in Our Communities* (New York: Touchstone, 1998), and Eli Silverman, *NYPD Battles Crime: Innovative Strategies in Policing* (Boston: Northeastern University Press, 1999).

17. *New York Times*, 17 February 1997.

18. Quoted in Smith, "Giuliani Time," p. 9.

19. Sharon Zukin, *The Culture of Cities* (Malden, MA: Blackwell, 1995).

20. *New York Daily News*, 13 August 2000.

21. *New York Times*, 18 May 1997.

22. Enzo Morabito, Interview with Author's Research Assistant, Southampton, NY, 12 December 1999.

23. For such celebrity-laden accounts of the supposedly "real" Hamptons see Peter Fearon, *Hamptons Babylon: Life among the Super Rich on America's Riviera* (Toronto: Birch Lane Press, 1998), or Dan Rattiner, *Who's Here: The Heart of the Hamptons* (Wainscott, NY: Pushcart Press, 1994).

24. Steven Gaines, *Philistines at the Hedgerows: Power and Passion in the Hamptons* (Boston: Little, Brown, 1998), p. 3.

25. Palen, "The Suburbs," pp. 113–115. See also Arthur Nelson, "Characterizing Exurbia," *Journal of Planning Literature* 6 (1991): 350–368; Lizbeth Pyle, "The Land Market beyond the Urban Fringe," *Geographical Review* 75, no. 1 (January 1985): 32–43; Dinker Patel, *Exurbs: Urban Residential Developments in the Countryside* (Washington, DC: University Press of America, 1980).

26. Alastair Gordon, *Weekend Utopia: Modern Living in the Hamptons* (New York: Princeton Architectural Press, 2001), p. 116.

27. Richard Lee Rigatz, "Vacation Homes in the Northeastern United States: Seasonality in Population Distribution," *Annals of the Association of American Geographers* 60, no. 3 (September 1970).

28. Chana Shoenberger, "Baby Boomers Movin' on Up: Boomers Reshape Real Estate," *Forbes* magazine (November 2002); Daniel G. Brown, "A Study of Land Ownership Fragmentation in the Upper Midwest," *Proceedings*, GIS/LIS 1996 Annual Conference and Exposition, Denver, CO, pp. 1199–1209.

29. Southampton College Institute for Regional Research, "Attitudes of the Southampton Town Population toward Various Subjects Addressed by the Master Plan" (Southampton: Author, 1995), p. 8.

30. Kevin McDonald and Nancy Nagle Kelley, "Recreation/Second Home Industry," in East End Economic and Environmental Task Force, *Blueprint for Our Future: Creating Jobs, Preserving the Environment* (New York: Newmarket Press, 1994), p. 89.

31. Robert Crease, "The History of Brookhaven National Laboratory: Part One," *Long Island Historical Journal* 3 (spring 1991): 167–188; Crease, "The History of Brookhaven National Laboratory: Part Two," *Long Island Historical Journal* 3 (spring 1992): 138–161; Francis Hession and Ann-Marie Scheidt, "Growing

the Region's Economic Future: The Long Island High Technology Incubator," *Long Island Historical Journal* 4 (fall 1991) 2: 14; Joshua Stoff, "Grumman versus Republic: Success and Failure in the Aviation Industry on Long Island" *Long Island Historical Journal* 1 (spring 1989): 113–127.

32. Southampton College Institute for Regional Research, "Attitudes," pp. 8–10.

33. Town of Southampton, "Southampton Tomorrow" (Southampton, NY: 2000).

34. Andrew Maykuth, "An Unwelcome Wave in the Hamptons," *Philadelphia Inquirer*, 9 August 1992.

35. Helen S. Rattray, "Connections," *East Hampton Star*, 2 August 2001.

36. Jane K. Dove, "McMansions: Love Them or Not, They Are Here to Stay," *Home Monthly* (February 2002).

37. Alex Williams, "Big Shack Attack," *New York* magazine (August 9, 1999).

38. Ibid.

39. Chip Ward, *Canaries on the Rim: Living Downwind in the West* (New York: Verso, 2001); Jane Martinson, "Tycoon at the Coal Face," *Guardian*, 11 September 2000; Paul Waldie, "The Mammoth Mansion," *Chicago Sun-Times*, 2 July 2000; Donna Giancontieri, "Permits for Rennert Estate Valid," *Southampton Press*, 1 February 2001; Elizabeth Collins, "Petition Drive for Sagaponack Incorporation Planned," *Southampton Press*, 11 March 1999. For more on Rennert's corporate crimes see Michael Moore's *The Awful Truth*, Episode 5.

40. Tom Daniels, "Community Development and the Challenge of Sprawl," paper presented at the International Community Development Society Conference, Spokane, WA, 28 July 1999.

41. Jennifer Henn, "Village Residents Talk Traffic and Trash the Town," *Southampton Press*, 16 November 2000. Bob Deluca, Interview with Author, Bridgehampton, NY, 25 January 2002; "The South Fork," Group for the South Fork homepage (www.thehamptons.com/group/south_fork/html). Deluca explains that increased specialization and expertise among upscale services for homeowners results in separate trips for the "doorknob man," the "bathroom grout man," "the tall tree specialist," and so on.

42. McDonald and Kelley, "Recreation/Second Home Industry," p. 89. Most town-planning documents and vision statements by local chambers of commerce, even builders' associations, speak of recognizing the commercial and economic importance of at least some environmental protection and preservation.

43. Available at www.nypost.com, 13 May 2001.

44. Hal Ross, "Two Wrongs," *Southampton Press*, 20 February 2003. Ross's letter opposed the building of a casino on the East End (see chapter 6).

45. As much as Whitman contributed to reifying such a duality of physical

nature and human civilization, he clearly understood his own role in constructing it. *From Montauk Point* conflates the untamed and eternal sense of "wild unrest" in viewing "nothing but sea and sky" with his own "inbound urge and
urge of waves, seeking the shores forever."

46. Wendy Chamberlain, Phone Interview with Author, Boston, MA, 8
May 2003.

47. Kathryn Szoka, "Vanishing Landscapes," lecture presented to the
Group for the South Fork, 3 April 2001.

48. *Southampton Press,* 28 June 2001; Interview with Kathryn Szoka, 9 June
2003.

49. Kathryn Szoka, Interview with Author, Southampton, NY, 7 September
2003.

50. *Newsday,* 4 October 1992.

51. *Southampton Press,* 4 November 1999.

52. *East Hampton Star,* 21 September 2000.

53. *East Hampton Star,* 5 November 1998.

54. *New York Times,* 26 August 1992.

55. *Southampton Press,* 4 November 1999.

56. T. H. Breen, *Imagining the Past: East Hampton Histories* (New York: Addison-Wesley, 1989), p. 252.

57. Melanie Ross, "President's Message" (Southampton: Cook Pony Farm,
1998).

58. Gaines, *Philistines,* p. 310.

59. Alex Williams and Beth Landman, "Reversal of Fortune," *New York*
magazine (August 30, 2001).

60. According to Gaines, Norman Jaffe's Hamptons houses made him famous because "nothing else looked like them, at peace with the land, each one
a sculpture, sweeping angles and low, low, overhangs, half walls of quarried
stone and slate, the landscaping built against the house like a verdant cushion."
(*Philistines,* p. 214). Here, the artist's or architect's dream of successfully infus-
ing not only one's creation but one's clients' lifestyle into the natural landscape
is fulfilled. It should be no surprise that his son positions himself as a "native"
in his comments on the destruction of the Hamptons.

61. Quotations and information taken from Web site www.nukethehamp-
tons.com, and articles appearing in the *Southampton Press,* 3 May 2001; *East
Hampton Star,* 3 May 2001; *Newsday,* 4 May 2001, and the *New York Post,* 13 May
2001.

62. Palen, *Suburbs,* p. xiv.

63. *Southampton Press,* 2 July 2002.

64. *Southampton Press,* 4 April 2002.

65. *Southampton Press,* 7 November 2002; 24 October 2002; 19 September
2002. More than 250 articles on homelessness appeared in the *Southampton Press*

during the three and a half years between March 2000 and June 2003. Stories about the shelters were in the Press's list of Top Ten stories for 2001 and 2002.

66. *East Hampton Star,* 2 August 2002.

67. *East Hampton Star,* 9 August 2001.

68. For information on the Sachem Quality of Life see www.sqlife.org or other organizations whose work SQL supports and has links to on its home page (e.g., Ranch Rescue and the American Border Patrol, two right-wing militia-type organizations that advocate the beating and murder of illegal aliens).

69. *East Hampton Star,* 22 March 2001.

NOTES TO CHAPTER 3

1. *Southampton Press,* 7 November 1996; *New York Times,* 24 November 1996.

2. T. H. Breen, *Imagining the Past: East Hampton Histories* (New York: Addison-Wesley, 1989), p. 10.

3. Ibid., p. 14.

4. Hal Ross, "Summary: The Case for Peconic County Now," 5 August 1996 (unpublished).

5. Robert Keeler, *Newsday: A Candid History of the Respectable Tabloid* (Hempstead, NY: Newsday, 1990), p. 256.

6. A local journalist, Karl Grossman, and Fred Thiele Jr. also imply that a loss of patronage was part of what Griffing and his cohort feared losing. Having less control over Suffolk County would mean having fewer opportunities to perform political favors and offer political appointments.

7. Lee Koppelman, "The Quest for a Suffolk County Legislature," *Long Island Historical Journal* 8, no. 2 (spring 1966).

8. Evans K. Griffing, Interview with Karl Grossman, Shelter Island, NY, 5 February 1979.

9. Robert Caro, *The Power Broker* (New York: Vintage, 1974), p. 945.

10. Karl Grossman, Interview with the Author, Sag Harbor, NY, 4 August 1998.

11. Karl Grossman, *Power Crazy: Is Lilco Turning Shoreham Into America's Chernobyl?* (New York: Grove Press, 1986), p. 267.

12. For more on growth coalitions and growth machines, see John Logan and Harvey Molotch, *Urban Fortunes: The Political Economy of Place* (Berkeley: University of California Press, 1988), and John Mollenkopf, *The Contested City* (Princeton: Princeton University Press, 1983). For more on William Casey's role in Long Island development during this period, see Herbert Meyer's edited collection, *Scouting the Future: The Public Speeches of William J. Casey* (Washington, DC: Regnery Gateway, 1989).

13. Griffing, Interview with Grossman.

14. Ibid.

15. Hector St. John de Crevecoeur, *Letters from an American Farmer* (New York: Viking Press, 1981), p. 70.

16. John Strong, *The Montaukett Indians of Eastern Long Island* (Syracuse: Syracuse University Press, 1999), p. 10.

17. Ronald Takaki, *A Different Mirror* (New York: Little, Brown, 1993), pp. 42–44. For more on the impact of the cultural clash between Yankee values of individual industry and development and Native American values of solidarity and subsistence see William Cronon, *Changes in the Land* (New York: Hill & Wang, 1983).

18. *Newsday*, 21 January 1972.

19. *Newsday*, 13 January 1972.

20. Ibid..

21. *Riverhead News Review,* 9 March 1967.

22. Peter F. Cohalan, "Impact of the Proposed Peconic County" (Hauppauge, NY: Office of the County Executive, 1980).

23. Fred Thiele Jr., Interview with the Author, Bridgehampton, NY, 29 March 2002.

24. Hal Ross, Interview with the Author, Southampton, NY, 20 February 2002.

25. Thiele, Interview with Author.

26. East End Economic and Environmental Task Force, *Blueprint for Our Future: Creating Jobs, Preserving the Environment* (New York: Newmarket Press, 1994), p. 89.

27. Ibid., p. 3.

28. Liz Granitz, Interview with Author, Southampton, NY, 18 February 2002.

29. "Peconic County Financial Feasibility Study" (Southampton, NY: East End Economic and Environmental Institute, 1995).

30. Ross, Interview with Author. For history of Group, see "Newsletter" 1, nos. 1–3 (1973), in possession of author. Bob Deluca, Interview with the Author, Bridgehampton, NY, 25 January 2002.

31. Nancy Goell, Interview with the Author, East Hampton, NY, 22 February 2002.

32. For more on Earth Day and its impact on the environmental movement see Kirkpatrick Sale, *The Green Revolution: The American Environmental Movement, 1962–1999* (New York: Hill & Wang, 1993), and Philip Shabecoff, *A Fierce Green Fire: The American Environmental Movement* (New York: Hill & Wang, 1994).

33. Group for America's South Fork, "Newsletter" 1, no. 3 (Bridgehampton, NY: 1973), in possession of author.

34. Ibid.

35. Group for America's South Fork, "Newsletter" 1, no. 2 (Bridgehampton, NY: 1979), in possession of author.

36. Bob Deluca, Interview with Author, Bridgehampton, NY, 24 July 1998.

37. Ibid.

38. Michael Zweig, Interview with the Author, Greenport, NY, 25 July 1998. For more on this type of agricultural strategy, see Michael Zweig, "The Wine Industry and the Future of Agriculture on Long Island's North Fork," Research Paper No. 290 (Stony Brook, NY, 1986).

39. Scott Carlin, Personal Communication, 16 June 2003.

40. Edward T. McMahon, "Community Appearance and Tourism: What's the Link?" reprinted in East End Economic and Environmental Task Force, *Blueprint for Our Future*, p. 192.

41. Roger Wunderlich, "Peconic County: To Be or Not to Be," *Long Island Historical Journal* 9, no. 2 (spring 1997): 142.

42. John J. Palen, *The Suburbs* (New York: McGraw-Hill, 1994), p. 7.

43. *New York Times*, 1 August 1999.

44. Ed Sharretts, Phone Interview with the Author, Boston, MA, 2 January, 2004.

45. Lee Koppelman, "The Myth and the Reality," *Long Island Historical Journal* 9, no. 2 (spring 1997): 157.

46. "Affordable Housing Seminar," filmed by LTV Studios, Wainscott, NY 11975.

47. For more on the difference between affordable and low-income housing, see David Smith, "Mark-to-Market: A Fundamental Shift in Affordable Housing Policy," *Housing Policy Debate* 10, no. 1 (1999): 142–183.

48. Lori Wehrner, Interview with the Author, Riverhead, NY, 15 February 2002.

49. *Southampton Press*, 13 December 2000.

50. *Southampton Press*, 23 August 2001.

51. Ibid.

52. Katherine Hartnett, Interview with the Author, Southampton, NY, 14 February 2002.

53. *Southampton Press*, 11 October 2001.

54. Ross, Interview with the Author.

55. Bob Deluca, Interview with the Author, Bridgehampton, NY, 25 January 2002.

56. Theile, Interview with the Author.

57. Mary Killoran, Interview with the Author, Sag Harbor, NY, 6 August 1998.

58. Lou Ware, Interview with the Author, Southampton, NY, 20 February 2002.

59. Melissa Arch Walton, Interview with the Author, Southampton, NY, 5 October 1997.

60. Everett Rattray, *The South Fork: The Land and the People of Eastern Long Island* (New York: Random House, 1979), p. ix.

61. In the early 1990s, the borough of Staten Island voted to secede from New York City. The state legislature blocked the move, arguing that the state's constitution requires that the city itself vote on whether to allow for secession. Despite numerous lawsuits and legislation filed by state representatives from Staten Island, the secession issue has remains unresolved. Following the Peconic County secession vote, Sheldon Silver, president of the state Assembly, explained that the same rules had to apply to the East End and that without a countywide referendum for secession, Peconic County would not be established.

62. *Southampton Press*, 9 June 1999.

63. Thiele, Interview with the Author.

64. William Mulvihill, *South Fork Place Names: Some Informal Long Island History* (Sag Harbor, NY: Brickiln Press, 1995), p. 95.

NOTES TO CHAPTER 4

1. The literature on globalization is vast and varied. For excellent work on the role of New York City in the process of globalization, see Janet Abu-Lughod, *New York, Chicago, Los Angeles: America's Global Cities* (Minneapolis: University of Minnesota Press, 2000); Saskia Sassen, *The Global City: New York, London, Tokyo* (Princeton: Princeton University Press, 2001); and Susan Fainstein, Ian Gordon, and Michael Harloe, *Divided Cities: New York and London in the Contemporary World* (London: Blackwell, 1992).

2. For more on telecommuting and its impact on the changing geographies of work and economic development see E. Boholin and S. L. Levin, *Telecommunications Transformation: Technology, Strategy and Policy* (Amsterdam: IOS Press, 2000); Krishan Kumar, *From Post-Industrial to Post-Modern Society: New Theories of the Contemporary World* (London: Blackwell, 1995); and Donald Tomaskovic-Devey and Barbara J. Risman, "Telecommuting Innovation and Organization: A Contingency Theory of Labor Process Change," *Social Science Quarterly* 74, no. 2 (1993): 367–385.

3. Corey Dolgon, "Ann Arbor, The Cutting Edge of Discipline: Postfordism, Postmodernism, and the New Bourgeoisie," *Antipode* 31, no. 2 (1999): 129–162; Neil Smith, *The New Urban Frontier: Gentrification and the Revanchist City* (New York: Routledge, 1996); and Sharon Zukin, *The Culture of Cities* (London: Blackwell, 1995).

4. Robert Rowthorn and Ramana Ramaswany, *Deindustrialization: No Cause for Alarm* (Washington, DC: International Monetary Fund, 1997); Ash

Amin, *Post-Fordism, A Reader* (London: Blackwell, 1994): Barry Bluestone and Bennett Harrison, *Deindustrialization of America: Plant Closings, Community Abandonment and the Dismantling of Basic Industry* (New York: Basic Books, 1982).

5. Saskia Sassen, *The Mobility of Labor and Capital: A Study in International Investment and Labor Flow* (Cambridge: Cambridge University Press, 1990); Sarah Mahler, *Salvadorans in Suburbia: Symbiosis and Conflict* (Boston: Allyn & Bacon, 1995).

6. Michel Chossudovsky, *The Globalisation of Poverty: Impacts of IMF and World Bank Reforms* (London: Zed Books, 2001); Jerry Mander and Edward Goldsmith, *The Case against the Global Economy and for a Turn toward the Local* (San Francisco: Sierra Club Books, 1997); Jean-Bertrand Aristide, *Eyes of the Heart: Seeking a Path for the Poor in the Age of Globalization* (Boston: Common Courage Press, 2000).

7. For the best discussions of the role of secondary circuit capital, see Henri Lefebvre, *The Production of Space* (New York: Routledge, 1991), and Joe Feagin's two books on urban political economy, *The Urban Real Estate Game: Playing Monopoly With Real Money* (Englewood Cliffs, NJ: Prentice Hall, 1983) and *The New Urban Paradigm: Critical Perspectives on the City* (Lanham, MD: Rowman & Littlefield, 1998), as well as his article "The Secondary Circuit of Real Estate Investment," *Urban Affairs Quarterly* 25 (June 1990): 138–144.

8. Steven Gaines, *Philistines at the Hedgerow: Passion and Property in the Hamptons* (Boston: Little, Brown, 1998), pp. 29–36.

9. Michael Thomas, "Bridgehampton's Golden Season," *Town and Country* (August 1998); Linda Miller Zellner, Interview by Author, Southampton, NY, 6 January 1999; Enzo Morabito, Interview with Author's Research Assistant, Southampton, NY, 12 December 1998.

10. Mark Gottdiener and Ray Hutchinson, *The New Urban Sociology,* 2d ed. (Boston: McGraw-Hill, 2000), pp. 143–149. For more on Allan Schneider and his impact on the Hamptons read Steven Gaines's brilliant opening chapter to *Philistines at the Hedgerow,* pp. 3–48; Vince Cannuscio, Interview with Author, Southampton, NY, 6 August 1998; Bob Deluca, Interview with Author, Bridgehampton, NY, 24 July 1998.

11. Jay Schneiderman, East Hampton town supervisor, argues that, for a variety of reasons, the census numbers may be off by as much as 50 to 75 percent and that the Latino population probably makes up between 30 and 40 percent of the town's population. Jay Schneiderman, Personal Communication, 9 December 2003.

12. Many advocates for and activists within the Latino community discussed the difficulty of getting accurate numbers for both legal and illegal immigrants on the East End. Kathi Kugler, Interview with Author, Southampton, NY, 22 July 1999; Katherine Hartnett, Interview with Author, Southampton, NY,

14 February 2002; Carlos Sandoval, Interview with Author, Amagansett, NY, 21 February 2002; Anthony Rosalia, Interview with Author, Southampton, NY, 3 August 1998. For data on history of immigrant undercounts in the U.S. census, see Harvey Choldin, *Looking for the Last Percent: The Controversy over Census Undercounts.* (New Brunswick, NJ: Rutgers University Press, 1994).

13. Editorial, *East Hampton Star,* 13 January 1990.

14. Jay Schneiderman, Interview with Author, East Hampton, NY, 20 July 1999.

15. Alejandro Portes and Manuel Castells, "World Underneath: The Origins, Dynamics, and Effects of the Informal Economy," in *The Informal Economy: Studies in Advanced and Less Developed Countries,* edited by Alejandro Portes, Manuel Castells, and Lauren Benton (Baltimore: Johns Hopkins Press, 1989).

16. John Strong, *The Algonquian Peoples of Long Island from the Earliest Times to 1700* (Interlaken, NY: Empire Books, 1997), pp. 116–121.

17. Jeffrey Kroessler, "Baseball and Blue Laws," *Long Island Historical Journal* 5, no. 2 (1992).

18. Jeanette Rattray, "Fifty Years of the Maidstone Club," in *Discovering the Past: Writings of Jeanette Edwards Rattray, 1893–1974, Relating to the History of the Town of East Hampton* (New York: Newmarket Press, 2001), pp.136–146; Nancy Hyden Woodward, *East Hampton: A Town and Its People, 1648–1992* (East Hampton: Fireplace Press, 1995), pp. 171–183; Dennis Amato, "Court Tennis on Long Island" *Long Island Forum* 53 (spring–summer 1991): 43–49.

19. Woodward, *East Hampton,* p. 180.

20. Woodward, *East Hampton,* pp. 191–203, 224–226; Mary Cummings, *Southampton: Images of America* (Dover, NH: Arcadia, 1996), p. 70.

21. Pierre Bourdieu, *Distinction: A Social Critique of the Judgement of Taste* (Cambridge, MA: Harvard University Press, 1984). Judith Sealander, *Private Wealth and Public Life: Foundation Philanthropy and the Reshaping of American Social Policy from the Progressive Era to the New Deal* (Baltimore: Johns Hopkins Press, 1997); E. Digby Baltzell, *The Protestant Establishment: Aristocracy and Caste in America* (New Haven: Yale University Press, 1987).

22. Bourdieu, *Distinction,* pp. 217–220.

23. Peter Matthiessen, *Men's Lives* (New York: Vintage, 1986), pp. 157–158.

24. T. H. Breen, *Imagining the Past: East Hampton Histories* (New York: Addison-Wesley, 1989), p. 11.

25. Helen Harrison and Constance Dyer Denne, *Hamptons Bohemia: Two Centuries of Artists and Writers on the Beach* (San Francisco: Chronicle Books, 2002), p. 86.

26. Alastair Gordon, *Weekend Utopia: Modern Living in the Hamptons* (New York: Princeton Architectural Press, 2001), pp. 40–68.

27. Paul Thompson, "The Fishermen's Tales: Men's Lives," *New Statesman and Society* (November 1988).

28. Bryan Carpenter, *The Classic Experience* (New York: Jostens, 1995), p. 118.

29. *Southampton Press,* 30 July 1998.

30. *New York Times,* 23 August 1998.

31. H. E. Chehabi and A. Guttmann, "From Iran to All of Asia: The Origin and Diffusion of Polo," in *Sport in Asian Society: Past and Present,* edited by Fan Hong (London: Frank Cass, 2003), p. 390.

32. Patricia Hill Everett, "Player Profile: Michael Caruso," *The Bridgehampton Polo Guide, 1998* (Stamford, CT: PCI, 1998), pp. 33–36.

33. "Sudsy Says," *Morning Line,* East End edition (August 9, 1998), pp. 5–9.

34. David Rubin, Interview with Author, New York, NY, 15 August 1999.

35. Peter Parkes, "Indigenous Polo and the Politics of Regional Identity in Northern Pakistan," in *Sport, Identity and Ethnicity,* edited by J. MacClancy (New York: Berg, 1996).

36. David Rubin, Interview with Author, New York, NY, 15 August 1999.

37. Ibid.

38. Everett, "Player Profile," p. 34.

39. Roland Barthes, *Mythologies* (New York: Farrar, Straus & Giroux, 1970).

40. Wini Brienes, *Young, White, and Miserable* (Boston: Beacon Press, 1993).

41. And while this initial wave of post–World War II familial populism characterized the settling of the 1950s suburbs, this new wave of hyper-bourgeois familial populism is now helping to write the story of exurbia. For more on the conflation of family and populist ideology see Michael Kazin, *The Populist Persuasion: An American History* (New York: Cornell University Press, 1998); Stephanie Coontz, *The Way We Never Were: American Families and the Nostalgia Trap* (New York: Basic Books, 2000).

42. Peter Fearon, *Hamptons Babylon: Life among the Super-Rich on America's Riviera* (Toronto: Birch Lane Press, 1998), p. 6.

43. Anthony Rosalia, Interview with Author, Southampton, NY, 3 August 1998; Quentin Dante, Interview with the Author, Bridgehampton, NY, 6 July 1998.

44. Peter Berger, "Steps toward a Small Theory of the Visible," *Left Curve* 21 (1997): 30.

45. *Dallas Morning News,* 18 August 1996.

46. *Morning Line,* 17 August 1999.

47. *Morning Line,* 24 August 1999.

48. Garry Whannel, *Fields in Vision: Television Sport and Cultural Transformation* (London: Routledge, 1992).

49. Lang Phipps, "Party Animals," *New York* magazine (August 18, 1997).

50. Quentin Dante, Interview with Author, Bridgehampton, NY, 6 July 1998.

51. Ibid.

52. Zukin, *The Culture of Cities*, p. 253.

53. Peter Berger, *Ways of Seeing* (London: Penguin, 1972), pp. 149–155.

54. Ibid.

55. Michael Thomas, "Bridgehampton's Golden Season," *Town and Country* (August 1998), p. 75.

56. Ibid., p. 104.

57. *New York Times*, 18 May 1997.

58. Southampton Town Board of Supervisors, *Southampton Tomorrow* (Southampton, NY: 1998).

59. Caldor went out of business in the Bridgehampton Commons in 2000 and has been replaced by K Mart.

60. *Newsday*, 2 August 1998.

61. *Newsday*, 24 August 1998.

62. *Southampton Tomorrow*, p. IIIA-1.

63. *Southampton Press*, 23 April 1998. Bob Zellner, Interview with Author, Southampton, NY, 21 February 1999. Tony Rosalia, Interview; Katherine Hartnett, Interview.

64. *Sag Harbor Express*, 7 August 2003.

65. *Dan's Papers*, 10 June 1999.

66. Carlos Vargas, Interview with Author, East Hampton, NY, 8 August 1998.

67. David Rodriguez, Interview with Author, Sag Harbor, NY, 9 August 1998.

68. Joel Gomez, Personal Communication, 18 July 1998.

69. Kathi Kugler, Interview with Author, Southampton, NY, 22 July 1999.

70. *Montauk Pioneer*, 16 July 1993.

71. Jay Schneiderman, Interview with Author, East Hampton, NY, 20 July 1999.

72. Interviews with soccer players.

73. *East Hampton Star*, 7 October 1993.

NOTES TO CHAPTER 5

1. George Harney, Interview with Author.

2. Louis Hartz, *The Liberal Tradition in America* (New York: Harcourt, Brace, Jovanovich, 1955).

3. Alan Dawley, *Class and Community: The Industrial Revolution in Lynn* (Cambridge, MA: Harvard University Press, 1976); Amy Bridges, "Becoming American: The Working Classes in the United States before the Civil War," in *Working-Class Formation: Nineteenth-Century Patterns in Western Europe and the United States*, edited by Ira Katznelson and Aristede Zolberg (Princeton: Princeton University Press, 1986); Sean Wilentz, *Chants Democratic: New York City and*

the Rise of the American Working Class, 1788–1850 (New York: Oxford University Press, 1986); David Montgomery, *Citizen Worker: The Experience of Workers in the United States with Democracy and the Free Market during the Nineteenth Century* (Cambridge: Cambridge University Press, 1993).

4. Frederick Jackson Turner's "frontier thesis" could be folded into this conception of an expanding marketplace, although the actual lived experience of this idea occurred much more in what Mike Davis conceives of as the "urban industrial frontier." Davis, *Prisoners of the American Dream* (New York: Verso, 1986).

5. David Roediger, *Wages of Whiteness: Race and the Making of the American Working Class* (New York: Verso, 1991); Gary Gerstle, *American Crucible: Race and Nation in the Twentieth Century* (Princeton: Princeton University Press, 2001); Michelle Fine, Lois Weis, Judi Addelston, and Julia Marusza, "(In) Secure Times: Constructing White Working-Class Masculinities in the Late 20th Century," *Gender and Society* 11, no. 1 (February 1997).

6. While I use class terminology broadly in this chapter, I base the discussion on the fairly dominant scholarly perspective, which holds that class should be defined as a primarily structural category based on individuals' relationships to economic, political, and social resources. The most basic element of class is one's relationship to property ownership and the means of production.

7. John Strong, *The Algonquian Peoples of Long Island from the Earliest Times to 1700* (Interlaken, NY: Empire Books, 1997). Strong has written that some local Indians did sell themselves and their children into indenture, but this seems to have been primarily for short periods of time, relatively infrequent, and mostly a short-lived practice.

8. Strong, *The Algonquian Peoples*, p. 274. See also Strong, "From Hunter to Servant: Patterns of Accommodation to Colonial Authority in Eastern Long Island Indian Communities," in *To Know the Place: Teaching Local History*, edited by Joann Krieg (New York: Long Island Historical Institute, 1986); Strong, "Shinnecock and Montauk Whalemen," *Long Island Historical Journal* 2 (fall 1989); Matt Villano, "Whaling: A Central Part of Long Island Indian Life," *Long Island Historical Journal* 5 (fall 1992); Nathaniel Howell, *Long Island Whaling* (Bayport, NY: Long Island Forum, 1888).

9. As quoted in T. H. Breen, *Imagining the Past: East Hampton Histories* (New York: Addison-Wesley, 1989), p. 175.

10. Grania Bolton Marcus, *Discovering the African American Experience in Suffolk County, 1620–1860* (Mattituck, NY: Amereon House, 1988), p. 22. See also Floris Barnett, "African American Whalers: Images and Reality," *Long Island Historical Journal* 2 (fall 1989).

11. Marcus, *Discovering the African American Experience*, p. 18.

12. Nancy Hyden Woodward, *East Hampton: A Town and Its People, 1648–*

1992 (East Hampton: Fireplace Press, 1995); Abe Frank, *Together but Apart: The Jewish Experience in the Hamptons* (New York: Shengold, 1966).

13. For more on schools and Americanization between 1880 and 1920 see John W. Meyer, David Tyack, Joane Nagel, and Audri Gordon, "Public Education as Nation-Building in America: Enrollments and Bureaucratization in the American States, 1870–1930," *American Journal of Sociology* 85, no. 3 (November 1979): 591–613; Cara-lynn Ungar, "Black and Jewish Working-Class (Im)migrant Women Speak to the Nation: Rhetoric and Pedagogy in Americanization Practices, 1890–1930," Ph.D. diss., University of Miami, 2000; Joel M. Roitman, *The Immigrants, the Progressives, and the Schools: Americanization and the Impact of the New Immigration upon Public Education in the United States, 1890–1920* (Starks, KS: DeYoung Press, 1997). For more on the role of civic culture in the Americanization process see Roy Rosenzweig, *Eight Hours for What We Will: Work and Leisure in an Industrial City* (Cambridge: Cambridge University Press, 1990). It is important to note that this process of Americanization was not a seamless one; it evolved as a contested process. Thus, the historian James Barrett reminds us that "immigrant workers constructed their own identities, embracing those perspectives and ideas that made sense to them, rejecting those that seemed at odds with what they recognized as reality." But, this self-selection was always made within the context of severe efforts at coercion that, according to Gary Gerstle, severely limited the choices that immigrants could make in constructing their identities. James Barrett, "Americanization from the Bottom Up: Immigration and the Remaking of the Working Class in the United States, 1880–1930," *Journal of American History* 79, no. 3 (December 1992); Gary Gerstle, "Liberty, Coercion, and the Making of Americans," *Journal of American History* 84, no. 2 (September 1997). The point I want to emphasize is that the intersection of coercive social and political structures and individual and collective agency were themselves circumscribed by changing economic conditions and the evolving cultural narrative of race.

14. While the liberal culture's more formal assimilation and identity-based functions won the struggle for the hearts and minds of Americans, this more mainstream identity was still heavily racialized, although within the discourse of national and local identity. For more on this issue see Roger Daniels, *Not Like Us: Immigrants and Minorities in America, 1890–1924* (Chicago: Ivan R. Dee, 1997).

15. This is not to imply that ethnic identities disappeared immediately or forever, just that they appeared less threatening and exclusionary over time and played nominal roles in lasting forms of institutional discrimination.

16. Samuel O'Neil, quoted in Calvin Tomkins and Judy Tomkins, *The Other Hampton* (New York: Grossman, 1974), p. 44.

17. Eddie Clark, quoted in Steve Wick, *Heaven and Earth: The Last Farmers of the North Fork* (New York: St. Martin's, 1996), p. 91.

18. George Harney, Interview with Author, Southampton, NY, 20 February 2002; Jerry Domatob, *African Americans of Eastern Long Island* (Charleston, SC: Arcadia, 2001).

19. Sharon Saunders, Interview with the Author, Southampton, NY, 6 August 1998. Mary Killoran, Interview with Author, Southampton, NY, 6 August 1998.

20. Tomkins and Tomkins, *The Other Hampton*, p. 8.

21. Mary Killoran, Personal Correspondence with the Author, 28 October 2003. Joanne Carter, Interview with Author, 19 February 2002.

22. Tomkins and Tomkins, *The Other Hampton*, p. 42.

23. Ibid., p. 39.

24. One minor caveat to these identities has been the constant intermarriage, especially among African and Native Americans. While these relationships have done little to alter class conditions between whites and people of color, it has created increased stratification among people of color in the working and middle classes in the region. For more on these identities, see John Strong, *We Are Still Here: The Algonquian Peoples of Long Island Today* (Interlaken, NY: Empire State Books, 2001), pp. 23–26.

25. Katherine Hartnett, Interview with Author, Southampton, NY, 14 February 2002.

26. Hartnett Interview; Carlos Sandoval, Interview with Author, Amagansett, NY, 21 February 2002.

27. Melissa Arch-Walton, Interview with Author, Southampton, NY, 5 October 1997.

28. *Southampton Press*, 3 June 1999.

29. *Southampton Press*, 9 July 1998; 6 June 1998; 3 June 1999; Robert Fischer, Phone Interview with Author, Boston, MA, 6 June, 2002.

30. For excellent descriptions of the economic, political and cultural corporatization of higher education, see Lawrence Soley, *Leasing the Ivory Tower: The Corporate Takeover of Academia* (Boston: South End Press, 1995); Cary Nelson et al., *Will Teach for Food: The Crisis in Academic Labor* (Minneapolis: University of Minnesota Press, 1997); Geoff White, *Campus, Inc.: Corporate Power in the Ivory Tower* (New York: Prometheus Books, 2001); and David Noble, *Digital Diploma Mills* (New York: Monthly Review Press, 2002). See also Roger Geiger, *To Advance Knowledge: The Growth of American Research Universities, 1900–1940* (Oxford: Oxford University Press, 1986); Geiger, *Research and Relevant Knowledge: American Research Universities since World War II* (Oxford: Oxford University Press, 1997); and Corey Dolgon, "Rising from the Ashes: The Michigan Memorial Phoenix Project and the Corporatization of University-Based Scientific Research," *Educational Studies* 24, no. 1 (April 1998).

31. Samuel Perry, "SFX Broadcasting Buys Concert Promoter," *Reuter Business Report*, 16 October 1996; Harry Hurt III, "The New King of Rock-and Roll

Concerts," *U.S. News and World Report*, 27 April 1998; Phyllis Furman, "SFX's Sillerman Builds Live-Entertainment Powerhouse," *New York Daily News*, 7 June 1999; Keith Alexander, "Mogul Muscles into Showbiz," *National Post*, 30 January 1999; Sallie Hofmeister, "Company Town," *Los Angeles Times*, 1 March 2000.

32. Robert Danziger, Phone Interview with Author, Boston, MA, 6 June 2002; Arnold Abrams, "He Works for $1 a Year," *Newsday*, 3 May 1994.

33. One of Sillerman's first major "achievements" was to bring in Kermit the Frog as the 1994 Commencement speaker. Despite numerous protests from faculty, many saw the event as a great success because the College gained national publicity. When challenged about the academic and intellectual credentials of the frog puppet, Sillerman argued that Kermit was a devout environmentalist who brought an important ecological message to campus.

34. Dan Rattiner, "Bob Sillerman," in Rattiner, *Who's Here: The Heart of the Hamptons* (Wainscott, NY: Pushcart Press, 1994), pp. 147–150.

35. Southampton College Website (www.Liu.edu). Bob Danziger confirms that coops and internships continue to be driven more by economic and business imperatives than by academic rigor, since faculty supervision has been reduced over the past decade. There have been many important critiques of the links between universities' increasing corporatization and the implementation of internship and coop programs. For examples, see Sam Marullo and Bob Edwards, "Service Learning Pedagogy as Universities' Response to Troubled Times," *American Behavioral Scientist* 43, no. 5 (February 2000); Corey Dolgon, "In Search of 'Cognitive Consonance': Humanist Sociology and Service Learning," *Humanity and Society* 26, no. 2.

36. For evidence of new immigration patterns in the 1980s and 1990s, especially immigration directly to the suburbs, see Saskia Sassen, *Globalization and Its Discontents: Essays on the Mobility of People and Money* (New York: New Press, 1999). For a study that focuses on the Long Island area in particular, see Sarah Mahler, *Salvadorans in Suburbia: Symbiosis and Conflict* (Boston: Allyn & Bacon, 1995).

37. Robert Winerip, "Blue-Collar Millionaire," *New York Times Magazine*, 7 June 1998.

38. Much has been written about the "global race to the bottom," but for good examples of its local effects, see Susan Clarke and Gary Gaile, "Local Politics in a Global Era: Thinking Locally, Acting Globally," *Annals of the American Academy of Political and Social Science* (May 1997); Jeremy Brecher and Tim Costello, *Global Village or Global Pillage: Economic Reconstruction from the Bottom Up* (Boston: South End Press, 1998).

39. George Harney, Interview with the Author, Southampton, NY, 15 February 2002.

40. Southampton Coalition for Justice Meeting tapes and notes, in possession of Author, 6 October 1997; 20 October, 1997; 3 December 1997; 2 February

1998; 16 February 1998; 4 August 1998. Cassie Watters, Interview with Author, Boston, MA, 13 June 2002.

41. Slave resistance to working and living conditions has been well studied and documented. For more about slaves' lasting impact on traditions of African American protest, see Robin D. G. Kelley, *Race Rebels: Culture, Politics, and the Black Working-Class* (New York: Free Press, 1994); Raymond Bauer and Alice Bauer, "Day-to-Day Resistance to Slavery," *Journal of Negro History* 37 (October 1942). For similar discussions of these dynamics in Long Island history, see Marcus, *Discovering the African American Experience.*

42. Minutes from CFS Meeting, 3 December 1998.

43. Michael Knight, Interview with Author, Southampton, NY, 5 October 1997.

44. Tony Smith, Interview with Author, Southampton, NY, 2 February 1998.

45. Minutes from CFJ Meeting, 6 October 1997.

46. Minutes from CFJ Meeting, 3 December 1997.

47. For the entire Friends World Mission statement, visit the FWP Web site at http://www.southampton.liunet.edu/fw/about. For more on the philosophy and activities of Friends World College, see Morris Mitchell, *World Education: An Emerging Concept* (Washington, DC: University Press of America, 1977).

48. Kathleen Modrowski, Interview with Author, Southampton, NY, 13 June 2002. For a more complete description of the distinction between Friends World and other programs based on experiential education, see Kathleen Modrowski, Corey Dolgon, and Hugh McGuiness, "From Local Community Involvement to a Global Curriculum: Friends World Model in Experiential Learning," unpublished paper presented at the Annual Meeting of the National Society for Experiential Education, New Orleans, November 1995.

49. John Dewey, *Experience and Education* (New York: Simon & Schuster, 1997); Paulo Freire, *Pedagogy of the Oppressed* (New York: Continuum, 1970); Frances Moore Lappe and Paul Martin DuBois, The *Quickening of America: Rebuilding Our Nation, Remaking Our Lives* (San Francisco: Jossey-Bass,1994); Myles Horton, *The Long Haul: An Autobiography* (New York: Doubleday, 1990).

50. Bob Zellner, Interview with Author, Southampton, NY, 12 August 2000.

51. Student journal, copies in possession of the author.

52. Student journal, copies in possession of the author.

53. Coalition for Justice papers in possession of the author.

54. Student journal, copies in possession of the author.

55. Ibid.

56. Charles Payne, *I've Got the Light of Freedom: The Organizing Tradition and the Mississippi Freedom Struggle* (Berkeley: University of California Press, 1995). For more on Ella Baker and the philosophy of collective leadership in organizing, see Joanne Grant, *Ella Baker: Freedom Bound* (New York: Wiley, 1999); Bar-

bara Ransby, "Ella Jo Baker: African American Radical and Intellectual," in *The American Radical*, edited by Paul Buhle, Mari Jo Buhle, and Harvey Kaye (New York: Routledge, 1994).

57. Bob Zellner, Interview with Author, Southampton, NY 10 October 1999; Cassie Watters, Interview with Author, Boston, MA, 13 June 2002.

58. Student journal, copies in possession of the author.

59. Brian Quist, *Orphans of the University*, video documentary, Southampton, NY, 2000.

60. Student journal, copies in possession of the author.

61. Student journal, copies in possession of the author.

62. *Southampton Press*, 3 February 2000.

63. *Southampton Press*, 13 January 2000.

64. Ibid.

65. Bob Zellner, Interview with Author, Southampton, NY, 12 August 2000.

66. Sharon Saunders, Interview with the Author, Southampton, NY, 6 August 1998.

67. Robin D. G. Kelley, "Finding the Strength to Love and Dream," *Chronicle of Higher Education* (June 7, 2002).

68. Robin D. G. Kelley, "The Proletariat Goes to College," in *Will Teach for Food: Academic Labor in Crisis*, edited by Cary Nelson (Minneapolis: University of Minnesota Press, 1997), 152.

NOTES TO CHAPTER 6

1. *New York Times*, 25 February 2000; *Southampton Independent*, 1 March 2000; *Southampton Press*, 2 March 2000. Bob Zellner and Rebecca Genia, in interviews with the author, used the terms "manhandled" and "brutalized." While upcoming court cases will determine the legal outcome of these claims, the photographs and videos of the incident seem to support the use of the terms.

2. *Newsday*, 1 August 2003.

3. Available at http://www.savetheeastend.org.

4. *Southampton Press*, 7 August 2003. Both Cannuscio and the long-time Democratic County legislator George Guldi supported the Shinnecock casino proposal, and both were defeated in the 2003 elections.

5. *Southampton Press*, 7 March 2003.

6. John Strong, "How the Land Was Lost: An Introduction," in *The Shinnecock Indians: A Cultural History*, edited by Gaynell Stone (Lexington, MA: Ginn, 1983), p. 54.

7. Ibid.

8. Francis Jennings, *The Invasion of America* (New York: Norton, 1976).

9. John Strong, *The Montaukett Indians of Eastern Long Island* (Syracuse: Syracuse University Press, 1999), pp. 33–34.

10. Quoted in ibid., p. 92.

11. Ibid., p. 101.

12. Ibid., pp. 112–113.

13. Jeanette Rattray, "Montauk: Three Centuries of Romance, Sport, and Adventure," in *Discovering the Past: Writings of Jeanette Edwards Rattray, 1893– 1974, Relating to the History of the Town of East Hampton* (New York: Newmarket Press, 2001), pp. 111–113. Vincent Seyfried, *The Long Island Rail Road: A Comprehensive History* (Garden City, NY: Seyfried, 1961).

14. Harvey Laudin, "The Shinnecock Powwow," in *The Shinnecock Indians: A Cultural History*, edited by Gaynell Stone (Lexington, MA: Ginn, 1983), pp. 345–366. For more general material on the powwow see David Whitehorse, *Pow-Wow: The Contemporary Pan-Indian Celebration* (San Diego: San Diego State University, 1988); Margaret Wilson, "What Is a Powwow?" *Cimarron Review* 36, no. 12 (July 1976).

15. Laudin, "The Shinnecock Powwow," p. 352.

16. Ibid.

17. Harriet Crippen Brown Gumbs, "The Land Defended: The Cove Realty Case," in *The Shinnecock Indians: A Cultural History*, edited by Gaynell Stone (Lexington, MA: Ginn, 1983).

18. Laudin, "The Shinnecock Powwow," p. 353. John Strong also cites this interview and makes a similar argument for the importance of the powwows. John Strong, *We Are Still Here: The Algonquian Peoples of Long Island Today* (Interlaken, NY: Empire State Books, 2001), pp. 36–42.

19. Harriet Brown, "We Hang in the Balance," p. 3.

20. Nancy Lurie, "The Contemporary American Indian Scene," in *North American Indians in Historical Perspective*, edited by Eleanor Burke Leacock and Nancy Ostereich Lurie (New York: Random House, 1971). Strong, *We Are Still Here*, p. 13. For more on the American Indian movement see Ward Churchill, *Struggle for the Land* (Monroe, ME: Common Courage Press, 1993); Paul Chaat Smith and Robert Allen Warrior, *Like a Hurricane: The Indian Movement from Alcatraz to Wounded Knee* (New York: New Press, 1996).

21. John Strong, "How the Land was Lost: An Introduction," in *The Shinnecock Indians: A Cultural History*, edited by Gaynell Stone (Lexington, MA: Ginn, 1983), pp. 60–63.

22. Ibid., pp. 61–63, and Nathan Cuffee testimony, pp. 112–113.

23. Strong, *We Are Still Here*, pp. 18–19; *New York Times*, 21 November 2003. Becky Genia, Interview with the Author, Southampton, NY, 9 July 2003; Elizabeth Haile-Davis, Interview with the Author, Southampton, NY, 9 July 2003.

24. *Southampton Press*, 5 September 2000.

25. Elizabeth Haile-Davis, Interview with the Author, Southampton, NY, 9 July 2003.

26. *New York Times*, 21 November 2003.

27. *New York Times*, 17 July 2000.

28. *Southampton Press*, 30 March 2000.

29. Becky Genia, Interview with the Author, Southampton, NY, 9 July 2003.

30. Joane Nagel, "American Indian Ethnic Renewal: Politics and the Resurgence of Identity," *American Sociological Review* 60, no. 6 (December 1995); Troy Johnson, *Contemporary Native American Political Issues* (Walnut Creek, CA: AltaMira Press, 1999).

31. John Wunder, *Recent Legal Issues for American Indians, 1968 to the Present* (New York: Garland, 1996); Thomas Biolosi, "Bringing the Law Back In: Legal Rights and the Regulation of Indian-White Relations on Rosebud Reservation," *Current Anthropology* 36, no. 4 (August–October 1995).

32. John Strong, *We Are Still Here*, pp. 45–56.

33. *New York Times*, 20 May 2001.

34. *New York Times*, 27 August 2000.

35. Bob Zellner, Interview with the Author, Southampton, NY, 10 October 2003; *Southampton Press*, 18 May 2002.

36. *Southampton Press*, 1 June 2000.

37. *Southampton Press*, 7 March 2002.

38. *Southampton Press*, 1 August 2002.

39. Bob Zellner, Interview with the Author, Southampton, NY, 10 October 2003.

40. Strong, *The Montaukett Indians*, p. 93.

41. Alvin Josephy, Joane Nagel, and Troy Johnson, eds., "Indian Gaming Regulatory Act" in *Red Power: The American Indians' Fight for Freedom* (Lincoln: University of Nebraska Press, 1999), p. 168.

42. Ian Frazier, *On the Rez* (New York: Farrar, Straus & Giroux, 2001), pp. 81–82.

43. Ibid., p. 84. Also see Kim Eisler, *The Revenge of the Pequots* (New York: Simon & Schuster, 2001); and Brett Fromson, *Hitting the Jackpot* (Atlanta: Atlantic Monthly Press, 2003).

44. Available at http://www.senate.gov/~schumer/SchumerWebsite/pressroom/press_releases/PR01442.html.

45. *Southampton Press*, 20 February 2003.

46. *Southampton Press*, 13 August 2003.

47. *Southampton Press*, 25 September 2003.

48. *Southampton Press*, 16 August 2003.

49. *Newsday*, 13 August 2003.

50. *New York Times*, 6 July 2003.

51. *New York Times*, 23 March 2003.

52. *Southampton Press*, 4 July 2003; *New York Times*, 23 March 2003.

53. *Southampton Press*, 7 August 2003.

54. *Southampton Press*, 29 May 2003.

55. *Southampton Press,* 14 August 2003.

56. Bob Zellner, Interview with the Author, Southampton, NY, 10 October 2003.

57. *New York Times,* 23 March 2003.

58. Available at http://www.stopcasino.net.

NOTES TO THE EPILOGUE

1. Karl Marx, "The Eighteenth Brumaire of Louis Bonaparte," in *Marx and Engels: The Communist Manifesto,* edited by Samuel Beer (New York: Meredith, 1955), p. 48.

2. Sharon Saunders, Interview with the Author, 6 August 1998.

3. *Southampton Press,* 16 July 1998.

4. *Southampton Press,* 31 July 2003.

5. *East Hampton Star* 20 July 2003.

6. *Southampton Press,* 1 May 2003.

7. *Southampton Press,* 30 October, 2003.

8. Kathryn Szoka, Interview with the Author, Southampton, NY, 9 July 2003.

9. South Fork Progressive Coalition Mission Statement, available at http://www.lipc.org/sfpc.htm.

10. *Southampton Press,* 22 January 2004.

Bibliography

Abu-Lughod, Janet. *New York, Chicago, Los Angeles: America's Global Cities.* Minneapolis: University of Minnesota Press, 2000.

Arian, Asher, et al. *Changing New York City Politics.* New York: Routledge Press, 1990.

Amato, Dennis. "Court Tennis on Long Island." *Long Island Forum* 53 (spring–summer 1991): 43–49.

Amin, Ash. *Post-Fordism, A Reader.* London: Blackwell, 1994.

Arian, Asher, Arthur S. Goldberg, John H. Mollenkopf, and Eugene Rugowsky. *Changing New York City Politics.* New York: Routledge, 1990.

Axtell, James. *The European and the Indian: Essays in the Ethnohistory of Colonial North America.* New York: Oxford University Press, 1981.

Baltzell, E. Digby. *The Protestant Establishment: Aristocracy and Caste in America.* New Haven: Yale University Press, 1987.

Barthes, Roland. *Mythologies.* New York: Farrar, Straus & Giroux, 1970.

Barnett, Floris. "African American Whalers: Images and Reality." *Long Island Historical Journal* 2 (fall 1989): 12–15.

Barrett, James. "Americanization from the Bottom Up: Immigration and the Remaking of the Working Class in the United States, 1880–1930." *Journal of American History* 79 (December 1992): 996–1020.

Bauer, Raymond, and Alice Bauer. "Day-to-Day Resistance to Slavery." *Journal of Negro History* 37 (October 1942).

Baxandall, Rosalyn, and Elizabeth Ewen. *Picture Windows: How the Suburbs Happened.* New York: Basic Books, 2000.

Beckert, Sven. *The Monied Metropolis: New York City and the Consolidation of the American Bourgeoisie, 1850–1896.* Cambridge: Cambridge University Press, 2001.

Beecher, Lyman. "A Sermon, Containing a General History of the Town of East Hampton, L.I. From Its First Settlement to the Present Time." Sag Harbor, NY: Alden Spooner, 1806.

Behrens, David. "The KKK Flares Up on LI." In *Long Island: Our Story.* New York: Newsday, 1998.

Berger, Peter. *Ways of Seeing.* London: Penguin, 1972.

———. "Steps toward a Small Theory of the Visible." *Left Curve* 21 (1997): 30.

Biolosi, Thomas. "Bringing the Law Back In: Legal Rights and the Regulation of Indian-White Relations on Rosebud Reservation." *Current Anthropology* 36, no. 4 (August–October 1995).

Black, John. "Robert Moses and the Ocean Parkway: An Environmental Retrospective." In *Evoking a Sense of Place*, edited by Joann Krieg. Interlaken, NY: Heart of the Lakes, 1988.

Bourdieu, Pierre. *Distinction: A Social Critique of the Judgement of Taste*. Cambridge, MA: Harvard University Press, 1984.

Bratton, William. *Turnaround: How America's Top Cop Reversed the Crime Epidemic*. New York: Random House, 1998.

Breen, T. H. *Imagining the Past: East Hampton Histories*. New York: Addison-Wesley, 1989.

Bridges, Amy. "Becoming American: The Working Classes in the United States before the Civil War." In *Working-Class Formation: Nineteenth-Century Patterns in Western Europe and the United States*, edited by Ira Katznelson and Aristede Zolberg. Princeton: Princeton University Press, 1986.

Brienes, Wini. *Young, White, and Miserable*. Boston: Beacon Press, 1993.

Buckles, Mary Parker. *Margins: A Naturalist Meets Long Island Sound*. New York: North Point Press, 1997.

Caro, Robert. *The Power Broker: Robert Moses and the Fall of New York*. New York: Vintage, 1974.

Carpenter, Bryan. *The Classic Experience*. New York: Jostens, 1995.

Cavioli, Frank. "The Ku Klux Klan on Long Island," *Long Island Forum* (May 1979): 100–106.

———. "An Incident at Eastport." *Long Island Forum* (November 1984).

———. "People, Places, and the Ku Klux Klan on Long Island." *Long Island Forum* (August 1986).

———. "The KKK Memorial Day Riot." *Long Island Forum* (winter 1992).

Ceci, Lynn. "Reconstructing Indian Culture on Long Island: Fisher's Study of the Montauks." In *The History and Archeology of the Montauk Indians*, edited by Gaynell Stone. Lexington, MA: Ginn, 1979.

———. *The Effect of European Contact and Trade on the Settlement Pattern of Indians in Coastal New York, 1524–1665*. New York: Garland, 1990.

Chehabi, H. E., and A. Guttmann. "From Iran to All of Asia: The Origin and Diffusion of Polo." In *Sport in Asian Society: Past and Present*, edited by Fan Hong. London: Frank Cass, 2003.

Chossudovsky, Michel. *The Globalisation of Poverty: Impacts of IMF and World Bank Reforms*. London: Zed Books, 2001.

Christman, Henry M. *Walt Whitman's New York: A Collection of Walt Whitman's Journalism Celebrating New York From Manhattan to Montauk*. New York: Macmillan, 1963.

Churchill, Allen. *The Upper Crust: An Informal History of New York's Highest Society.* Englewood Cliffs, NJ: Prentice Hall, 1970.

Churchill, Ward. *Struggle for the Land.* Monroe, ME: Common Courage Press, 1993.

Clarke, Susan, and Gary Gaile. "Local Politics in a Global Era: Thinking Locally, Acting Globally," *Annals of the American Academy of Political and Social Science* 551 (May 1997): 28–43.

Colacelleo, Bob. *Studios by the Sea: Artists of Long Island's East End.* New York: Harry N. Adams, 2002.

Crease, Robert. "The History of Brookhaven National Laboratory: Part One." *Long Island Historical Journal* 3 (spring 1991): 167–188.

———. "The History of Brookhaven National Laboratory: Part Two." *Long Island Historical Journal* 3 (spring 1992): 138–161.

Cummings, Mary. *Southampton: Images of America.* Dover, NH: Arcadia, 1996.

Daniels, Roger. *Coming to America: A History of Immigration and Ethnicity in American Life.* New York: Harper, 1991.

———. *Not Like Us: Immigrants and Minorities in America, 1890–1924.* Chicago: Ivan R. Dee, 1992.

Daniels, Tom. "Community Development and the Challenge of Sprawl." Paper presented at the International Community Development Society Conference, Spokane, WA, 28 July 1999.

Davis, Mike. *Prisoners of the American Dream.* New York: Verso, 1986.

———. *City of Quartz.* New York: Verso, 1990.

———. *Ecology of Fear: Los Angeles and the Imagination of Disaster.* New York: Metropolitan Books, 1998.

———. *Dead Cities and Other Tales.* New York: Norton, 2002.

Dawley, Alan. *Class and Community: The Industrial Revolution in Lynn.* Cambridge, MA: Harvard University Press, 1976.

Day, Lynda R. *Making a Way to Freedom: A History of African Americans on Long Island.* Interlaken, NY: Empire State Books, 1997.

De Crevecoeur, Hector St. John. *Letters from an American Farmer.* New York: Viking Press, 1981.

DeKay, Charles. "Eastern Long Island: Its Architecture and Art Settlements." *American Architect* (April 1908).

Dewey, John. *Experience and Education.* New York: Simon & Schuster, 1997.

Dolgon, Corey. "Rising from the Ashes: The Michigan Memorial Phoenix Project and the Corporatization of University-Based Scientific Research." *Educational Studies* 24, no. 1 (April 1998).

———. "Building Community amid the Ruins: Strategies for Struggle from the Coalition for Justice at Southampton College." In *Forging Radical Alliances across Difference: Coalition Politics for the New Millennium,* edited by Jill

Bystydzienski and Steven Schacht. New York: Rowman & Littlefield, 2001.

———. "Ann Arbor, The Cutting Edge of Discipline: Postfordism, Postmodernism, and the New Bourgeoisie." *Antipode* 3 (1999).

East End Economic and Environmental Task Force, *Blueprint for Our Future: Creating Jobs, Preserving the Environment*. New York: Newmarket Press, 1994.

Everett, Patricia Hill. "Player Profile: Michael Caruso." *The Bridgehampton Polo Guide, 1998*. Stamford, CT: PCI, 1998.

Featherstone, Drew. "Waves of Immigrants." In *Long Island: Our Story*. New York: Newsday, 1998.

Feagin, Joe. *The Urban Real Estate Game: Playing Monopoly with Real Money*. Englewood Cliffs, NJ: Prentice Hall, 1983.

———. *The New Urban Paradigm: Critical Perspectives on the City*. Lanham, MD: Rowman & Littlefield, 1998.

Fearon, Peter. *Hamptons Babylon: Life among the Super-Rich on America's Riviera*. Toronto: Birch Lane Press, 1998.

Fine, Michelle, Lois Weis, Judi Addelston, and Julia Marusza. "(In) Secure Times: Constructing White Working-Class Masculinities in the Late 20th Century." *Gender and Society* 11, no. 1 (February 1997).

Fishman, Robert. *Bourgeois Utopias: The Rise and Fall of Suburbia*. New York: Basic Books, 1987.

Fitch, Robert. *The Assassination of New York*. New York: Verso, 1993.

Foster, Neston Sherrill. "Boarders to Builders: The Beginnings of Resort Architecture in East Hampton, Long Island, 1870–1894," M.A. thesis, State University of New York, Binghamton, 1977.

Frank, Abe. *Together but Apart: The Jewish Experience in the Hamptons*. New York: Shengold, 1966.

Frazier, Ian. *On the Rez*. New York: Farrar, Straus & Giroux, 2001.

Freire, Paulo. *Pedagogy of the Oppressed*. New York: Continuum, 1970.

Fuchs, Lawrence. *The American Kaleidoscope: Race, Ethnicity and the Civic Culture*. Boston: University Press of New England, 1991.

Gaines, Steven. *Philistines at the Hedgerow: Passion and Property in the Hamptons*. Boston: Little, Brown, 1998.

Geiger, Roger. *To Advance Knowledge: The Growth of American Research Universities, 1900–1940*. Oxford: Oxford University Press, 1986.

———. *Research and Relevant Knowledge: American Research Universities since World War II*. Oxford: Oxford University Press, 1997.

Gerard, Helene. "And We're Still Here: 100 Years of Small Town Jewish Life." *Long Island Forum* (October 1981): 204–208.

Gergen, Joe. "Three of a Kind: Brown, Erving, Yaz Grew Up on LI, Then Grew into Legends." LIHistory.com, available at http://www.lihistory.com/specspor/stars.htm.

Gerstle, Gary. *American Crucible: Race and Nation in the Twentieth Century.* Princeton: Princeton University Press, 2001.

Gordon, Alastair. *Weekend Utopia: Modern Living in the Hamptons.* New York: Princeton Architectural Press, 2001.

Groocock, Gwendolyn. "Seventy Years of Polish Politics." *Suffolk Times* (April 2002).

Grossman, Karl. *Power Crazy: Is Lilco Turning Shoreham into America's Chernobyl?* New York: Grove Press, 1986.

Gumbs, Harriet Crippen Brown. "The Land Defended: The Cove Realty Case." In *The Shinnecock Indians: A Cultural History,* edited by Gaynell Stone. Lexington, MA: Ginn, 1983.

Harrison, Helen, and Constance Dyer Denne. *Hamptons Bohemia: Two Centuries of Writers and Artists at the Beach.* San Francisco: Chronicle Books, 2002.

Hartz, Louis. *The Liberal Tradition in America.* New York: Harcourt, Brace, Jovanovich, 1955.

Hefner, Robert J. *East Hampton's Heritage.* New York: Norton, 1982.

Hession, Francis, and Ann-Marie Scheidt. "Growing the Region's Economic Future: The Long Island High Technology Incubator." *Long Island Historical Journal* 4 (fall 1991): 14.

Hinderaker, Eric. "The Four Indian Kings and the Imaginative Construction of the First British Empire." *William & Mary Quarterly* 53, no. 3 (1996).

Howell, George Howell. *The Early History of Southampton, L.I., New York with Genealogies.* Albany: Weed, Parsons, 1887.

Howell, Nathaniel. *Long Island Whaling.* Bayport, NY: Long Island Forum, 1888.

Hurt, Harry, III. "The New King of Rock-and-Roll Concerts." *U.S. News and World Report* (27 April 1998).

Jackson, Kenneth. *Crabgrass Frontier: The Suburbanization of the United States.* London: Oxford University Press, 1987.

Jacobs, Wilbur. "Wampum: The Protocol of Indian Diplomacy." *William & Mary Quarterly* 6, no. 4 (1949).

Jennings, Francis. *The Ambiguous Empire: The Covenant Chain Confederation of Indian Tribes with English Colonies from Its Beginnings to the Lancaster Treaty of 1744.* New York: Norton, 1990.

Johansen, Bruce. *Native American Political Systems and the Evolution of Democracy: An Annotated Bibliography.* Westport, CT: Greenwood Press, 1995.

Johnson, Troy. *Contemporary Native American Political Issues.* Walnut Creek, CA: AltaMira Press, 1999.

Josephy, Alvin, Joane Nagel, and Troy Johnson, eds. "Indian Gaming Regulatory Act." In *Red Power: The American Indians' Fight for Freedom.* Lincoln: University of Nebraska Press, 1999.

Keeler, Robert. *Newsday: A Candid History of the Respectable Tabloid.* Hempstead, NY: Newsday, 1990.

Kelly, Robin D. G. *Race Rebels: Culture, Politics, and the Black Working-Class*. New York: Free Press, 1994.

―――. "The Proletariat Goes to College." In *Will Teach for Food: Academic Labor in Crisis*, edited by Cary Nelson. Minneapolis: University of Minnesota Press, 1997.

―――. "Finding the Strength to Love and Dream." *Chronicle of Higher Education* (June 2002).

Kontos, Louis. "Review of *Turnaround*." *Humanity and Society* 24, no. 4 (November 2000): 421–425.

Koppelman, Lee. "The Quest for a Suffolk County Legislature," *Long Island Historical Journal* 8, no. 2 (spring 1996): 24–48.

―――. "The Myth and the Reality." *Long Island Historical Journal* 9 (spring 1997).

Krieg, Joann. *Robert Moses: Single-Minded Genius*. Interlaken, NY: Heart of the Lakes, 1989.

Kroessler, Jeffrey. "Baseball and Blue Laws." *Long Island Historical Journal* 5 (1992).

Kuentzel, Walter, and Thomas Heberlein. "Social Status, Self-Development, and the Process of Sailing Specialization." *Journal of Leisure Research* 29, no. 3 (1997): 300–319.

Kumar, Krishnan. *From Post-Industrial to Post-Modern Society: New Theories of the Contemporary World* London: Blackwell, 1995.

Laffan, William Mckay. The *New Long Island: A Handbook of Summer Travel*. New York: Rogers & Sherwood, 1879.

LaGomina, Salvatore. "Long Island Italians and the Labor Movement." *Long Island Forum* (January 1985): 34–37.

―――. "Fullerton and the Italians: Experiment in Agriculture." *Long Island Forum* (February 1989): 12–20.

Laudin, Harvey. "The Shinnecock Powwow." In *The Shinnecock Indians: A Cultural History*, edited by Gaynell Stone. Lexington, MA: Ginn, 1983.

Lepore, Jill. *The Name of War: King Phillips War and the Origins of American Identity*. New York: Vintage, 1998.

Lurie, Nancy. "The Contemporary American Indian Scene." In *North American Indians in Historical Perspective*, edited by Eleanor Burke Leacock and Nancy Ostereich Lurie. New York: Random House, 1971.

Mackay, Robert. *Long Island Country Houses and Their Architects*. New York: Norton, 1997.

Mahler, Sarah. *Salvadorans in Suburbia: Symbiosis and Conflict*. Boston: Allyn & Bacon, 1995.

Marcus, Grania Bolton. *Discovering the African American Experience in Suffolk County, 1620–1860*. Mattituck, NY: Amereon House, 1988.

Marullo, Sam, and Bob Edwards. "Service Learning Pedagogy as Universities'

Response to Troubled Times." *American Behavioral Scientist* 43, no. 5 (February 2000).

Marx, Karl. *The German Ideology.* In *The Marx-Engels Reader,* edited by Robert C. Tucker. New York: Norton, 1972.

Marx, Leo. *The Machine in the Garden: Technology and the Pastoral Idea in America.* New York: Oxford University Press, 1964.

Matthiessen, Peter. *Men's Lives.* New York: Vintage, 1986.

McDonald, Kevin, and Nancy Nagle Kelley. "Recreation/Second Home Industry." In *Blueprint for Our Future: Creating Jobs, Preserving the Environment.* New York: Newmarket Press, 1994.

Meyer, John W., David Tyack, Joane Nagel, and Audri Gordon. "Public Education as Nation-Building in America: Enrollments and Bureaucratization in the American States, 1870–1930." *American Journal of Sociology* 85, no. 3 (November 1979): 591–613.

Miller, Christopher, and George Hamell. "A New Perspective on Indian-White Contact: Cultural Symbols and Colonial Trade. *Journal of American History* 73 (1986).

Miller, Robert. "The Long Island Motor Parkway: Prelude to Robert Moses." In *Robert Moses: Single-Minded Genius,* edited by Joann Krieg. Hempstead, NY: Long Island Studies Institute, 1989

Mitchell, Morris. *World Education: An Emerging Concept.* Washington, DC: University Press of America, 1977.

Mollenkopf, John. *A Phoenix in the Ashes.* Princeton: Princeton University Press, 1994.

Montgomery, David. *Citizen Worker: The Experience of Workers in the United States with Democracy and the Free Market during the Nineteenth Century.* Cambridge: Cambridge University Press, 1993.

Moses, Robert. "Parks, Parkways, Express Arteries, and Related Plans for New York City after the War." New York City, 1943.

Mulvihill, William. *South Fork Place Names: Some Informal Long Island History.* Sag Harbor, NY: Brickiln Press, 1995.

Murphy, Robert Cushman. *Fish-shape Paumanok; Nature and Man on Long Island.* Philadelphia: American Philosophical Society, 1964.

Nagel, Joane. "American Indian Ethnic Renewal: Politics and the Resurgence of Identity." *American Sociological Review* 60, no. 6 (December 1995).

Naylor, Natalie. *Exploring African American History.* Hempstead, NY: Long Island Studies Institute, 1991.

Nelson. Arthur. "Characterizing Exurbia." *Journal of Planning Literature* 6 (1991): 350–368.

Nelson, Cary. *Will Teach for Food: The Crisis in Academic Labor.* Minneapolis: University of Minnesota Press, 1997.

Newfield, Jack, and Wayne Barrett. *City for Sale: Ed Koch and the Betrayal of New York*. New York: Harper & Row, 1988.

Palen, John J. *The Suburbs*. New York: McGraw-Hill, 1994.

Parkes, Peter. "Indigenous Polo and the Politics of Regional Identity in Northern Pakistan." In *Sport, Identity and Ethnicity*, edited by J. MacClancy. New York: Berg, 1996.

Patel, Dinker. *Exurbs: Urban Residential Developments in the Countryside*. Washington, DC: University Press of America, 1980.

Payne, Charles. *I've Got the Light of Freedom: The Organizing Tradition and the Mississippi Freedom Struggle*. Berkeley: University of California Press, 1995.

Perry, Samuel. "SFX Broadcasting Buys Concert Promoter." *Reuters Business Report* (16 October 1996).

Portes, Alejandro, and Manuel Castells. "World Underneath: The Origins, Dynamics, and Effects of the Informal Economy." In *The Informal Economy: Studies in Advanced and Less Developed Countries*, edited by Alejandro Portes, Manuel Castells, and Lauren Benton. Baltimore: Johns Hopkins University Press, 1989.

Pyle, Lizbeth. "The Land Market beyond the Urban Fringe." *Geographical Review* 75, no. 1 (January 1985): 32–43.

Rattiner, Dan. *Who's Here: The Heart of the Hamptons*. Wainscott, NY: Pushcart Press, 1994.

Rattray, Everett. *The South Fork: The Land and People of Eastern Long Island*. New York: Random House, 1979.

Rattray, Jeanette. *Discovering the Past: Writings of Jeanette Edwards Rattray, 1893–1974, Relating to the History of the Town of East Hampton*. New York: Newmarket Press, 2001.

Rigatz, Richard Lee. "Vacation Homes in the Northeastern United States: Seasonality in Population Distribution." *Annals of the Association of American Geographers* 60, no. 3 (September 1970).

Roediger, David. *Wages of Whiteness: Race and the Making of the American Working Class*. New York: Verso, 1991.

Roitman, Joel M. *The Immigrants, the Progressives, and the Schools: Americanization and the Impact of the New Immigration upon Public Education in the United States, 1890–1920*. Starks, KS: DeYoung Press, 1997.

Sale, Kirkpatrick. *Wages of Whiteness: Race and the Making of the American Working Class*. New York: Verso, 1991.

Salisbury, Neal. "The Indians' Old World: Native Americans and the Coming of Europeans." *William & Mary Quarterly* 53, no. 3 (1996): 435–458.

Sassen, Saskia. *The Mobility of Labor and Capital: A Study in International Investment and Labor Flow*. Cambridge: Cambridge University Press, 1990.

———. *Globalization and Its Discontents: Essays on the Mobility of People and Money*. New York: New Press, 1999.

————. *The Global City: New York, London, Tokyo.* Princeton: Princeton University Press, 2001.

Sealander, Judith. *Private Wealth and Public Life: Foundation Philanthropy and the Reshaping of American Social Policy from the Progressive Era to the New Deal.* Baltimore: Johns Hopkins University Press, 1997.

Seyfried. Vincent. *The Long Island Railroad: A Comprehensive History,* Part 6, *The Golden Age, 1881–1900.* Garden City, NY: Newsday, 1968.

Shefter, Martin. *Political Crisis, Fiscal Crisis: The Collapse and Revival of New York City—The Columbia History of Urban Life Series.* New York: Columbia University Press, 1992.

Sites, William. "The Limits of Urban Regime Theory: New York City under Koch, Dinkins, and Giuliani." *Urban Affairs Review* (March 1997).

Smith, Louise Carter. "Long Island Motor Parkway." *Nassau County Historical Journal* 22 (spring 1961).

Smith, Neil. *The New Urban Frontier: Gentrification and the Revanchist City.* New York: Routledge, 1996.

————. "Giuliani Time." *Social Text* 57 (1998): 1–20.

Smith, Paul Chaat, and Robert Allen Warrior. *Like a Hurricane: The Indian Movement from Alcatraz to Wounded Knee.* New York: New Press, 1996.

Snyderman, George S. "The Functions of Wampum." *Proceedings of the American Philosophical Society* 98 (December 1954).

Soley, Lawrence. *Leasing the Ivory Tower: The Corporate Takeover of Academia.* Boston: South End Press, 1995.

Stoff, Joshua. "Grumman versus Republic: Success and Failure in the Aviation Industry on Long Island." *Long Island Historical Journal* 1 (spring 1989): 113–127.

Stone, Gaynell. *The History and Archeology of the Montauk Indians.* Lexington, MA: Ginn, 1979.

————. *The Shinnecock Indians: A Cultural History.* Lexington, MA: Ginn, 1983.

Strong, John. "How the Land Was Lost: An Introduction." In *The Shinnecock Indians: A Cultural History,* edited by Gaynell Stone. Lexington, MA: Ginn, 1983.

————. "From Hunter to Servant: Patterns of Accommodation to Colonial Authority in Eastern Long Island Indian Communities." In *To Know the Place: Teaching Local History,* edited by Joann Krieg. New York: Long Island Historical Institute, 1986.

————. *The Algonquian Peoples of Long Island from the Earliest Times to 1700.* Interlaken, NY: Empire State Books, 1997.

————. *The Montaukett Indians of Eastern Long Island.* Syracuse: Syracuse University Press, 1999.

————. *We Are Still Here: The Algonquian Peoples of Long Island Today.* Interlaken, NY: Empire State Books, 2001.

Suarez-Orozco, Marcelo M., and Mariela Paez. *Latinos: Remaking America.* Berkeley: University of California Press, 2002.

Tabb, William K. "The New York City Fiscal Crisis." In *Marxism and the Metropolis: New Urban Perspectives,* edited by William K. Tabb. New York: Oxford University Press, 1978.

Thomas, Michael. "Bridgehampton's Golden Season." *Town and Country* (August 1998).

Thompson, Paul. "The Fishermen's Tales: Men's Lives." *New Statesman and Society* 1 (November 1988).

Tomaskovic-Devey, Donald, and Barbara J. Risman. "Telecommuting Innovation and Organization: A Contingency Theory of Labor Process Change." *Social Science Quarterly* 74, no. 2 (1993): 367–385.

Tomkins, Calvin, and Judy Tomkins. *The Other Hampton.* New York: Grossman, 1974.

Twomey, Tom. *Awakening the Past: The East Hampton 350th Anniversary Lecture Series, 1998.* New York: Newmarket Press, 1999.

Villano, Matt. "Whaling: A Central Part of Long Island Indian Life." *Long Island Historical Journal* 5 (fall 1992).

Vincent, Stuart. "Long Island's Founding Jews." In *Long Island: Our Story.* New York: Newsday, 1998.

Ward, Chip. *Canaries on the Rim: Living Downwind in the West.* New York: Verso, 2001.

Wesler, Kit. "Trade Politics and Native Peoples in Iroquoia and Asante." *Comparative Studies in Society and History* 25, no. 4 (October 1983).

White, Geoff. *Campus, Inc.: Corporate Power in the Ivory Tower.* New York: Prometheus Books, 2001.

Whitehorse, David. *Pow-Wow: The Contemporary Pan-Indian Celebration.* San Diego: San Diego State University, 1988.

Wick, Steven. *Heaven and Earth: The Last Farmers of the North Fork.* New York: St. Martin's, 1996.

Williams, Alex. "Big Shack Attack." *New York* magazine (9 August 1999).

Williams, Alex, and Beth Landman. "Reversal of Fortune." *New York* magazine (30 August 2001).

Williams, Raymond. *The Country and the City.* New York: Oxford University Press, 1973.

Wilson, Margaret. "What Is a Powwow?" *Cimarron Review* 36 (July 1976): 12.

Winerip, Robert. "Blue-Collar Millionaire," *New York Times Magazine,* 7 June 1998.

Wolfe, Tom. *The Bonfire of the Vanities.* New York: Bantam, 1987.

Woodward, Nancy Hyden. *East Hampton: A Town and Its People, 1648–1992.* East Hampton: Fireplace Press, 1995.

Wunder, John. *Recent Legal Issues for American Indians, 1968 to the Present.* New York: Garland, 1996.

Wunderlich, Roger. "Peconic County: To Be or Not to Be," *Long Island Historical Journal* 9 (spring 1997).

———. "Go East, Young Man: Nineteenth-Century Farm Life on the South Fork of Long Island." *Long Island Historical Journal* 13 (fall 2000).

Zukin, Sharon. *The Culture of Cities.* London: Blackwell, 1995.

INTERVIEWS

Mae Anderson, Interview with the Author, Southampton, NY, 15 February 2002.

Melissa Arch-Walton, Interview with the Author, Southampton, NY, 5 October 1997.

Vince Cannuscio, Interview with Author, Southampton, NY, 6 August 1998

Scott Carlin, Personal Communication, 16 June 2003.

Joanne Carter, Interview with Author, Southampton, NY, 19 February 2002.

Wendy Chamberlain, Phone Interview with Author, Boston, MA, 8 May 2003.

Quentin Dante, Interview with the Author, Bridgehampton, NY, 6 July 1998.

Robert Danziger, Phone Interview with Author, Boston, MA, 6 June 2002.

Bob Deluca, Interview with the Author, Bridgehampton, NY, 25 January 2002; 24 July 1998.

Robert Fischer, Phone Interview with Author, Boston, MA, 6 June, 2002.

Becky Genia, Interview with the Author, Southampton, NY, 9 July 2003.

Nancy Goell, Interview with the Author, East Hampton, NY, 22 February 2002.

Joel Gomez, Personal Communication, 18 July 1998.

Liz Granitz, Interview with Author, Southampton, NY, 18 February 2002.

Evans K. Griffing, Interview with Karl Grossman, Shelter Island, NY, 5 February 1979.

Karl Grossman, Interview with the Author, Sag Harbor, NY, 4 August 1998.

Elizabeth Haile-Davis, Interview with the Author, Southampton, NY, 9 July 2003.

George Harney, Interview with the Author, Southampton, NY, 15 February 2002.

Katherine Hartnett, Interview with Author, Southampton, NY, 14 February 2002.

Mary Killoran, Interview with the Author, Sag Harbor, NY, 6 August 1998.

Michael Knight, Interview with Author, Southampton, NY, 5 October 1997.

Kathi Kugler, Interview with Author, Southampton, NY, 22 July 1999.

Enzo Morabito, Interview with Author's Research Assistant, Southampton, NY, 12 December 1999.

David Rodriguez, Interview with Author, Sag Harbor, NY, 9 August, 1998.

Anthony Rosalia, Interview with Author, Southampton, NY, 3 August 1998.
Hal Ross, Interview with the Author, Southampton, NY, 20 February 2002.
David Rubin, Interview with Author, New York, NY, 15 August 1999.
Carlos Sandoval, Interview with Author, Amagansett, NY, 21 February 2002.
Sharon Saunders, Interview with the Author, Southampton, NY, 6 August 1998.
Jay Schneiderman, Interview with Author, East Hampton, NY, 20 July 1999.
Ed Sharretts, Phone Interview with the Author, Boston, MA, 2 January 2004.
Tony Smith, Interview with Author, Southampton, NY, 2 February 1998.
Kathryn Szoka, Interview with Author, Southampton, NY, 9 July 2003; 7 September 2003.
Fred Theile, Interview with the Author, Bridgehampton, NY, 29 March 2002.
Carlos Vargas, Interview with Author, East Hampton, NY, 8 August 1998.
Lou Ware, Interview with the Author, Southampton, NY, 20 February 2002.
Cassie Watters, Interview with Author, Boston, MA, 13 June 2002.
Lori Wehrner, Interview with Author, Riverhead, NY, 15 February 2002.
Bob Zellner, Interview with Author, Southampton, NY, 21 February 1999; 10 October 1999; 12 August 2000; 10 October 2003; 18 October 2003.
Linda Miller Zellner, Interview by Author, Southampton, NY, 6 January 1999.

MISCELLANEOUS

Cohalan, Peter F. "Impact of the Proposed Peconic County." Suffolk, NY: Office of the County Executive, 1980.
Group for America's South Fork. "News" 1, nos. 2–3, Bridgehampton, NY, 1979.
Peconic County Financial Feasibility Study. Southampton, NY: East End Economic and Environmental Institute, 1995.
Quist, Brian, Orphans of the University, video documentary. Southampton, NY, 2000.
Southampton College Institute for Regional Research. "Attitudes of the Southampton Town Population toward Various Subjects Addressed by the Master Plan." Southampton, NY: Author, 1995.
Szoka, Kathryn. "Vanishing Landscapes." Lecture presented to the Group for the South Fork, 4 April 2001.
Town of Southampton, "Southampton Tomorrow." Southampton, NY: Author, 2000.
Zweig, Michael. "The Wine Industry and the Future of Agriculture on Long Island's North Fork." Research Paper No. 290. Stony Brook, NY, 1986.

Index

About the Author

Corey Dolgon is associate professor and chair of sociology at Worcester State College and the editor of *Humanity and Society,* the journal of the Association for Humanist Sociology.